Children Learning Outside
the Classroom

.va
and r..

Education at SAGE

SAGE is a leading international publisher of journals, books, and electronic media for academic, educational, and professional markets.

Our education publishing includes:

- accessible and comprehensive texts for aspiring education professionals and practitioners looking to further their careers through continuing professional development

- inspirational advice and guidance for the classroom

- authoritative state of the art reference from the leading authors in the field

Find out more at: **www.sagepub.co.uk/education**

Children Learning Outside the Classroom
From Birth to Eleven

Edited by
Sue Waite

SAGE

Los Angeles | London | New Delhi
Singapore | Washington DC

First published 2011. Reprinted 2011

SAGE Publications Ltd
1 Oliver's Yard
55 City Road
London EC1Y 1SP

SAGE Publications Inc.
2455 Teller Road
Thousand Oaks, California 91320

SAGE Publications India Pvt Ltd
B 1/I 1 Mohan Cooperative Industrial Area
Mathura Road
New Delhi 110 044

SAGE Publications Asia-Pacific Pte Ltd
33 Pekin Street #02–01
Far East Square
Singapore 048763

Library of Congress Control Number: 2010930659

British Library Cataloguing in Publication data
A catalogue record for this book is available from the British Library

ISBN 978-0-85702-047-5
ISBN 978-0-85702-048-2 (pbk)

Typeset by Dorwyn, Wells, Somerset
Printed in Great Britain by the MPG Books Group
Printed on paper from sustainable resources

To
my granddad, lifelong learner outside the classroom
my mum, for wildflower naming
Dick, for walks in wild places
and
Katie and Rory, for loving nature and experiential learning
Long may such learning continue

Contents

About the editor and contributors   xi
Acknowledgements   xvii
Key for icons   xviii

Introduction   xix

1   Theoretical perspectives on learning outside the classroom:
    relationships between learning and place   1
    Sue Waite and Nick Pratt

    Developing a personal theory for understanding learning in
    different contexts   2
    Concepts of learning and different focal planes   5
    A broader concept of learning   6
    Towards a relational model for learning outside
    the classroom   6
    A psychological plane   10
    A socio-cultural plane   13
    Using different planes for different purposes   15

Section 1   Early Years Practice – Reaching Out   19

2   Crawling and toddling in the outdoors: very young
    children's learning   20
    Valerie Huggins and Karen Wickett

    Why is it important for very young children to have
    substantial experience of the outdoor environment?   22
    Dealing with risk   31

3   Using the local community as part of the early years
    learning environment   35
    Karen Wickett and Valerie Huggins

Starting from children's interests 37
Involving parents and carers 43
The children's culture 45
Some issues 46

4 A time of change: outdoor learning and pedagogies of
transition between Foundation Stage and Year 1 50
Sue Waite, Julie Evans and Sue Rogers

Play-based and playful pedagogies 57
Spaces: intentions and tensions 59

**Section 2 Learning Outside the Classroom Across the
Curriculum for Primary Aged Children 65**

5 English and language outside the classroom 66
Howard Cotton

English as a medium for learning in and out of school 66
The role-play area 68
Environmental print 72
In support of equity 78

6 Mathematics outside the classroom 80
Nick Pratt

What mathematics is – and isn't 81
A model for mathematical thinking 84
The role of the outdoors 86

7 Science and technology outside the classroom 94
Beth Gompertz, Julia Hincks and Rachael Hincks Knight

Developing a sense of belonging – Earthwalks 95
Finding out about the world around us 99
Identifying ways to reduce impact on the environment 102

8 Understanding places and society through history and
geography outside the classroom 106
Orla Kelly and Roger Cutting

Learning *for* a landscape 108
Drama as a pedagogy for outdoor integrated humanities 110
Research in drama education 116

9   The Arts outside the classroom   119
    Jeff Adams, Martin Ashley and Ian Shirley

    Taking music outside   120
    Becoming sensitive to spaces – engaging the aesthetic   121
    Making up music   122
    Musical development   126
    Land and environmental art   128
    Context and subjectivity   129

10 Physical development, health and well-being: the role of
    physical education 'outside'   133
    Emma Sime and Liz Taplin

    Learning 'outdoors' and 'outside the classroom'   134
    Physical education and the concept of physical literacy   135
    Learning 'outdoors' and 'outside the classroom' through
    outdoor and adventurous activities (OAA)   137
    Overcoming the barriers to learning in the outdoors   142
    Reading the environment   144

Section 3   Outside the Box   **147**

11 Residential centres: desirable difference?   148
    Tony Rea

    Outdoor centres: the historical and cultural background   149
    The first pillar: Learning to know – the cognitive domain   152
    The second pillar: Learning to do – skills acquisition   154
    The third pillar: Learning to live together – social skills
    development   154
    The fourth pillar: Learning to be – self-awareness and
    greater autonomy   154
    Why are centres becoming like school?   156
    Examining learning at outdoor education centres critically   158

12 School gardens and Forest Schools   162
    Rowena Passy and Sue Waite

    School gardens and lessons for life   163
    Forest Schools and dispositions for learning   166
    Summary of similarities and differences   172
    Some critical thoughts   173

13 Environmental education in the National Park: case
   studies on Exmoor   176
   Dave Gurnett, Linda la Velle, and Sue Waite

   Pedagogical approach   177
   The Exmoor Model: real experience environmental
   education   183
   Implications for policy and practice   186

14 Managed learning spaces and new forms of learning
   outside the classroom   188
   Alan Peacock

   New forms of educational enterprise: learning spaces   190
   The impact of micro-contexts   192
   New forms of learning   194
   The importance of collaborative engagement   195
   Implications for LPs   196

15 Making a difference: learning on a grand scale   201
   Sue Waite

   How does learning (outside the classroom) happen?   203
   Why learn outside the classroom?   206
   What might be learned outside the classroom?   208

Useful websites   213
References   214
Index   229

About the editor and contributors

Editor

Sue Waite is Faculty Research Fellow in the Faculty of Education, University of Plymouth, where she has been a researcher since 1998. She is also a qualified primary school teacher. She has carried out research for local authorities and national bodies in the field of policy, continuing professional development, inclusion and outdoor learning, including Forest Schools. She leads the university's outdoor and experiential learning research network and was awarded an Economic and Social Science Research Council grant for research looking at 'Opportunities afforded by the outdoors for alternative pedagogies in children's transition from Foundation Stage to Year 1'. Within a BIG Lottery Research Programme award, she is currently developing research capacity in third sector organisations to investigate 'Social cohesion and well-being deriving from woodland activities'. She is a member of the Editorial Boards of *Pastoral Care in Education* and *Education 3–13*. She co-edited with Tony Rea a special edition of *Education 3–13* on 'International Perspectives on Outdoor Learning' in 2009. She has published widely in academic and practitioner journals and edited books.

Contributors

Jeff Adams is a Reader in the Faculty of Education at Edge Hill University, where he is leader of the faculty's doctoral studies unit. Prior to this he worked at Goldsmiths College, University of London, leading the MA Artist Teachers and Contemporary Practices programme. Before joining Goldsmiths he coordinated the PGCE Art and Design course at Liverpool John Moores University, and tutored in modern art history for the Open University. Jeff's earlier career was spent teaching in secondary comprehensive schools in Yorkshire and Cumbria. He is principal editor of the *International Journal of Art and Design Education*. His recent publications include *Documentary Graphic Novels and Social Realism* (2008, Peter Lang), and *Teaching through Contemporary Art*

(2008, Tate; coauthored with Goldsmiths and Tate colleagues).

Martin Ashley is Professor and Head of Research in the Faculty of Education at Edge Hill University. Trained initially as a music teacher, he enjoyed a broad and eclectic career for seventeen years in state and independent primary and middle schools. Since moving into higher education some fourteen years ago he has researched and published widely on boys' education and boys' engagement with music. He established the Sounding Edge music education project at Edge Hill University and is a consultant for SingUp, the National Singing Programme.

Howard Cotton leads the language and literacy team in the Faculty of Education, Plymouth University. He has worked in primary schools, secondary schools and universities in Devon, France and Chile. His idea of fun is climbing volcanoes, which may account for his interest in outdoor learning!

Roger Cutting spent many years teaching Environmental Sciences in both the FE and HE sectors. Originally a wetland ecologist, an area in which he has been widely published, he has more recently become interested in environmental education. This has led to research in the areas of both Education for Sustainability and the teaching of Science. He teaches in the Faculty of Education in Environmental Education and is presently a Research Fellow with the Centre for Sustainable Futures at the University of Plymouth.

Julie Evans is a senior lecturer in sociology and programme Leader for the BA Early Childhood Studies course at the University College Plymouth St Mark and St John. Julie's PhD research focused on children, consumer culture and social inequalities. Julie has worked on a range of research projects and is currently a co-investigator on an ESRC project entitled 'Opportunities afforded by the outdoors for alternative pedagogies in children's transition from Foundation Stage to Year 1'. Julie has published in the areas of Early Years education, children's consumption, and widening participation in HE.

Beth Gompertz is a Lecturer in Science Education and is responsible for the management of the PGCE programme at the University of Plymouth. As a former science and school grounds co-coordinator and primary school teacher, she has a particular interest in engaging children in the outdoors. Her PhD research is centred on children as co-researchers and she is also engaged in research on the use of Earthwalks.

Dave Gurnett is a qualified teacher with an MSc in health education. Having spent four years teaching and playing serious rugby, he joined Exmoor National Park in a ranger/education role. Twenty years and many fantastic experiences later, leading over 25,000 children on forays into the countryside, he considers there is a greater need than ever to re-connect with nature through 'real experiences'. He has conducted research at the University of Plymouth looking at the impact of National Parks on children's views and suggests National Parks to be well worth a visit either for experiencing the 'wow' of the countryside or a more curricular-orientated educational study.

Julia Hincks is an experienced primary school teacher, FE lecturer in creative craft, and freelance textiles artist based in Brighton. She is passionate about education for sustainable development and reducing human impact on the environment.

Rachael Hincks Knight is a Lecturer in Education at the University of Plymouth, having previously taught in both mainstream and special schools. Her research interests lie within the field of inclusive education, particularly looking at roles of support staff and also in considering the place of practical and experiential learning in science.

Valerie Huggins is a Lecturer in Early Childhood Studies at the University of Plymouth. She is an experienced Early Years teacher and worked for several years as a consultant for a local authority. Before taking up her current post she spent some time with VSO training teacher educators in Ethiopia. Her research interests centre on different approaches to effective Early Education, including the use of the outdoor environment, using digital media to share children's interests and Early Years provision in the developing world. She is currently studying for an EdD with a focus on the professionalisation of the Early Years workforce.

Orla Kelly PhD, BSc is a Lecturer in Science Education and Drama Education at the University of Plymouth. Her research interests include using problem-based learning to support science understanding and using drama to teach across the primary curriculum. Use of the outdoors has been embedded in her practice both within schools and now with student teachers, enriching their scientific experience and understanding.

Miles Opie is a Lecturer in Primary ICT at the University of Plymouth. Having originally specialised as a geographer, his experience in primary schools led him to become an ICT Coordinator. He is passionate about outdoor education and combining his strengths in both ICT and geography. He is enjoying seeing how new technology is opening up the world of geography.

Rowena Passy is a Research Fellow in the Faculty of Education at the University of Plymouth. She was previously Senior Research Officer at the National Foundation for Educational Research, where she led the project commissioned by the Royal Horticultural Society to assess the impact of school gardening. She has been involved with a number of qualitative research projects in primary schools since completing her doctoral studies, and is particularly interested in values in education.

Alan Peacock is currently Honorary Research Fellow at the Graduate School of Education, University of Exeter, where he was Course Director for the Primary Science PGCE programme until 2004. He has a degree in Chemistry and a doctorate in Environmental Education, and has been a teacher, teacher educator, researcher and author for over 40 years. As well as a career in schools and universities in England, he has worked in Scotland, Northern Ireland, India and various African countries, notably Kenya, Botswana, Namibia and South Africa. He has carried out consultancy/evaluation work for a range of environmental organisations, and conducted research in textbook design and development, which led to chairing a UNESCO working group on 'Textbooks for International Understanding'. Recently, his work has taken him to New Zealand, Ireland and Chile. He is also editor of *Primary Science*, the ASE's professional journal for primary teachers, and his latest book is *Eco-literacy for Primary Schools* (Trentham Books).

Nick Pratt has taught in Higher Education for the past 14 years, having previously taught in primary schools in Exeter. His first degree was in Engineering Science from Oxford University and he subsequently gained a PGCE at Exeter University and then, in 2004 his PhD, which was in the field of interaction in maths classrooms. Nick was a member of the mathematics education team at the Faculty of Education of the University of Plymouth for 12 years, working with BEd and PGCE students. He now works with teachers on a Masters programme, running taught modules and regular Masters-level INSET for schools in the Devon area. Nick has previous writing experience, including *Interactive Maths Teaching in the Primary School* with SAGE.

Tony Rea is Principal Lecturer in Education at the University of Winchester, Hampshire and is external examiner on the Adventure Education degree course at the University of Chichester. He has presented and written widely on the subject of outdoor education and learning, and his PhD is based on an ethnography of a residential outdoor education centre. In his spare time Tony enjoys sailing and hill walking.

Sue Rogers is a Senior Lecturer at the Institute of Education, University of London. A qualified primary school teacher and experienced researcher, Sue has worked in Higher Education since 1995, completing her PhD in 2000. Her research interests include early educational policy and play pedagogy. She has published widely in the field of early childhood including two recent books, *Inside Role Play: Researching children's perspectives* with Julie Evans and *Rethinking Play and Pedagogy: Concepts, contexts and cultures* (both Routledge).

Ian Shirley is Senior Lecturer in Primary Music Education at Edge Hill University. He is editor of *Primary Music Today* and he has produced a number of materials to support music education in initial teacher training. He was co-project manager for the Canterbury HEARTS project funded in part by Esme Fairbairn and Paul Hamlyn to explore the pedagogy of arts education in primary schools. He is a musician, choral conductor and a tutor for the national choral organisation Sing for Pleasure.

Emma Sime is a lecturer in physical education at the University of Plymouth. She originally trained as a primary school teacher with a specialism in physical education and has taught in a number of primary schools throughout Devon. Through her work, and her role as subject leader for physical education, she has developed research interests in the role of outdoor adventure education in the development of an individual's self-concept and the facilitation of communities of practice during initial teacher education.

Liz Taplin trained as a physical educationist and taught in secondary schools during the early part of her career, before moving into the primary sector where she focused on developing a physical education programme for Early Years. Liz has worked at the University of Plymouth for two years and has responsibility for teaching on the PGCE and BEd programmes. She is leader of the Outdoor Adventurous Activities module taken by the 2nd Year physical education specialists and previously pioneered a successful OAA residential visit for Year 2 children when she worked in schools. Liz has been the editor of *Physical Education Matters* for 10 years and is a regular contributor in this journal. Liz is currently studying for her PhD, researching the concept of physical literacy and, in particular, what this might feel like for a 7-year-old child.

Linda la Velle has a career spanning 35 years in teaching, centred on Science Education. Her wide-ranging research includes aspects of Biology education, with a particular interest in ethical implications. She also has research interests in e-learning. A recent research project with partners from the Exmoor National Park has been in the use of drama in environmental education.

Karen Wickett is a part-time Lecturer in Early Childhood Studies at the University of Plymouth and a part-time Children's Centre teacher in Somerset. She has many years of experience working in a range of Early Years settings, as a manager and teacher. Within her role as the teacher in a Sure Start local programme she has supported settings in the development of their outdoor learning opportunities for the under-5s. Her research interests lie in understanding the child's motivations in his/her own individual learning journey and developing learning communities for adults and children alike.

Acknowledgements

Thank you to all my fellow contributors for the fascinating and innovative approaches they have shared, to the many practitioners and settings that enabled us to paint this colourful and detailed composite picture of learning outside the classroom. Above all, many thanks to the children, whose sparkle and delight in contexts beyond the classroom stimulated this book.

In particular, the authors of Chapter 12 would like to express their thanks to Norbridge Primary School, in particular George Huthart and Jenny Brad, with the latter being the inspiration for all the school's work on the school garden project, as well as the Royal Horticultural Society who funded this research.

Key for icons

Chapter objectives

Points for practice

Case study

Thoughts on theory

Summary

Further reading

Introduction

Sue Waite

My earliest memories are of being outside: accidentally disturbing a nest and getting stung by angry wasps as a tiny toddler and playing all day and every day in the summer with my cousin on our 'Chocolate Island' in local woods. I began my statistical education learning about bar charts in my rural primary school of only 60 pupils by live trapping and identifying small mammals in our surroundings. These childhood experiences influenced how I brought up my own children. Poking about in the garden and investigating ponds and beaches, muddiness and curiosity were everyday occurrences for them. My own schooling also encouraged me to plan learning outside the classroom in my teaching, with walking tours around the town leading to historical and geographical awareness of the locality and rainy days allowing us to model the formation of rivers and erosion in the school grounds. Yet, I don't think that I really questioned where these impulses came from or what might underpin them until I began to research this area about six years ago. I discovered that, despite evangelical texts extolling the benefits of the outdoors for very young children and a research literature on outdoor education, there was relatively little theory underpinning *how* and *why* learning outside the classroom might be beneficial and for *what*. This book is intended to probe these questions and, crucially, to help you, the reader, to develop your own theories about this. While the majority of the book uses examples that are 'outside' both in the sense of 'not in the classroom' and 'outdoors', the *points for practice* and *thoughts on theory* with proper regard for context could be applied across all forms of learning outside the classroom from museums to marshes.

In Chapter 1 Nick Pratt and I consider several ways in which the relationship between learning and place can be theorised. We think that this may help to gain a better understanding of how learning in contexts within and outside the classroom occurs. We think it is important that the core consideration is how best to facilitate learning for different purposes in these contexts and to acknowledge that places have certain possibilities shaped by cultural expectations. We hope you will return to this chapter to interrogate some of the ideas that are presented throughout the book. All the chapters include case studies to bring theory to life and some focused *thoughts on theory* and *points for practice*. Miles Opie has contributed some of the *ideas for ICT* featured in the main primary age phase chapters.

Following this introduction and the chapter on theory, the book is organised in two ways: by age phase and by types of provision. First, in Section One there are three chapters on early years practice in learning outside the classroom from babies to children aged four/five years old. In the second section of the book the Primary National Curriculum is addressed through clustered areas of learning in a variety of contexts beyond the classroom and these chapters are principally concerned with provision for children in the primary years, aged five to eleven. Deliberately these chapters focus on broader understandings of disciplinary areas than subjects as this approach to learning is most suited to learning outside the classroom where 'subjects' are naturally encountered all together; subjects studied in isolation from how they occur outside school often fit more neatly *inside* the classroom. Furthermore, this breadth allows teachers and schools to provide more continuity with the way in which early years children are taught and learn and capitalise on children's curiosity about the world. The chapters do not attempt to cover all the ways that these areas might be addressed; the case studies represent exemplar innovative approaches to stimulate your thinking. They draw on aspects of theory outlined in Chapter 1, but are also an invitation to the reader to apply and evaluate their own theories. There are references to published texts that have further ideas for practice at the end of the book or included in the Further Reading sections after each chapter. The third section of the book then looks 'outside the box' of schooling with examples of learning outside the classroom with less direct curricular links, such as residential centres, National Parks and other organisations. These chapters offer some food for thought about how external providers and schools can negotiate potentially different aims and practices. The final chapter reflects upon how learning outside the classroom might 'make a difference' to children's lives, not just in the short term but on a grander scale.

Early Years is the most well provided age phase for books on outdoor learning, but I think you will find that the approaches taken in this first section are fresh and thoughtful about theory. A distinctive feature of the book is the inclusion of very young children's need for outdoor experiences from birth. Valerie Huggins and Karen Wickett in Chapter 2 draw on psychological theories of learning and argue that outdoor experiences are essential for very young children for their holistic development as independent learners. They also offer some useful insights into the challenges of a risk-averse culture, so linking to broader socio-cultural influences on our practice. In Chapter 3 Karen and Valerie develop this idea, showing how practitioners can extend children's interests and learning needs using the local community. They discuss how a carefully thought out approach, both respecting and extending family and community values, can strengthen partnership with parents, with corresponding benefits for learning within the family and setting.

Outdoor learning is generally more established in the early years because it is part of curriculum guidance for practitioners, but in Chapter 4 Julie Evans, Sue Rogers and I focus on different ways teachers and children in Foundation Stage and Year 1 approach their outdoor spaces as contexts for learning. We highlight how practitioners' teaching and learning intentions may be received by children in different places and how transition from Foundation Stage play-based learning to the demands of the primary curriculum might be smoothed by pedagogies that are more commonly practised outdoors.

The chapters that follow in Section Two are each concerned with curriculum areas and how learning outside the classroom might contribute in these. Howard Cotton in Chapter 5 demonstrates the interrelationship of language within and beyond the classroom. He suggests that attention to the uses of language for life beyond the classroom setting can increase children's criticality of environmental print, a sometimes taken-for-granted medium of communication, and also acknowledges how cultural factors affect learning.

Socio-cultural theory also underpins Chapter 6, where Nick Pratt argues that the political demands of schooling constrain the potential for teachers to use the outdoors. Careful planning that includes exploratory grounded (horizontal) with disciplinary focused conceptual (vertical) learning is seen as a more appropriate way to teach an essentially abstract discipline such as mathematics outside the classroom rather than with a random set of conceptually diverse activities. Doing, knowing and using are all important elements in understanding mathematics, which can naturally occur within well-planned learning outside the classroom.

In Chapter 7 Beth Gompertz, Julia Hincks and Rachael Hincks-Knight give some wonderfully detailed examples of how school grounds can offer opportunities to explore, observe and carry out scientific investigations in a practical context. The combination of technology and science in this chapter particularly seems to offer the chance to *apply* learning and, as we argue in Chapter 1, an active embodied aspect of learning is an important feature of outdoor learning theory.

Orla Kelly and Roger Cutting advocate the use of drama-based activities in Chapter 8, to teach children about historical, geographical and social aspects of landscapes. Their case study, like the example in Chapter 5 for English, reinforces how role-play used productively beyond the Foundation Stage can enhance children's empathy, understanding and critical thinking, all vital social skills for lifelong learning. Drama-based and narrative pedagogies call for imagination and creativity in teachers, which can be stimulated in and by novel outdoor contexts. These pedagogies coupled with environments rich in variety and lived experience appear eminently well suited to engaging cross-curricular work.

In Chapter 9, while the subject disciplinarity of different arts is acknowledged as important by Jeff Adams, Martin Ashley and Ian Shirley, they also believe primary teachers should inculcate aesthetic appreciation *across* the disciplines through an understanding of how young children develop, relate to others and perceive the world. The case studies essentially advocate child-centred practice and suggest that personal meaning derives from children's experiences beyond the classroom setting. Their examples are a long way from any simplistic notion of art outside the classroom being about 'sketching'. Jeff, Martin and Ian argue that affective education that respects and includes children's lives outside the classroom will tend to encourage intuitive and creative faculties.

The contribution of the outdoors to physical development, health and well-being is discussed by Emma Sime and Liz Taplin in Chapter 10. They draw attention to how 'outside' is in many senses a 'classroom' for PE teachers, which brings us back to question whether it is 'place' in physical terms or 'place' as cultural practices that matters. They also point out that PE may be the child's only regular experience of learning outside, thus it might be pivotal in terms of attitudes for learning outside the classroom across the rest of the curriculum. Emma and Liz use the concept of physical literacy to show progression. They demonstrate how challenge can extend children by gradually moving them outside their comfort zones, and developing skills in understanding the demands and risks of different environments.

In the next set of chapters distinct types of learning outside the classroom are considered. Clearly this book cannot hope to include the vast range available, but Section Three gives a flavour of how some external partners interface with mainstream settings. Tony Rea in Chapter 11 charts the historical background of residential outdoor centres and the cultural position they occupy in the British education system. Outdoor education as offered by many centres has a richer seam of research literature associated with it but its applicability to the learning that is currently privileged in schools and its close cousin 'learning outside the classroom' is somewhat untested. Tony argues that centres are constrained by three main issues: risk aversion regarding health and safety of children; financial pressures on schools; and neo-liberalism and the drive to raise attainment. He sees these acting together to make centres increasingly similar in their pedagogies and purposes to schools.

The question of pedagogies and purpose is also raised in Chapter 12. Rowena Passy and I compare the educational offer of school gardens and Forest Schools. School gardens are accessible and have closer links to school cultural norms, while Forest Schools have developed their own specific training and pedagogical principles, but, like residential centres in Chapter 11, may be becoming increasingly aligned with schools, reinforcing the argument that schooling is dominating broader ideas of education. Both school gardens and Forest Schools vary according to the communities they serve and the individuals running them, so a critical evaluation of their aims and pedagogical approaches for different learning purposes is essential.

Such sensitivity to culture, place and purpose is a recurrent theme in chapters throughout the book. For example, Dave Gurnett, Linda la Velle and I in Chapter 13 report how Exmoor National Park has a distinct culture, framed by an innovative model of 'real experience environmental education'. The first case study details how children's emotional response to experiences of living and dead wildlife forms lasting memories; the second introduces ideas about how physical engagement with historical aspects of local places can enrich multi-curricular learning opportunities. Dave suggests that this form of experiential learning involves the engagement of learners' emotions and senses and leads to increasing knowledge, understanding, responsibility and action regarding environmental issues over time, an essentially psychological perspective.

Repeated and sustained experience over time is also a theme of the last chapter in this section, Chapter 14 by Alan Peacock. Alan provides a valuable overview of several successful examples of how school learning can mesh with the opportunities and objectives of other managed learning spaces. He suggests that staff, both in school and at the learning space outside the classroom, need to understand the value of ongoing collaborative engagement in the planning, preparation and organisation of visits. Other organisations such as Learning through Landscapes and the Eco-schools initiative, which we did not have space to address here, are also well worth investigating online as they have many ideas for practical activities using school grounds. Some example websites are listed on page 213.

The final chapter of the book, Chapter 15, looks at the difference that learning outside the classroom can make and offers me an opportunity to revisit some beliefs and hopes derived from my own experiences in the light of theories we have examined in the book:

▓ that learning outside the classroom is a 'good thing';

▓ that nature and community can contribute to children's lives now and in the future;

▓ that the politically shaped educational landscape may at last be beginning to acknowledge that schooling alone cannot *educate* a child.

1

Theoretical perspectives on learning outside the classroom: relationships between learning and place

Sue Waite and Nick Pratt

Chapter objectives

- A framework for developing a set of personal theories for teaching and learning outside the classroom
- An awareness of different learning theories that might help to understand learning outside the classroom
- An appreciation of the complexity of learning in relation to place: psychological, social, cultural, geographical and historical factors

A head teacher was recently asked to say why practical science, including the use of the outdoors – apparently under threat from health and safety concerns and science experiment videos – was so important to pupils. How would you have responded?

It might, or might not, come as a surprise to you that the head teacher with 30 years' experience was in certain respects unable to answer the question. She gave a fluent response that pointed to her conviction that 'pupils learn more' because it is 'hands-on', 'experiential' and 'enjoyable and engaging', but none of these go very deeply into *how* it makes a difference. Actually, such an explanation appears hard to provide; just how does 'the outside' and 'experience' make learning different? To begin to respond to the challenge of making sense of the relationship between place and learning – the central purpose of this chapter – let us return to the head teacher's comments above and think about what they represent. Pointing to practical science being 'hands-on' shows an implicit sense that *embodiment* is important; we use our bodies in practical activities, but why might this be beneficial? The conviction that pupils learn *more* might suggest that practical science is important to raise school outcomes. However, interestingly, it also points to an implicit model of learning that relates to the acquisition of knowledge in terms of cognition and which probably therefore values how much we know (quantity), rather than its form and its worth (qualities). Claiming that pupils learn more does not address the equally interesting question of more 'what'. The use of the term *experiential* might suggest that the *way* in which we come into contact with phenomena – rather than simply whether we do or not – might have a bearing on *what* is learnt. *Engagement* as the relationship between the learner and the focus of learning is important, and might again point to the need to consider *what* is being learnt and *how*; reinforced perhaps by *enjoyment*.

This analysis demonstrates that any conception of learning, particularly taking account of place and experience, is inevitably complex.

Developing a personal theory for understanding learning in different contexts

In this chapter we suggest that place plays an active part in learning and that developing a personal theory of learning outside the classroom that includes consideration of place can help planning for rich learning opportunities.

 Points for practice

- Consider the 'places' available to you for different learning purposes.
- Think about what meanings these 'places' have for staff, children, community.
- Consider what sorts of learning opportunities would be well supported by these places.

All the space beyond the four walls of the classroom is not a homogeneous 'other' to be regarded simply in contrast to what happens indoors and generally 'a good thing'. Although the UK government's Learning Outside the Classroom Manifesto appears to support this view, it does not go on to explain *why*:

> Learning outside the classroom is about raising achievement through an organised, powerful approach to learning in which direct experience is of prime importance. This is not only about *what* we learn but importantly *how* and *where* we learn. (DfES, 2006a: 3)

In fact, these questions form a useful shorthand evaluation of the appropriateness of place and pedagogy:

- *What* are we trying to teach/learn?
- *How* will this best be supported?
- *Where* is most likely to provide those conditions?
- *Why* is this so?

Different subjects bring particular cultural expectations, applicable regardless of where learning in that discipline takes place, but it might also be reasonable to assume that particular spaces are suitable for different kinds of learning because of the functions and activities that they support. For example, handling different materials can be beneficial in understanding their qualities. If materials are brought into the classroom, while the children may learn about some of their features through direct experience, they do not also learn where they occur in the world. Experiences outside the classroom may therefore seem more 'authentic' and grounded in 'reality' and certainly some of the children in our own research (Waite, 2011) have talked of knowing that something is 'real' in the sense of 'believable' through first-hand experience rather than just being told. Perhaps then, reference to 'reality' and 'authenticity' is understood in relation to *life beyond the educational setting*.

Nevertheless, this does not necessarily mean that the experiences are also 'relevant', another common claim for learning outside the classroom. Relevance comes from the meanings with which people imbue objects and spaces and from how activity fits with cultural expectations. Children in the Western world live their lives and learn both in and outside of formal education; perhaps their learning in both contexts is more easily linked and developed if the boundaries between the two are blurred by application of their learning in either context in the other, so that they see a purpose beyond the expectations of teachers as arbiters of their education. In some cultures such a distinction between places for formal and non-formal learning is less clear-cut and yet we see 'relevance' operating in their play (non-formal learning), where skills to be adopted later in their life are practised through play and participation (Smith, 2010). But the Learning Outside the Classroom Manifesto (DfES, 2006a) seems to yoke education outside the classroom to outcomes valued in schooling, saying it is about '*raising achievement* through an *organised*, powerful approach to learning in which direct experience is of prime importance' (p. 3, emphasis added).

So the opportunities inherent in places for 'relevance' and 'authenticity' to life beyond the educational setting are sometimes not taken up because of cultural transfers. Julian Sefton-Green (2006) notes that 'out-of-school learning' often actually takes place *within* schools in the form of clubs and after-school activities. Many are led by teachers. Although some of these activities are run in a less formal way, the cultural expectations of 'in-school' mean that many are simply 'extensions of the formal curriculum and function like study groups' (p. 4). They are only 'out-of school' in a temporal sense.

Other researchers in outdoor education (such as Brookes, 2002 and Stewart, 2006) argue strongly for awareness of cultural and historical meaning in place-based education. So in addition to emotionally mediated personal responses, students also learn how places have become as they are. However, relevance for the individual, or broader socio-cultural understandings of place, are often subservient to imposed demands, such as raising standards in learning. Yet, Greenwood (2008: 239) believes that the best place-based education 'emerges from the particularities of places, the people who know them best ... and the people who wonder about all the opportunities that might arise from action-oriented place study'. Such place-based learning refers to contexts that have long-term effects through long association with them. Ward Thompson et al. (2008: 132), in a study about how adults use green places, found that children who had not had access to outdoor environments in childhood were unlikely to spend time in the outdoors as adults, with consequent impacts on adult health and well-being.

Other ways of learning may be stimulated by novelty and adventure. Min and Lee (2006), indeed, suggest outdoor spaces for learning need a balance between challenge and security, private and public and meeting current and future, as yet unpredicted, needs. This suggests a high degree of flexibility in the resourcing and landscaping of such areas (Armitage, 1999). However, places may be better understood not simply as areas with geographical boundaries, but rather as places with particular social relations and understandings, which transcend time and space. Consideration of intersubjective experiences is vitally important when thinking about pedagogy and place (McKenzie, 2008), and there are several ways that we can consider learning to take account of subjectivity, culture and place.

Concepts of learning and different focal planes

Learning may be viewed using different focal planes, offering complementary ways to make sense of this complex process that defies any one single explanation. Zooming in tightly, one sees learning in terms of individuals. This is how the head teacher viewed the acquisition of knowledge by learners and echoes Cannatella's (2007) belief in the centrality of *self* in engaging with learning. Often this leads to a focus on the mind and claims that learning takes place through affective associations and (increasingly) reasoned thought, brought about through some conceptual challenge which requires the learner to rethink their conception of something. This is the basis of constructivism and represents a psychological plane of focus.

We cannot look inside the individual but we can take into account what that individual shows us through behaviour. The body is therefore one way we might gain insight into the learning process. How do we know how to adjust our teaching and planning to meet the needs of our children? It is not through X-ray vision of children's mental processes but what their behaviour tells us about how that teaching is being received. Are the children misbehaving, looking blank, fiddling with something? Beard and Wilson (2007: 5) put forward a psychologically based explanation of this conceptualisation in the form of a learning combination lock, where a series of tumblers represent the external environment, senses and internal environment as the person is seen as internalising the environment through their senses. Another way of looking at this positioning of self within the world is that through the mind *and* the social we come to 'know' and 'be' in relationship with our bodies and places and that culture is constructed from the interactions between these. In the model shown in Figure 1.1 this relationship is portrayed in a way that reflects an understanding of place as culturally constructed.

Using different ways of looking at learning in a context-sensitive way, this chapter aims to make more explicit some of the components of the 'holism' claimed for outdoor learning; how terms like *hands-on*, *experiential* and *practical* and the interplay between learning and place might be understood using these planes of focus.

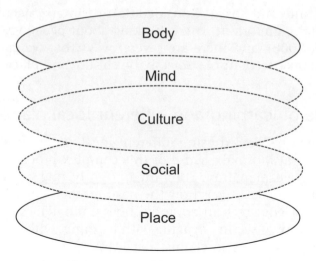

Figure 1.1 The embodiment of place: an individual's interaction in the construction of culture in place

A broader concept of learning

In considering concepts of learning, however, we need to be aware that we are also talking about concepts of education and schooling. Schooling implies a deliberate attempt to learn specific things that are valued within our society, so education can been understood as the manner in which this is organised and managed. Indeed, one of the prime motives for undertaking this book is a desire amongst the authors to unpick something new about how the wider education system has come to shape learning and what contribution 'place' might make to this. More specifically it stems from a shared concern with the way in which 'the classroom' tends to encourage a rather narrow view of what learning might involve and a desire to open up new ideas about this. An opportunity to revisit values for determining curriculum and pedagogy may be a possibility over the next few years. The UK coalition government claims that their invitation to all schools to become academies is 'offering them greater independence and freedom' (DFE, 2010), but since testing in the Primary National Curriculum is set to continue, it remains to be seen whether this 'freedom' and 'independence' is somewhat illusory. However, this is only one of the contributory factors that shape learning in and out of school.

Towards a relational model for learning outside the classroom

One way of reflecting upon the learning environment considers the interaction between the programme, facilitator, group, individual, culture, environment (place) and activity (Neill, 2008). Figure 1.2 illustrates the relationship between the national context of curriculum, standards and guidance, the cultural norms and expectations of the local context and the child, place and 'others' – adults and children – involved in their schooling. It is in the white space between these that pedagogic activity is enacted. Learning opportunities are created in this space through interactions between the three corners of the triangle (child, others and place); all in mutual interaction with the activity. Place will have new meanings and therefore new potentials as a learning context; the child and others will have learnt from the interactions and return to the place with developed expectations. Thus a micro-culture of that particular learning space may be co-constructed. Activity theory is one possible method for working with this conceptualisation. (For further details of activity theory, see Engeström, Miettinen and Punamäki, 1999.)

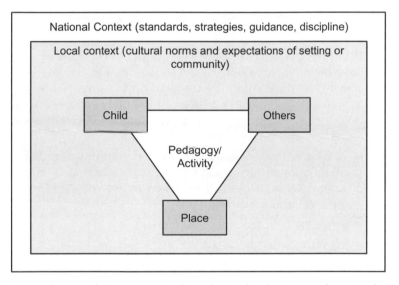

Figure 1.2 The possibility space in the relationship between place, pedagogy and learning (adapted from Waite et al., 2008)

Place in this relational model is an active partner in the learning activities in which the child engages and the pedagogies employed, but this model only captures a snapshot in a dynamic system of interactions. Spaces have particular possibilities, history and associations for children and adults that make them meaningful 'places' and these are constantly being revised by ongoing experiences in them. Repeated visits may result in the establishment of a different set of cultural expectations such as within Forest School programmes (see Chapter 12). On the other hand places that offer some novelty and unpredictability may be valuable in exciting a revision of our ideas (Jarvis, 2009). This might be why wild places lend themselves to transformative learning according to some researchers (Senge et al., 2005). If we accept that place contributes to cultural norms, an unusual context may reduce reliance on 'custom and practice' from the more usual site of learning and open another possibility space. Another explanation might be that power runs through teaching and learning, predominantly from teacher to taught, but if this usual distribution of power is disrupted in new places, different opportunities for learning may arise. Furthermore, if these places are not regularly revisited or stable, teaching and learning practices in them are likely to be more fluid. We therefore need to be alert to different sorts of places, what they make possible and how they are likely to interact with learning intentions.

 Points for practice

A framework for planning learning outside the classroom

Using the diagram in Figure 1.2, consider occasions where you have been teaching both in the classroom and elsewhere. Note down how these might be understood in terms of the model, as well as any implications for planning and practice. The questions below will prompt points to consider. Reflect how they cluster around certain aspects of this model.

- What are the powerful influences on your practice? How might you wish to change your practice to match your values? What theoretical perspectives are you using to interpret your pedagogy?
- What are your teaching intentions?
- Why are these important?
- What places are most suited to this sort of teaching and learning?
- How does the place particularly support the learning?
- What might the place mean to the children?
- What other valuable learning might therefore take place?
- How does this relate to priorities within the setting and nationally?

Review after activity

- What learning have you observed?
- How has the experience contributed on individual, local and national levels?
- Where to next – in learning and spaces?

We now turn to an example of learning outside the classroom taken from Economic and Social Research Council funded research (Waite, Evans and Rogers, 2008) to provide an illustration of how different focal planes allow us to take different perspectives on events and so can enhance our understanding.

Case Study 📁

Pushes and pulls: forces at work in the play park

Laura feels some trepidation in taking this Year 1 class outside. As a supply teacher, she does not know the children very well, although certain ones have already been pointed out to her. The children gather around her on the carpet as she sets out the plans for the lesson on Forces, looking for examples of pushes and pulls in the play park. Nearly all the talking is done by the teacher. In fact, there are nearly twenty behavioural injunctions, principally about how they should *not* behave, and several of these remarks are targeted at the identified children directly; seven teacher comments are about practical arrangements such as who will hold the clipboard and pencil; a mere six relate to the substantive topic of the activity, why they are going out to the play park, and that they will need to put on their 'science hats'. The children are *very* excited about their trip.

In the play park the children are in their assigned groups with a leader (chosen by the teacher and indicated by possession of a clipboard) but they are pulled by the attractions of play in this context that they associate so much with freedom. They debate if play is allowed. One child says: 'We must be doing work, because I have a pencil.' Others are not so sure and lark about, making the most of their surroundings. The group leader adopts the teacher's role, while trying to get them to cooperate in compiling a group list of pushes and pulls in the environment. She herself has to be pushy to try to achieve this, but the interaction is very unidirectional, as it was in the classroom beforehand. 'If I see any silly behaviour!' she admonishes the boys throwing grass. Eventually, she calls on the teacher to reinforce behavioural control in this ambiguous area. 'Right,' says the teacher, 'we're coming away from this play area because you're all playing.' The child replies, 'I'm not playing. I'm just looking.' But the leader of the group rejoins, 'You *was* playing'.

How are we to make sense of what is happening here? The predominant way of thinking about learning is to consider how individuals make sense of the learning objects (forces in this case) and how interactions with others (usually teachers) can help them to develop this sense-making. In this situation though what is most noticeable is that pupils do not engage in the kind of conceptual thinking about forces that the teacher had hoped for. It is tempting to think that this is just misbehaviour, but it is also possible to make sense of it in other terms by looking at it on a wider plane.

First, we might consider why the supply teacher was perhaps more anxious about taking the children out of the classroom. Classrooms are associated with rules (explicit ones certainly, but also many more implicit ones) that allow teachers to control physical and intellectual behaviour, making everyone feel safe, but also strongly affecting what is deemed appropriate for learning. Leaving this haven affords the possibility that the children might 'misbehave' and show up both her and the school in public, perhaps accounting for her heavy emphasis on behaviour in the introduction. She may also have been given the lesson plan. Not only does this mean that she may not have thought through what specific learning points she wanted to support by the experience, but the practice of having 'plans' implies that there is specific learning to be achieved – and hence pressure to achieve it. This may then account for her organisation of pupils and resources. In setting up the groups, she chose children she thought would behave in ways that she deemed appropriate for schooling (mini-teachers), based on well-established social, cultural and historical patterns of 'school' behaviour. Ironically, this left the less motivated children with no symbols of work and perhaps confused therefore as to how this task was meant to operate, leaving them more likely to be seduced by the playful opportunities. Rather than becoming a 'new' experience that offered pupils the chance to appreciate forces in new ways, the group work didn't function as such but became a microcosm of the classroom. Children were not in fact free to engage in novel learning, but were implicitly required to learn in the same ways as a classroom would require. In effect, the class took 'the classroom' out there with them – and even increased the number of teachers! As a result, although the activity took place outside, it was not experiential or hands-on, and the relevance for the children (play) was seen as counterproductive because of the cultural norms that were exported with them from the classrooms.

This is just one of many possible readings of the situation. The learning itself does not differ but application of different focal planes, according to our own beliefs about learning and the questions we want to answer, can help make sense of how to set up and understand appropriate learning opportunities. We therefore turn now to a more detailed examination of these various planes.

A psychological plane

Cumulative learning refers to situations where there is no prior experience, so it is suggested this is how very young children may learn, like a sponge soaking up knowledge. However, anyone who has spent time with a baby is likely to agree that they are far from passive in their learning, encouraging repetition of actions and events that they find interesting. Although ideas of empty vessels to be filled may still linger in instrumental ticking off of 'things to be learnt', the most common form of learning found in schooling is probably *assimilation,* where the learner (and her teacher) incrementally build on existing knowledge. The knowledge that is taught or skills that are shown do not disrupt the expected progression from an existing and relatively circumscribed body of knowledge. However, *accommodative* learning also comes into play where a greater leap is needed to make sense of the new and is more likely to be present where challenge and complex problem-solving is required which calls on prior knowledge, understanding and skills *across* disciplines. It is this type of learning, where the learner makes more prolific and diffuse links with other experience, contexts and knowledge, which may be more easily transferred between situations. This is not to say that a 'piece of knowledge' is carted unchanged from one situation to another but that the many links made enable aspects of the original learning to be re-combined in and for new situations. (For more discussion of this, see Illeris, 2009.)

Jarvis (2009) argues that after initial experiences the cultural meaning rather than the experience is attended to by the learner, so that assimilation may be more likely. This has particular implications for outdoor and experiential learning which often offers opportunities to approach learning anew through novelty. However, we need to take care that such experience isn't understood as culture-free; even 'new' situations are only understood through reference to the past and anticipation of the future. Accommodative learning, though, is especially important for the rapid changing work/life contexts for which we prepare our children and ourselves, where many situations are 'new' to us. The apparent unpredictability of outdoor contexts therefore may afford a better preparation for real-life problem-solving than classrooms that conform to standard regular rituals, including perhaps 'taking the teacher's word for it'!

Reflective practice, which is drawn from one of the most common theories of learning used in outdoor education, Kolb's experiential learning cycle (1984), provides another theoretical vehicle for further engagement of the individual in making a learning opportunity their own. The simplest models of the cycle have been criticised for not taking the situated nature of learning into account and for portraying each 'stage' as discrete (Illeris, 2007: 55); in fact, we are constantly reflecting, planning and doing as we experience. (For further discussion and critique of Kolb's theory, see Jarvis and Parker, 2007: 6–7.) Another aspect of learning which is somewhat overlooked in this tidy model is that sometimes the experience is so out of the normal run of experience that it requires a drastic re-appraisal of what we think we know. A shake-up of our existing ways of thinking can lead to *transformative* learning (Jarvis, 2009). These are the occasions where experience or reflection leads to a re-adjustment not only to our previous ways of thinking but also to our understanding of ourselves, a sort of learning often claimed for wilderness experiences and adventure education.

Meanings may also be different for the individual and 'others' and it is therefore important that all children have an opportunity to be active in their learning, so that they can link these prior meanings to their present and to wider social and cultural meanings. If an adult takes control, the relevance to the child may be reduced, as the learning is mediated through the adult's cultural position (see Chapter 4 for an example of this). Sometimes the local context's cultural influences may be 'exported wholesale' to particular learning spaces, as we saw in the case study earlier. This is to be expected given teachers' investment in establishing norms for behaviour and relationships within schools. However, this practice may also jeopardise capitalising on the unique ways in which different places could shape learning. For example, imagine children being expected to ignore the 'distractions' of the outside world and listen to the teacher while they stand at the edge of the pond in order to learn about frogs, when supported direct observation would be a far more effective way of using that place.

We also know from our research that learning outside the classroom often allows the practitioner opportunities for close observation of children's natural behaviour. This is assessment that is not tied to a particular learning outcome but incorporates a rounded view of social and emotional aspects of learning for children, the holistic aspect mentioned earlier. In child-led activity, the teacher is able to observe and contingently develop the child's own interests enhancing the child's enjoyment. We see some particularly good examples of this in Chapter 3. This endeavour is worthwhile as *engagement* and *enjoyment* have both been found to be valuable in supporting motivation for learning from Early Years to Higher Education (e.g. Carver, 2003; Waite and Davis, 2006; Waite et al., 2009).

Another key question that must be asked in planning and observing learning outside the classroom is *what* is being learnt? Adopting a socio-cultural plane of focus can assist with this question.

A socio-cultural plane

A socio-cultural plane of analysis is not a common way for teachers to think about their work because of the deeply rooted emphasis in our education system on individual cognition (albeit with some social activity involved). There is no single social theory of learning (Jarvis and Parker, 2007), but the central ideas that we want to focus on here are twofold:

- the notion that people participate in activity that is socially orientated and organised;

- the idea that 'understanding' need not be viewed as an individual affair in which people (pupils) 'acquire' knowledge and carry it around with them, but can be seen as being linked more closely to context and experience.

Socially orientated activity

To illustrate further what we mean by activity that is socially orientated, we might ask you a question: have you been behaving normally today? Though we cannot access your answer, the fact that we can ask this and you can consider it points to the idea that there are 'normal' ways to behave within whatever social context you find yourself. We go about our life using well-established practices/behaviours. These practices are embedded in the social context in which we live and work, and are cultural (what we do round here) and historical (we always do it this way).

Schooling is no different. Pupils and teachers operate in customary patterns; one need only watch young children 'playing' schools or consider the behaviour of the leader of the group in the case study above to know this. One way to make sense of classrooms therefore is to think about them in terms of:

- the common *practices* involved (people's actions);

- the *norms* involved (what is usual practice; what it is normal to do);

- the *discourses* involved (how people communicate meaning, both implicitly and explicitly, through language, action and symbolic means, such as clothing, status etc.).

As part of these ideas one can also consider 'rules' that operate within a situation (implicit as much as explicit), the notion of who does what (often referred to as the division of labour) and also the resources one has available to support activity. In thinking then about learning outside the classroom we can consider ways in which taking learning out of the normal environment encourages these practices, norms, discourses, rules and divisions of labour to change in ways that are desirable. If the value of working outside the classroom is in providing pupils with experiences that are different from those inside it, we need a framework and language that allow us to analyse and talk about such experience. So, returning to the class that goes outside to find frogs in the environmental area rather than simply reading books, this may be because we want them to learn to behave in ways that are different to classroom behaviour (as young environmentalists perhaps), as well as to learn 'about' frogs.

Understanding and experience

This example of youngsters learning to behave as environmentalists brings us to our second point about socio-cultural perspectives on learning; the idea that understanding need not always be thought of as an individual affair. This is more than simply saying context matters. The argument is that knowledge cannot be separated from the situation in which it is developed. Children learning about frogs through experiencing them around a pond don't learn 'more' or 'less' about frogs than children whose access is through books or a video; they learn a qualitatively different thing, a different way of 'knowing frogs'. This view of learning, which is often referred to as 'situated understanding', is not 'better' than an individualised, cognitive and affective view but it does offer ways to make sense of learning in terms of context, which is important in thinking about the role of place.

While culture itself is the product of social construction, the meaning of culture is continually being interpreted through our learning and enacted in our lives. So, in practice, it is not a question of nailing one's colours to the mast of socio-cultural or psychological/psychosocial theories of learning, but rather developing a personal theory about how these shed light and operate in the contexts in which one lives and works. Using different planes of focus helps us to approach different questions we may have about children's learning and our own teaching, but as Wenger (2009: 215) says: 'A perspective is not a recipe; it does not tell you what to do. Rather it acts as a guide about what to pay attention to, what difficulties to expect, and how to approach a problem.' In this book we hope that the stories we tell of practice and the theories we link with these in the following chapters will help readers each to make personal sense of what will help and guide them as practitioners.

Using different planes for different purposes

In terms of learning outside the classroom, our research leads us to think that cultural pressures associated with schooling (such as meeting standards, conforming to agreed targets, following plans) may be more intense where the social and institutional are more established, such as *within* schools. After all, where there are guidance documents, strategies and institutional policies, 'culture' is made more manifest. This is not to say that these outward signs are *the* 'culture' in any straightforward, unambiguous way; you probably hold your own views about what elements you agree with in these externally acknowledged policies and your personal beliefs (invisible culture) will inevitably colour the impacts of these policies (visible culture) on your practice. However, it is possible that novel situations, such as some of those outside the classroom, may represent a greater freedom for personal resistance to and inter- pretations of general norms. It is worth bearing in mind too that this freedom may not just be experienced by you as practitioner but also by learners. They too bring their own socio-cultural and historical values constructed from the histories of their family, community and peer group to the party!

Thus, our responses shape learning inside and outside the formal context of the classroom. Thinking of our own lives and of the children we have taught, we remember very different attitudes being shown to apparently identical sets of resources or places. This awareness of individual response may explain why the idea of 'personalisation' in learning is seductive. It is championed by government in a challenging and sometimes puzzling dynamic with recommendations for more objective-led teaching. Personalisation may be partly attributable to the uniqueness of experience through the distinct psychological understanding that each of us brings to our social and cultural worlds. Clearly it follows that places or learning opportunities are not always viewed in a standard fashion. On a psychological plane, our personality shaped by processes of socialisation throughout our lives means that we all experience events with potential for learning in different ways – what is offered is different to what is received because the learner brings her own past, present and aspirations for the future to bear on that. This personal response may be the 'engagement' that the head teacher spoke of, making links or 'engaging' with the learner's prior experience, and future hopes in the learning of the present and actual. Each child will ask (consciously or unconsciously): 'What does this (experience) **mean *to*** (in relation to my past and present) and *for* (in relation to my future) me?' Meaning and purpose are central for valuing what is learnt and, for that learning to be enduring, forging many links with other memories is helpful.

On the other hand, a wider lens suggests a problem with this tighter analysis. Although at the micro level each individual has experiences that are clearly different, at the macro level there is a strong sense of commonality between people, rooted in the social discourses within which they operate. The pupils in the play park mentioned earlier might, on the surface of things, have appeared to be free to 'see' anything they liked, but what is valued, and therefore what is valuable to see, is bounded by the social expectations of schooling, even when the children are not in the classroom. The trip was about forces and schooling dictates that objectives are met; issues of 'playing' therefore are only problematic because schooling is culturally and socially required to be about 'learning' and school learning means making focused, articulated observations about the issue under study. Interestingly, this plane of analysis is also always a political (small 'p') one in the sense that it asks questions about values. This is illustrated in considering notions of 'ability'. The main way we measure ability in schools is in the way pupils write and talk about ideas, but if outdoor learning offers pupils the chance to engage with the world in more tacit, experiential ways, then we need to reconsider this. An expert environmentalist is not expert because of his or her ability to talk about the environment. Rather, it is the ability to *do* the things that are central to expertise in the world of environmental science and indeed many other occupations. This mismatch between measures of achievement and desirable abilities brings into question how appropriate schooling in its current form might be for supporting vocational aspects of learning, but also implies that whilst working outdoors might seem like a good idea, it may conflict with other priorities within a teacher's professional life.

Returning to our head teacher's explanation for the value of practical learning, being 'hands on' makes learning potentially more direct and less mediated by another's meanings. An important skill as a teacher is in facilitating; after all, no one but the learner can learn *for* them. As learners, we implicitly call on our rich history of associations to forge links to make new knowledge, skills or understandings particularly meaningful, relevant and therefore more memorable for us. Involvement of the body in learning is another way in which more links are constructed. Children in our research have commented that 'hands-on' first-hand experience makes the learning more real and believable (Waite et al., 2006), but whether this leads to learning in a form that is useful for schooling remains an issue – and a challenge perhaps to develop new ways of understanding (and assessing) learning.

Furthermore, the head teacher's idea of 'enjoyment' is not simply a general hope that the learner will enjoy school but is underpinned by empirically evidenced associations, first from research into motivation (Hufton et al., 2002; Waite and Davis, 2006) and secondly from brain research which shows how important affect and emotional loading of memories are in their application in future situations (Carver, 2003; Waite, 2007). So the fact that children often mention wanting more outdoor and practical activities should indicate to us that it is worthwhile accommodating their preferences if we want them to remember. It may therefore be helpful to consider both emotional loading (psychological) and 'belonging' (psychosocial) in considering how to make learning experiences memorable. And so we come full circle to the value of personal theories employing various planes of focus in negotiating the relational complexity of learning and place.

 Thoughts on theory

- How do you conceptualise learning: as principally psychological, psychosocial, socio-cultural or a mixture of all three? [Your personal theory of learning.]

- Are some aspects more emphasised than others in your setting? [The local context.]

- What aspects of learning do you place the most/least value on? [Your personal values.]

- How could you better accommodate your personal concept of learning in your own practice? [Reconciliation of local context and personal values and theory.]

- What are the implications of this personal view for the way you choose to teach and use spaces beyond the classroom and for changes that might need to be made at the wider policy level of your teaching context? [Your plans.]

Summary

This chapter has outlined a number of ways in which learning and place can be viewed and has encouraged you to consider what your personal understandings are. Using different ways of looking may help to gain a better understanding of how learning in contexts within and outside the classroom occurs and this should support your thinking about how best to facilitate learning for different purposes. Clearly in a short chapter, we cannot hope to address this wide theme in great depth but we have provided pointers to further reading if aspects have caught your attention. The chapter should also be a useful resource to return to as you dip into the chapters that follow pursuing your own interests in supporting learning outside the classroom.

Further reading

Illeris, K. (ed.) (2007) *Contemporary Theories of Learning*. London: Routledge.

Jarvis, P. and Parker, S. (2007) *Human Learning: An Holistic Approach*. London: Routledge.

Nabhan, G.P. and Trimble, S. (1994) *The Geography of Childhood*. Boston: Beacon Press.

Section 1

Early Years Practice –
Reaching Out

The following three chapters concern early years provision in learning outside the classroom for children aged from birth to 5 and 6 years of age. The section starts with some thoughts about outdoor provision for very young children in Chapter 2, moves in Chapter 3 to a consideration of community visits for a broader age range of pre-school children and in Chapter 4, within a school context, focuses on the particular challenges of moving from rich play-based outdoor learning opportunities in the Foundation Stage to sharp reductions of these in Year 1 of primary school.

2

Crawling and toddling in the outdoors: very young children's learning

Valerie Huggins and Karen Wickett

Chapter objectives

- An understanding of the importance of outdoor learning experiences for children aged under 3

- An appreciation of the important constituents of appropriate outdoor activities

- An awareness of the issues around risk to children under 3 in the outdoor environment

---

By the time children are 3 years old they have learned much about the nature of the world they live in, how to behave within it and how to react in different situations. Clearly, this has been shaped by the attitudes and behaviour of those around them, but a major part of the learning has come from their active investigation of the physical world (Jarvis, 2009).

In much of the developing world, it is taken for granted that for children aged 0–3 a great deal of this learning will take place outdoors, whether carried by relatives going about their work, or with siblings/peers playing in the vicinity of their home (Forbes, 2005; Gottlieb, 2004; Lindon, 2005). The natural world is a familiar part of their growing experience and understanding. However, today this is less and less true of children in countries of the developed world, such as the UK. Many of us fondly remember going 'out to play', the opportunities it offered in terms of the freedom away from adults for significant lengths of time, the chance to get messy and dirty in a natural environment and to be with friends (Tovey, 2007; Waite, 2007), yet it seems that there have been significant changes in recent years that are restricting children's exposure to the natural world (Hope et al., 2007; Waters and Begley, 2007).

Nowadays the opportunities for children to play outside their homes or to walk around in their local community appear much more limited, due to changes in lifestyle and parental work patterns (Fjørtoft, 2004; Waller, 2007). Even when they do go outside the home they are often pushed in a buggy, to help the journey to go quicker than walking at a toddler's pace, or cocooned in a car. Children are separated from the natural world, often enveloped in plastic and protective clothing. Much more of their time is now spent in man-made environments and with bought toys and equipment. Heightened concerns about children's safety have compounded this and many young children are now in danger of having very little contact with the outdoor environment.

Alongside these changes, a significant number of children under 3 now spend a large proportion of their time in early years settings (Brooker, 2009), due to the pressure on mothers to return to work. In theory, they are entitled there to a full range of learning experiences, both inside and out, as laid down by the Early Years Foundation Stage framework.[1] The Practice Guidance document (DfES, 2007: 5) states that 'the environment plays a key role in supporting and extending children's learning and development' and that effective practice should provide 'opportunities to be outside on a daily basis all year round' (Practice Card 3.3). However, the framework does not lay down national standards for outdoor provision and in many settings outdoor opportunities for our youngest children are still very restricted (Tovey, 2007).

1 The Early Years Framework in England (DfES, 2007) has a series of Practice Cards in its Guidance document that articulate key principles and points for practice.

Why is it important for very young children to have substantial experience of the outdoor environment?

 Thoughts on theory

- A key element of the learning within the 0–3 age group is how they make sense of first-hand experience gained from their active investigation of the immediate environment (e.g. Doherty and Hughes, 2009; Forbes, 2005; Lindon, 2005).

- Underpinning this is investigation, movement and the use of all their senses – hence Piaget's description of the sensori-motor stage.

- Particularly powerful in the process is when they encounter novel, disconcerting and difficult situations, which force them to adapt and extend their existing skills and knowledge. Due to the novelty of large parts of their experience in the 0–3 age group, this involves more substantial levels of accommodation than the predominantly assimilative later stages of educational provision noted in Chapter 1.

- It is also vital that they are able to set up their own challenges so that these are well matched to their ability and interests, and that they are able to end or withdraw from them if they feel uncomfortable. This in turn will aid independence and self-regulation in their learning.

All this suggests that there may be important aspects of learning and development that children aged 0–3 are in danger of missing out on if restricted in their contact with the outdoors. One reason for this may be because their agenda is much less to do with being taught specific things that are valued in our society (see Chapter 1) and more about discovering the nature of their world. The focus therefore is much more centred on the triangle in Figure 1.2, see page 7, interacting with significant others and their immediate locale. Davis, Rea and Waite (2006) would argue that there is important learning to be gained in the 0–3 age group because even children that young have innate predispositions to values shaped by aspects of the natural world. If young children are kept away from the natural world and given the message that it is messy, dirty, even dangerous, then this restricts their development and instils negativistic values.

Although the man-made indoor environment is undeniably rich in learning possibilities, outdoor experiences promote a child's cognitive, emotional and physical development (Harding, 2005) in particular ways that are different from, or significantly extend, the experiences available indoors. Take the activity of picking up small objects and dropping them into a bucket, something most toddlers find engrossing. This can be done inside, e.g. with plastic construction bricks provided by an adult, but such materials are standardised and sanitised. Independently finding and picking up stones or pebbles outside is enormously more varied, unpredictable and interesting. The underside of the stone may be moist or muddy, may even conceal a minibeast. The bucket may contain some rain water or mud. Learning how to avoid getting wet and muddy (or trying to get wetter!) and how to clean oneself afterwards becomes a significant part of the learning. It is very important to emphasise that since most outdoor learning for this age group has to be grounded in first-hand experience, it is inevitable for them sometimes to get wet, muddy, dirty and to graze themselves or prick their fingers. This is all part of the learning. Preventing it happening hugely inhibits their learning.

Learning about the nature of the physical world

Being in an outdoor environment gives very young children the opportunity to experience more aspects of the natural world (Harding, 2005) and stimulates all their senses, for example, being able to listen to a wide range of sounds, from the gentle rustle of the leaves to the engine of a jet plane overhead, and to encounter a range of textures, from the gossamer of a spider's web to the sliminess of a snail's trail to the roughness of tree bark. It is an environment full of surprises and wonders – imagine watching for the first time the intricacy of a spider spinning a web. This provides a range of concrete, sensori-motor knowledge that can only be fully learned outside. It is this sense of change in the natural world that can so excite their curiosity.

Case Study

Seasons in the sand

On a very cold winter day in January Max and Ellie were busy banging the sand with sticks in the outside sand pits. The water in the sand had frozen. It made a cracking sound as it was banged and bits of ice and sand were chipped away. The sand could be picked up in large lumps. It did not crumble but stayed solid and icy cold in the children's hands.

(Continues)

(Continued)

Two weeks later the weather had warmed up. The ice melted and the rain came. This time Ellie was in her welly boots standing in the water-logged sand pit. She bent down carefully so as not to let the water into her boots. Using a spade she scooped the sand from the bottom of the sand pit. As she lifted the sand out of the water the sand was smooth, slimy and dark in colour. Holding the spade filled with sand in front of her she watched as the water dripped from the spade. First the drips were quick and then they slowed down.

Six weeks later, the sand pits had dried out and the sun was warm. This time Max, exploring the sand, had removed his shoes and trousers. He had a brush, which he dipped into the shallow water feature (a river), and then rubbed into the dry sand. The dry sand stuck to the brush and marks were made in the sand. When he had decided there was enough sand on the brush he would paint a wood railway sleeper with the sandy, watery paint. He repeated this sequence for about an hour until the railway sleeper was covered in a fine layer of sand.

This case study illustrates that frequent access to the outdoor environment exposes the children to the variations of the natural world and gives them direct experience of the changing weather and seasons, together with the impact of these on the environment. This variety and unpredictability challenges and extends their thinking and understanding and enhances their developing skills.

Learning through movement

Movement underpins all other areas of early development (Doherty and Hughes, 2009), whether physical, intellectual or social, and is essential for young children. Between 0 and 3 they grow more rapidly than at any other stage of life, and in this very short space of time the majority progress from lying to sitting to crawling to toddling to running, jumping and swinging. Smith (2010) describes very clearly the importance of gross locomotor movement to children's physical development, starting at the end of the first year and peaking at around 4–5 years of age. When they are deprived of it for a while they tend to overcompensate for lost time, which is one reason why when the door to a setting's outside area is opened children often explode outside and initially run around wildly.

The outdoor environment gives children wider spaces in which to move more freely, hopefully without the risk of adult disapproval. It also offers less predictability as things may not be what they seem. Toddlers mostly learn to walk inside, but having got used to walking on a flat surface, the varied terrain outside provides challenge and risk, and opportunities to learn and develop the skill in different ways. A gentle slope for a toddler can seem like a mountain for a crawling baby. The same applies to stairs. Uneven steps and stepping stones outside help the children to develop their climbing skills. A path that is easily negotiated when dry becomes slippery in the rain, or hard to stand up on in a strong wind, causing physical disequilibrium, and the toddler learns that things cannot be taken for granted in the same way as they can indoors. This forces them to revisit and extend their learning. Even some 3-year-olds may need this kind of extension of learning, as shown in the case study below

Case Study

The ups and downs of gross motor skill development

Billy, a physically confident and lively 3-year-old boy, brought up in a very level urban area, was visiting his new preschool setting for the first time. On arrival he excitedly ran into the undulating landscape outside area. Being unaware of how a downhill slope would speed him up, he lost control and tumbled head-over-heels. He was shocked and upset. But during his first week he was seen running down the same slope over and over, at first tentatively, then with growing skill and confidence. Eventually, he progressed to practising his recently mastered forward roll on the slope, clearly enjoying the acceleration imparted by the slope.

Developing attitudes

Learning is intrinsically linked to motivation, and the sense of well-being, freedom and enjoyment that the children gain from being outdoors aids that motivation, as outlined in Chapter 1. They are often constrained in adult-controlled environments, and so benefit from the sense of being free which the outdoors can offer. Indeed it has strong associations for all of us with a sense of freedom and openness (Waite, 2007). Jumping, bouncing and splashing water, as well as opportunities to be boisterous and noisy, are usually more possible and more acceptable in an outdoor context than indoors.

Another positive feature of the outdoors is its unforgiving but non-judgemental nature. A puddle of water will not make allowances for a toddler who does not realise that her trainers are not waterproof, but nor will it be disapproving of her getting her feet wet! It is an

excellent context for young children to learn about the consequences of their actions; to set their own challenges rather than have
them artificially set (and then judged) by adults, and, like Billy in the
preceding case study, to set their own timetable for meeting them. In
doing so they will develop the ability to deal with frustration, temporary difficulty and painful experiences, even 'failure' at times, and
develop their confidence, resilience, persistence and endurance.

Case Study

Challenge and persistence

Jill, wearing a long apron, filled a bucket to the top with water from the
outside tap. She carefully carried the water up and down the hillock. This
was challenging as she had to make sure she did not step on the apron
as it dragged on the ground on her way up the mound. She persevered
walking up and down the hillock. As she went, she watched the water
intently in her bucket, trying not to spill any. However, initially some
water was spilt. This made the surface slippery which meant climbing
became even more of a challenge. Despite these adverse climbing conditions she persisted with this activity for 20 minutes until she had
mastered travelling up and down the terrain.

It is also vital for young children to feel at home in the natural world
and that they belong there (Davis et al., 2006). This can only come
with familiarity and lots of opportunities to explore and experience
it from a very young age, which will provide an important basis for
subsequent learning, for instance about the significance of conservation and sustainability. Children's need for such frequent and
continuing experience should also remind us of a vital point.
Although we are focusing in this chapter on the particular importance of these experiences for children under 3 they should continue
to be offered throughout the EYFS and into the primary phase.
Opportunities to explore the world outside the home and the classroom promote positive dispositions towards lifelong learning,
mentioned in Chapter 1.

Characteristics of an enabling environment for outdoor learning for babies and young children

If we are saying that outdoor learning experiences are essential to
young children's learning and development, what do we need to
provide and how? What is the role of the adult, and how can we
enhance the quality of the experiences?

Given a choice, children will very often choose to be outside, yet allowing young children to do so in an early years setting frequently poses some particular challenges. It is often easier to minimise their exposure in order to avoid difficulties, rather than giving babies and toddlers these opportunities and organising a rich and stimulating provision for them.

Availability of physical space

Ideally every setting would have access to a substantial outdoor space, but many settings have a very limited space. However, even a small area can offer considerable opportunities for movement and sensory exploration if well planned. There needs to be a variety of levels and textures for children to experience, whether sitting, crawling or walking. It is therefore very important that significant parts of the area should be natural and not simply covered in a safety surface and resourced with bought toys and equipment.

It is also important not to over-sanitise the area. Slipperiness, muddiness, dampness are all desirable sensory resources. Cut grass, fallen leaves and twigs, stones, should not be quickly tidied away. They can offer endless opportunities for exploration, as well as props for imaginative play.

Very young children also enjoy being out of sight, from early games of peek-a-boo to hide and seek and den building, so, as Tovey (2007) suggests, a range of small hiding places need to be provided. Children will feel these places to be intimate and hidden even though an adult may still be able to see into them.

Careful consideration also needs to be given to the timing of children's access to the outdoors. One of the messages from the Early Years Foundation Stage framework (DfES, 2007) is that there should be a free flow between the outside and inside environments throughout the day. For children who are not yet mobile, the practitioners need to ensure that the children are taken outside at different times during the day, and as they start to crawl and toddle the children should be encouraged to go outside independently.

The practitioners should also avoid restricting access to a range of experiences. Tovey (2007) gives a lovely example of a crawling baby who wants to explore the wet grass and the practitioner who wants her to stay dry and clean. Tovey suggests the solution to the dilemma is some waterproofs but this raises the question of whether such clothing would restrict her investigation of the wetness. Direct physical experience is so very important.

Another aspect of access is that young children need extended time to explore their ideas, develop their understanding, and overcome their own set challenges, so restricting access to short timetabled slots in the outdoor area is not desirable. There should be flexibility in the routines.

The role of the adult

The crucial underpinning aspect of the role of the adult is to have a clear personal theory about young children's learning, without which practitioners are likely to make limited and tokenistic attempts at providing for outdoor learning and at worst may restrict access and instil negative attitudes in the children.

In setting up the environment   Practitioners with a deep knowledge of child development and an understanding of the ways that very young children learn most effectively will be able to see the unique potential in any outdoor learning environment, however limited it may appear. The notion of what the environment can 'afford' to different children at different stages of development can be a very useful tool when considering what to provide in terms of resources and adult support. Thus a tree stump can afford a tactile experience for a sitting baby, a solid base for a pull to standing for an older baby and a place for climbing and jumping by the time the child is 3. Nevertheless, practitioners should avoid the trap of deciding in advance what the environment can offer; they need to be aware that there is always an ongoing interaction between the environment and the child. The changing elements and contexts in the natural world transform the child's responses and play behaviours, while the individual child can transform the environment through their choices from all the possibilities that it offers. The outdoor learning environment is constantly changing and so the children can try out the same ideas in different contexts, as we saw in Billy's case study.

The provision needs to be matched to the mental and physical abilities of the children, which again is a challenge when one considers how diverse these are between 0 and 3. Practitioners need to pay particular attention to planning experiences that meet the unique developmental needs and interests of babies and toddlers

(Wellhousen, 2002), since these can be overlooked in making provision for a mixed-age group.

During a very short period of time, most children progress from rolling over, sitting, crawling, standing, to walking, and go on to move up and down steps, kick, catch, slide, run, jump and climb. This range of movement opportunities should also offer an element of 'scariness' to develop their sense of overcoming challenges. The outside area also offers the potential for young children to be a lot noisier than inside, not only by allowing them to experiment with their voices, but also to move at the same time. A wide range of resources can be provided to shake, rattle and bang in different parts of the area.

Whilst physical movement and exercise play is vital for this age group, it is not the only important aspect of being outside. The children need to be encouraged to move freely in the space, transporting resources, changing the pace and flow of their play without feeling the constraints of being able only to do certain things in a particular place. Thus a wide range of transportable, open-ended resources is much more appropriate than fixed, predetermined ones. Infants can progress from functional play to pretend play as young as 12 months old and the outdoor environment gives them space to be animals, vehicles and so on. These pretend play experiences happen naturally and are often unpredictable but access to a wide range of natural resources supports the children's imaginations as they move towards using more abstract objects. Thus, for example, stones, leaves and twigs can become food or money in the game. The variety of levels and spaces within an outdoor area (Harding, 2005) can also provide the backdrop for a range of role play scenarios and encourage children to move. All this adds richness to the possibilities within the outside space.

The Early Years Foundation Stage framework (DfES, 2007) advocates that the learning environment should be integrated in and out, with free flow between them. This gives opportunities for children to make connections in their learning, e.g. between small marbles in paint in a tray inside, and large balls in a bucket of water outside. Both will make tracks and patterns when rolled around, splash when bounced, but as the children explore them they will notice differences and similarities themselves. It also promotes the idea of providing for the six areas of learning outside as well as in. Some settings have interpreted this as having to have 'learning bays' for each area in the outdoor space, distinct from each other, but as Tovey (2007) points out, this can be restricting. Certainly, with the

Early Years Foundation Stage framework now also applying to the under-3s there is a real concern that infants and toddlers in a setting may be provided with a scaled-down version of provision for older children. There may also be more adult-directed activities outside. The result of this could be that children are constantly organised, supervised and monitored, with no 'adult-free' zones.

In interacting with the children   With children 0–3 the adult role will largely be supporting and extending the child's own focus of exploration. This support should always be informed by the adults' knowledge of the child's capabilities and interests, based upon observations. They will also need at times to manage the child's anxieties and frustrations. At this young age children are very limited in experience and prone to try out things that may be beyond their reach. They want to be independent and do things for themselves, and so may get frustrated when they are not able to. The adults need to be patient, supportive and yet firm in the face of the often unexpected eruptions of rage and fury that can occur during the day.

Each setting needs to discuss and establish a shared effective pedagogy for the outdoor learning environment consistent with the approach inside. A shared community of practice is needed within the setting, whereby a range of opportunities are provided for the children to explore as a group and as individuals, based on focused observations (Luff, 2009). For example, if you observe a group of children playing with water, each will be sharing the experience, but also pursuing their own exploration. Even their emotional responses will be different, with some thrilled to be getting wet, others not noticing, and a few distressed by it. This need for personalised contingent responses by the facilitator of learning in a group context extends the individually based model in Figure 1.2 in Chapter 1, as illustrated in Figure 2.1.

Sensitive adults, tuned in to these children (Brooker, 2009), can support, extend, console with language, gesture, physical contact, and so on, but need initially to have a good understanding of child development, of the children in their care and of the potential for learning for the individual in the given context. This is complex, and requires high-order thinking.

Attempts to 'teach' directly should be limited, and always reviewed very carefully to consider their suitability. The adults may also need to overcome instinctive and cultural urges to over-supervise, over-direct and over-protect these very young children. Although the children need to be closely supervised, the adults must balance the responsibility to keep them safe with the responsibility to give them the freedom to explore and learn. All too often concerns about health and safety take over when outside and the adults become much more supervisory and controlling.

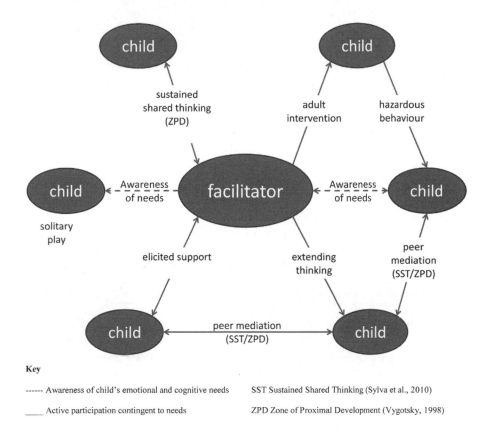

Key

------ Awareness of child's emotional and cognitive needs

_____ Active participation contingent to needs

SST Sustained Shared Thinking (Sylva et al., 2010)

ZPD Zone of Proximal Development (Vygotsky, 1998)

Figure 2.1 Contingent facilitation and diverse possibility spaces in a group activity (diagram developed by Waite based on Huggins)

Dealing with risk

There are several barriers to providing a range of stimulating and exciting outdoor learning experiences for babies and toddlers in a setting. These include settings with very limited outdoor resources, the downward pressures from the Early Years Foundation Stage framework, the tendency of adults to underestimate and belittle the competence of 0–3s and a cultural tendency within early years to equate caring with protection, restriction and prevention.

However, the largest element of this barrier is the recent growth of a

'risk-aware' and 'risk-averse' culture in the UK. Penn (2010) stresses that the expectations and norms of childhood are vastly different across the world. This was brought home recently to a group of teacher trainees from the UK when they saw 3-year-olds in a suburb of a town in The Gambia being let out of the nursery school gate and allowed to walk home alone at the end of the day. Sandster and Tovey presented papers at a 2006 conference (cited in Waters and Begley, 2007) which strongly suggested that Norwegian teachers, whilst concerned about risk, were more willing to allow children to engage in risky activities than their English colleagues. UK practitioners, under pressure from many parents, and anxious about their liability if anything goes wrong, are increasingly concerned to avoid risk. But an element of risk cannot and should not be eliminated or prevented because research into young children's risk-taking strongly suggests that it can have huge benefits (Waters and Begley, 2007).

 Thoughts on theory

- A clear distinction can (and should) be made between *risk-taking* behaviour 'in which there is uncertainty about the outcomes' (Little, 2006: 3) and *hazardous* behaviour, which can reasonably be predicted to result in harm or damage (Stephenson, 2003).

- Risk-taking is part of children's normal development and needs to be viewed positively (Maynard, 2007). Children need the opportunity to take risks and evaluate them, so that they will become able to identify and manage risks for themselves.

- Children actively seek out and enjoy physical challenges in their play (Stephenson, 2003), including the excitement of feeling a bit scared (Little, 2006), and their willingness to take risks in the physical domain leads on to taking risks emotionally, intellectually and socially (Waters and Begley, 2007).

- As taking risks and meeting challenges is enjoyable for young children, there may be links between young children's risk-taking and a subsequent positive disposition towards learning (Waters and Begley, 2007).

Thus practitioners' supporting positive risk-taking is important, and Little (2006) argues that they need to have a good understanding of the range of factors that affect risk-taking behaviours, such as the child's gender, temperament and sensation-seeking tendencies.

Points for practice

- Provide INSET to clarify the difference between risk and hazard.
- Monitor situations/environments to predict/eliminate serious hazards.
- Calculate carefully the balance between permission and protectiveness. Tend to err on the side of permission.
- Examine critically with colleagues your own instinctive responses to risk, which may well tend to over-restrict.
- Negotiate with the staff team and families to establish agreement over such matters as acceptable levels of risk.
- Accept that unforeseeable accidents will always occur. The closest possible adult supervision cannot prevent them, but will certainly hugely restrict children's learning.

Case Study

Protection from learning?

The Reception class outdoor area had been covered in safety surface. Large and heavy cylinders from a building site had been provided. Often a child would climb into the lying down cylinder and their friends would push them along.

One day these cylinders were in the school playground, where the surface was tarmac. A child came up to the adult looking very upset and holding his hand. She bent down and he told her he had hurt his fingers in the cylinder. After listening to him, they discussed what had happened. He said his fingers were holding on the outside of the cylinder as it rolled along. This was when he hurt his fingers. Using the cylinders only on the safety surface had almost set the children up to hurt themselves when playing on other surfaces. This child had not thought about the consequences and that playing on tarmac would be different than on a safety surface.

It is also very important to recognise that the early years setting should be an optimal situation for children aged 0–3 to take risks, being more organised and safer than the wider environment. Also, at this age the children have a range of self-protective instincts and strategies. Very young children move more slowly, are instinctively cautious and are light, flexible and close to the ground. A toddler tripping and falling hits the ground with a fraction of the force of the adult in a similar accident. Thus the overwhelming majority of their injuries are minor and usually beneficial in learning terms.

Of course, practitioners and parents need a shared consensus about what is acceptably risky and what is unacceptably hazardous, sometimes involving tricky negotiations. But in arriving at a consensus, we should all bear in mind Stephenson's powerful statement:

> The discourses that surround us tend to focus us on the 'darker' side of risk – seeing the uncertainty, the possibility of failure, of injury. As teachers, however, it is important that we ensure that the positive aspects of risk are also acknowledged – the possibility of discovering that one is adventurous, daring, brave, strong, confident and successful. (2003: 4)

 ## Summary

In this chapter we have put forward arguments drawing on psychological theories of learning that outdoor experiences are essential for very young children in order to promote their holistic development. We have also discussed the difficulties that practitioners have in operating within a risk-averse culture, even though children benefit from exposure to risky activities that challenge them, so linking to broader socio-cultural influences on our practice. We conclude that it is imperative for settings to provide a wide range of opportunities for babies and toddlers to explore the natural world in order to encourage and develop self-directed learning.

Further reading

Little, H. (2006) Children's risk-taking behaviour: implications for early childhood policy and practice. *International Journal of Early Years Education*, 14 (2): 141–154.

Tovey, H. (2007) *Playing Outdoors: Spaces and Places, Risk and Challenge.* Maidenhead: Open University Press.

3

Using the local community as part of the early years learning environment

Karen Wickett and Valerie Huggins

Chapter objectives

■ An awareness that the setting's learning environment includes resources and experiences within the local community

■ An awareness of how children's interests and learning needs can inform and shape the focus of visits within the community

■ An appreciation of the benefits to children from making links and building on children's learning experiences beyond the setting

---

Barbara Rogoff tells an illuminating story about 'a child of 3 years from a Mayan community in Guatemala who was more interested in church than was the rest of her family; every evening, she put on her shawl over her head and went to services at a church four blocks from her home, returning about 2 hours later' (1990: 9). It is evident within this scenario that this child recognises the possibilities beyond her home and has a strong identity in her local community. Rogoff later comments that if a child is 'free to navigate in their own community, they often choose to be where the action is' (1990: 91). For us this has important implications for early years settings. We are not suggesting that children should be able to leave and return from the setting as and when they please – our concerns over health and safety would prevent that. However, we consider that there are significant benefits to using the resources offered by the local community although we also recognise that there can be barriers between the setting, the home and the community which may significantly reduce possibilities for the children's learning.

As practitioners we are strongly encouraged to use the setting's local community. Within the Learning Outside the Classroom Manifesto it states that settings need to 'identify ways of encouraging parents, carers and the wider community in learning outside the classroom activities' (DfES, 2006a: 20). Within the Early Years Foundation Stage (DfES, 2007), practitioners are required to recognise the wider context of a child's learning and development, such as their home life and local community. In this chapter, we define the local community as the range of people, places, facilities, businesses and institutions with which the setting has meaningful contact. Therefore each setting's provision will be different because of its geographical location and the diversity of the population within the surrounding community.

It is now also widely recognised that every child has his/her own unique experiences (DFES, 2007; Fisher, 2008) within the community which he/she will bring to their setting. Early Years practitioners should be considering the child's 'current interests, development and learning' (DfES, 2007: Card 3.1), as influenced by contacts within the local community, when planning the next steps for his/her learning and development. These experiences outside the setting shape the child's understanding of themselves and the world around them and enable them to practise and develop skills.

For many settings, 'within the community' is simply a matter of the whole class/setting being taken on one or more 'visits', which may only happen at certain times of the year. Often the focus of these visits is determined by the adults to fit in with a theme or an event during the year and so 'designed explicitly for the socialization or education of the child' (Rogoff, 1990: 87). For instance, an urban setting may go on a one-off visit to the beach, planned because the children do not often have these experiences. Rennie and McClafferty (1996) coined the term 'edutainment' for such visits. Although these types of visits do have benefits, they do not recognise the 'uniqueness' of each child, or build on their individual interests and learning needs, or recognise the culture of the community in which the children live.

Instead, we explore in this chapter how practitioners can use the local community as a resource when meeting children's learning needs, by involving them individually and in small groups within their community which relate to their particular interests, and by making such interests the central focus of visits. We will also consider the benefits arising for the children, their families and the community, as well as several challenges that this approach throws up.

 Thoughts on theory

- What were your immediate responses to Rogoff's scenario? What do these tell you about your own cultural position?
- Consider the range of people, places, facilities, businesses and institutions that your setting has meaningful contact with. How do you use them as a resource for children's learning?
- Our beliefs and attitudes are informed by the culture of the community to which we belong, for example, our family. These in turn are influenced by 'the institutions of culture' (Rogoff, 1990: 43), which include government, schools, churches, welfare systems, the media and so on. Which have been the strongest influences on your view of your local community?

Starting from children's interests

Before planning a visit for a child or a small group of children it is necessary for practitioners to gain an insight into each child's understanding of the world and their current preoccupations or interests. In order for babies and young children to reveal and share their understanding of the world and their current preoccupations, practitioners need to provide an environment that is rich with opportunities to do so. In the previous chapter we focused on aspects of an enabling outdoor learning environment. Following other writers (Bilton, 2010; Ouvry, 2003; Tovey, 2007), we argue that children should have access to a range of open-ended resources and they need long periods of uninterrupted time in order for them to become engrossed in their play and learning. But many elements of this enabling environment should also be reflected in the learning environment inside and there should be a flexible interaction between the two. For example, a group of boys were often observed playing inside with the train track, building trains with a variety of construction toys and reading books about trains. Observing this, the practitioner planned an adult-led activity for this group of children. It started inside designing the trains to be constructed.

Outside, these designs were used to build the engines and carriages, using boxes, cylinders and bicycle wheels. As the activity progressed, designs were modified by the resources available; flower pots were used for the coal, as the train became a steam engine. A group of girls joined in with this play and the children developed their construction into a role-play as they went on a trip to the seaside. The whole activity lasted two and a half hours, even resuming after the passengers and train engineers had had lunch.

This play episode revealed much about the children's interests and significantly was one in which they became highly involved. Laevers (1993) and Pascal and Bertram (2001) argue that during such periods of intense involvement children are having high-quality learning experiences that will be meaningful and have positive long-term effects. They thus offer practitioners significant pointers to what may be powerful learning.

 Thoughts on theory

The following theorists offer practitioners interesting lenses through which to examine the nature of children's powerful long-term learning experiences.

- Csikszentmihayli (1979) talks of the 'state of flow' when learners (whether adults or children) are in deep concentration and the gap between the activity and themselves is narrow. You may have observed this high level of concentration when children are so absorbed in what they are doing that they are unaware of what is happening around them.

- Athey found that babies and young children would use schemas to make sense of their worlds. Schemas are 'a pattern of repeatable behaviour into which experiences are assimilated' (1990: 37). You have probably seen young 'scientists' in your care engaged in testing their developing views of the world by replicating 'experiments' to check out their ideas.

- Laevers (1993) suggests that a learner needs to have high levels of well-being and involvement in order to have a long-term learning experience. If children are not comfortable, feeling positive and engaged by what they are doing, they are less likely to take in what they are learning.

- Pascal and Bertram (2001) identified some signs of high levels of involvement – including concentration, satisfaction, creativity, energy, posture, persistence and precision. Their Effective Early Learning scale offers a way to try to assess these factors.

Therefore, it is especially valuable for sensitive practitioners to tune in, listen to and observe the child during such periods of high involvement to establish his/her possible interests and learning needs before planning visits. The EYFS states that 'all planning starts with observing children in order to understand and consider their current interests, development and learning' (DfES, 2007: Card 3.1) in order that the children may lead the learning process and contribute to an individual curriculum, rather than this being determined by the Development Matters, the Early Learning Goals or a class topic.

Observing and recording the children's learning helps 'us to bring learning into view, so that it can be seen, reflected upon and discussed' (Luff, 2008: 192). Analysing and discussing the observations 'sharpens the focus on important features of children's learning' (Carr, 2001: 137), enabling practitioners to listen to the children, gain a fuller picture of the children, and then plan visits into the local community which are informed by their interests.

Points for practice

Observing children:

- Are there opportunities in your setting for individual practitioners to have time to analyse observations, reflect on them and plan the children's next steps?
- Are there opportunities for the whole team to meet and share their knowledge about children's learning and plan their next steps?
- What kind of visits into the local community would you arrange for the children engaged in the train play?
- What other resources/people could you call upon to extend their learning?

Case Study

Shaun's interest, the motorbike shop and his dad

Several practitioners had been documenting Shaun's learning as he played. He had been observed spending a considerable time squirting water from syringes, making water and ball runs using guttering, playing football, running and jumping on and off the steps and resources in the garden and lots of chasing games with his friends. Then, during a conversation Shaun's father told the key person that he often took his son to watch rally bikes racing.

(Continues)

(Continued)

At the next planning session the practitioners shared this information with the rest of the team. They discussed Shaun's levels of well-being and involvement and his possible schemas and they were able to identify patterns in Shaun's learning. They decided Shaun had a strong trajectory schema but was also interested in wider aspects of movement, including the movement of water and balls and what determined them to move fast or slowly. For example, when the pump on the syringe was pushed the balls and water moved down the guttering if the guttering was tilted at an angle. Shaun also relished the feel of movement in football and in jumping and chasing games.

The practitioners first ensured that he had plentiful opportunities to make paper aeroplanes, kites, parachutes and to play games of football. Pulleys and buckets were set up, and tubes were fixed to climbing frames so he could climb up and pour water into them; coloured water was provided, as was soapy water (since soapy water flows differently to the water on its own). All these resources were organised within the outdoor learning environment. This information was recorded on Shaun's PLOD (possible lines of direction), a system developed by Margy Whalley (2007) and her team at Pen Green Children's Centre, which is used in some settings/schools as a method of providing personalised plans for individual children's learning.

Figure 3.1 Shaun's *possible lines of direction* (PLOD): how preference and preoccupation lead to learning

Subsequently, the information from Shaun's father about the motorbike interests was followed up by a visit to a motorbike shop within the community for Shaun and a group of boys identified as having similar interests. During the visit the boys took photographs of the bikes and were given motorbike magazines and leaflets, some of which were left at

(Continues)

(Continued)

the setting and some taken home. The outdoor role play area was then developed into a motorbike shop and old motorbike parts were provided as well as the pictures, magazines and leaflets. Providing these resources after the visit enabled the children to revisit and extend their experiences. A practitioner stated that 'they used the resources as an aid to reflect upon the experience and further their understanding of motorbikes during their play' (Pavey and Wickett, 2008: 10). Within their outside role-play they were observed using progressively more technical language and the story line became increasingly complex as elements of the visit were incorporated in the play. For instance, the shop assistant was able to explain to the person buying the motorbike about the differences between the bikes that were for sale in the shop. The boys had learnt to extend their repertoire and were learning accordingly.

A huge benefit was that these activities enabled the children to access the six Areas of Learning and Development (DfES, 2007: Card 4.4) in a holistic way, embedded in a context that made sense to them (Donaldson, 1978). For instance, a practitioner participating in the role-play might look through a motorbike brochure and discuss a possible purchase with the children. Questions such as 'What type of bike is this on the front cover?', 'What is the number of the page where I will find helmets?' will extend their thinking. As they play the children will be learning how to use reference books and also realising that they can be a source of information. It is the skill of the practitioners that enables the provision of the resources, language and questioning to promote sustained shared thinking (Sylva et al., 2010) and to support all the areas of learning and development.

Their powerful interests, informed by their experiences beyond the setting, were acknowledged and extended by practitioners and other children both within the setting and back into the local community. The significance of such a dynamic is recognised in the Learning Outside the Classroom Manifesto when it claims that the 'learning outside the classroom builds bridges between theory and reality, schools and communities, young people and their futures' (DfES, 2006a: 4). If contributing to life-long learning is an important goal of Early Years provision, then using the local community and the children's lives beyond the setting must be a powerful strategy (see Chapter 1 for discussion of this from psychological and socio-cultural perspectives).

Point for practice

■ Consider which of the aspects from each of the Areas of Learning and Development the children were able to experience during their visit to the motorbike shop and in their play after the visit.

Case Study

Ringing the changes: Jasprit, Kayleigh and jewellery

Within this second case study, we show reciprocity at work in how a parent built upon another visit within the local community. Some years ago, when they were in the garden of the setting, Kayleigh and Jasprit showed great interest in the rings a practitioner was wearing and asked to look at them. They were encouraged to sit and try them on. The team recognised that the girls had often been observed during their role-play taking different roles, dressing up as princesses in sparkly outfits, playing hairdressers. As a result, a trip to a jewellery shop was planned for the two girls. In the shop they looked at the many necklaces, rings, brooches and pairs of earrings, discussing the different shapes, patterns, stones etc. The shop manager asked each girl which was their favourite piece of jewellery and they chose their favourite necklace. One chose a pink crystal heart and the other chose a necklace with a teddy on it. Photographs were then taken of both girls wearing their favourite necklace.

Figure 3.2   The pink heart

(Continues)

(Continued)

On return to the setting the pictures of the girls were printed and given to them so they could tell their parents their stories. The next day the mother of the child who had worn the pink heart told us that 'everyone had to look at her picture, even the postman!' It was evident that the mother was delighted and amused by the story as, a week later, having searched high and low to find a pink heart necklace, parent and child called into the setting to show us a plastic heart necklace they had found in the supermarket. A photograph of the mother holding her daughter wearing this pink necklace was taken and a copy was added to the child's learning journey.

Several years later the practitioner met the child when walking around the community. She came up and asked 'Do you remember when we went to the jewellery shop and then mum bought me a pink necklace?' The practitioner said that she remembered it well and the child then shared that though her brother had broken the chain, she still had the heart.

This scenario supports Waite's (2007) suggestion that experiences with positive affect that occur outside settings are particularly memorable and have a positive impact on children's learning.

Involving parents and carers

It must be clear from these case studies that involving families goes far beyond merely reporting to parents and carers what their child is learning at school or in the setting. Talking with Shaun's father provided the setting with further insight into the boy's interests and learning needs. The subsequent visit to the motorbike shop gave the father the powerful message that he had been listened to, that his contribution was valued and respected and that the family interest in motorbikes was worth exploring further. Again, sharing with the parents of Kayleigh and Jasprit information about the visit to the jewellers enabled the family to extend the child's learning experience. As mentioned previously, the EYFS expects practitioners 'to build respectful and caring relationships with all children and their families' (DfES, 2007: Card 2.3) and 'to identify ways of engaging parents, carers and the wider community' (DfES, 2006a: 20). Such involvement of parents in shaping their children's learning can be powerful in achieving these goals and in building bridges between the learning in the community and the learning in the setting.

Points for practice

Parents as partners:

- How do you as a staff team value informal discussions with parents?
- How do the setting's systems enable you to use the information that parents share with you?

Another important aspect of this approach is that in both case studies the parents shared information with the practitioners during an informal chat as they dropped off and picked up their child from the setting. Duncan et al. (2006) found that parents preferred informal interactions with practitioners rather than formal contacts such as open evenings or parent literacy workshops. Informal chats on a day-to-day basis enabled relationships to develop and information to be shared in an easy yet respectful manner. Previously the parent in the second case study had been asked to join the 'Sharing Learning Sessions' with the child's key person and the teacher. The parent did not attend these sessions. This did not mean the parent was not interested in their child's learning. There are a variety of reasons why some parents are unwilling or unable to attend such sessions. A more formal session may not appeal, the commitment of time may be difficult due to other commitments (work, caring for elderly as well as children) and so on. But it is evident that Kayleigh's mother was interested and was able to take the learning further. But when the mother and daughter came to show us their purchase it was on their terms, and, despite the informality, it was an extremely powerful moment for the practitioners as they realised the meaningful links that were being established between the child's world within and beyond the setting. Practitioners need to value the times and conversations they have with parents/carers at the beginnings and ends of sessions as a vital bridge to the learning in the world beyond the setting.

 Points for practice

What other opportunities for parents to share their child's learning outside the setting can be offered? Here are two examples:

- In New Zealand Margaret Carr (2001) developed the idea of 'Learning Stories' to document and share children's learning between the home and the setting, with both parents and practitioners making contributions. All parties recognise and value each other's perspectives on the child's learning.

(Continues)

(Continued)

- Pen Green Children's Centre (Whalley, 2007) is renowned for its work with parents, for instance practitioners provide parents with video cameras to record the child's learning experiences at home and out in the community. These are then shared with the setting.

Such partnerships will erode the frequent perception that children's learning only happens in the setting with the practitioners. Indeed, as Easen et al. argue, 'professional experience and parents' everyday experience are seen as complementary but equally important' (1992: 285). During these case studies it was not only the children who were learning but also the practitioners and the parents. All were gaining an understanding of each other and their worlds. All (adults and children alike) were learning as members of a learning community both within and outside the setting.

The children's culture

The local community does not just mean the geographical location of the setting. It is a 'place' in the broader understanding discussed in Chapter 1; it also includes the diverse values, beliefs, attitudes and norms of behaviour within that community. These change over time, as does the community of the setting as children and practitioners come and go. As Smidt points out 'the child makes culture' and 'living within a community she will learn from all those around her through interaction, watching, listening, being an apprentice and being a teacher' (2006: 15) capable of producing change in the various contexts she is involved in. This means that rigid topic-based curriculum planning for all the children is not appropriate and they should be actively involved as co-constructors of their curriculum (see Chapter 1, Figure 1.2 and Chapter 2, Figure 2.1).

By using the community as a resource and planning the visits from the child's interests, this informs the unique culture within the setting. Bruner (1996) argues that practitioners should no longer perceive children as deprived of a culture but instead as active members who are constructing the culture within the family, the setting and the community. He suggests that practitioners should provide children with opportunities and 'a place for re-inventing, refurbishing and refreshing the culture in each generation' (Bruner, 1996: 13). When the children in the case studies were telling each other stories about their visits or sharing resources in their play they were actively constructing their shared cultural understandings which were then reflected within the setting; for instance, the children using the language of the bike culture.

Although responding to children's interests is often a vital starting point for visits, there are occasions when practitioners need to introduce new ideas and experiences that the children may not have encountered before in order to develop their learning.

Case Study

Young children being artists

The team within a Children's Centre had been developing their understanding of creativity and employed a resident artist. The Children's Centre team developed links with a local arts organisation. The arts organisation built in the idea of the resident artist (RA) and employ him as their RA for a weekly drop in session, a day a week to work with the children, practitioners and the parents in the nursery. To further extend the children's and practitioners' experiences, the teacher took children and a practitioner each week to the Arts Centre to work with the artist. This provided an opportunity to build bridges between the Arts Centre and the setting, as well as reflecting the culture of each of these settings within each other. It also offered the possibility of other experiences to the parents to access a cultural space with their children. Parents rarely accessed these independently or considered the possibilities of creative activities. As discussed in Chapter 1, this experience of 'being an artist' led to incredibly rich art work from the young 'artists' and opened the practitioners' eyes to the sophistication of aesthetic instincts even at this young age. (See also Chapter 9 on the Arts.)

Some issues

We have presented some of the benefits of dissolving barriers between setting and community to create powerful learning environments for young children and of using their interests in shaping and motivating their learning. However, this practice must be approached with criticality, perhaps using the questions suggested in Chapter 1: what are we trying to achieve; how would it best be addressed; where would serve best to meet those intentions; why will it be beneficial, applying appropriate lenses to understand the process and outcomes.

We should always unconditionally respect a child's interests as an expression of individual identity, but we may need to be more reserved in our evaluation of them for educational purposes. What they are interested in may not always be appropriate within a setting or in their best interests. This is highlighted for many practitioners by aspects of some children's interest in gun and weapon play. Some early years writers (Browne, 2004, 2009; Holland, 2003; Paechter, 2007) have identified benefits that may be gained from such play, but many practitioners feel uncomfortable engaging with it and it can marginalise the play of other children when it becomes very noisy and active.

Having accepted and identified a powerful interest on the part of certain children, the practitioners remain responsible for choosing and shaping any resulting visit and deciding upon the appropriateness of provision and follow-up back in the setting in terms of educational benefits to the children. It may be that the practitioners would prefer a visit to a martial arts class, with its emphasis upon control and self-discipline as the setting is likely to share these values, to going to a gun shop.

A further complication may arise. In the two case studies, parents fully shared and approved of their children's interests but what if this is not the case? If Shaun's interest had been jewellery, how might this have been linked to his father's motorbike hobby? Might parents, including other families, and indeed practitioners have been less supportive? Such concerns are not frequent but are certainly not unknown in early years settings. The two (real life) case studies fit closely with commonly accepted gender stereotypes:

Boys → father → action/movement/machinery → motorbikes

Girls → mother → sitting/dressing up/ornament → jewellery

Such patterns of interest are highly likely to emerge from many children given the strength of gender-stereotyped views in society. However, they raise the serious question of how far settings should be seen to give tacit support and encouragement to such patterns, given that they are charged with countering stereotyping. Such 'single-sex' visits should be the exception rather than the rule, and both boys and girls generally included.

Practitioners too have their own powerful views, beliefs and feelings shaping their practice and potentially affecting the children who are 'still influenced by the opinions and views of people to whom they are close' (Browne, 2009: 63). As Huggins (2008) points out, some might have labelled Shaun and his friends' chasing games as naughty, out of control and inappropriate (Jarvis, 2007) and so failed to acknowledge his significant learning schema. Equally, a boy might show interest in a practitioner's rings, but the interest might not be taken up with the child or shared with colleagues because it was deemed inappropriate. What we choose to notice and act upon is selective and subjective.

Practitioners may also be unwilling to take children out of the setting, due to their concerns over issues of ratios, risk, and health and safety procedures. The introduction of the National Standards for Under Eights (DfES, 2003a) appears to have lead to a severe tightening up of procedures around taking children out of the setting, even for short walks, and so many settings now avoid doing this altogether. However, practitioners should reflect upon the benefits and how problems might be overcome. Planning visits may be seen as too time-consuming, but the case study teams involved in organising these responsive visits found it could be carried out during quieter times of the day and did not take as much organising as a large group whole-day visit.

These issues show that it is vital for practitioners in a setting to develop a shared vision and agreed ways of working that establish their setting as an integral part of the community, and that enable them to feel safe to challenge, innovate and be open and enthusiastic with each other. Sharing the processes of documenting, analysing and reflecting upon children's learning will enable them to understand and appreciate more fully and accurately the potential for learning and to plan the next steps. It will also enable them to share these ideas consistently with members of the community.

Summary

Within this chapter we have shown how practitioners can extend children's interests and learning needs using resources within the local community, and considered the benefits of making links and building on children's learning experiences beyond the setting. There are benefits for all, children and adults alike, when responsive visits are planned and carried out using the community as a resource. As stated in the Primary National Strategy:

When we receive encouragement for our efforts and know that our ideas are valued, our feelings acknowledged and our discoveries recognised, we come to see the world as a safe place, and ourselves as competent and capable agents within it. (2007: 3)

(Continues)

(Continued)

This is true for the children and for their significant adults, and inclusion is founded upon such respect.

But it is not always straightforward. Practitioners may need to handle disagreements and conflicts between different views and interests; moreover they must be alert to the danger, however small, that an uncritical use of this approach may narrow the learning possibilities for their children and perhaps reinforce values and attitudes that they feel undesirable. They have a professional responsibility as educators to counter stereotyping; to offer alternatives to beliefs and values which, though widely accepted within the community, may restrict the life-chances of children; and always to look to enlarge the children's experiences and their horizons.

Further reading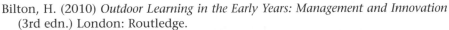

Bilton, H. (2010) *Outdoor Learning in the Early Years: Management and Innovation* (3rd edn.) London: Routledge.

Luff, P. (2009) Written observations or walks in the park? Documenting children's experiences. In: J. Moyles (ed.), *Early Years Foundations: Meeting the Challenge*. Maidenhead: Open University Press, pp. 185–196.

A time of change: outdoor learning and pedagogies of transition between Foundation Stage and Year 1

Sue Waite, Julie Evans and Sue Rogers

Chapter objectives

■ An awareness of how Foundation Stage and Year 1 teachers view outdoor learning

■ An appreciation of the child's view of outdoor learning

■ Ideas for how transition between Foundation Stage and Year 1 might be smoothed by pedagogies used in outdoor contexts

In Chapters 2 and 3 we saw how learning outdoors and more broadly learning outside the classroom are relatively well-established practice in the early years. The Early Years Foundation Stage (DfES, 2007) endorses outdoor play and learning because it has a positive impact on children's sense of well-being, supporting all aspects of children's development. Moreover, outdoor environments offer children freedom to explore, use their senses, and be physically active and exuberant. However, a sea change occurs for children as they enter the first year of the national curriculum. Yet, Every Child Matters policy states:

that every young person should experience the world beyond the classroom as an essential part of learning and personal development, whatever their age, ability or circumstances. (DCSF, 2009a)

Children need to experience some continuity in the way they learn and active play-based learning should be continued into Year 1. Furthermore, as later chapters will argue, experiential learning is a valuable pedagogical tool throughout the primary phase and beyond. As we will demonstrate in this chapter and throughout the book, learning outdoors is valued by adults and children and can encourage enjoyment and motivation, different child/adult interactions, the use of stimulating contingent pedagogies and so address wider purposes for learning.

So what is it like to be a child aged 5 or 6 moving between two phases of education from Foundation Stage to Year 1? Do reduced opportunities to play and learn outside (Waite, 2009) indicate wider differences in the learning and teaching they experience? Some of our earlier research suggested that the outdoors may offer opportunities for more self-directed forms of learning, whether through the natural context, novelty or alternative ways of teaching (Davis et al., 2006; Waite and Davis, 2007) or because teachers tend to direct learning outcomes less closely in outdoor contexts (Rogers and Evans, 2007). Drawing on two studies funded by the Economic and Social Science Research Council (Rogers and Evans, 2007; Waite et al., 2008), this chapter considers how continuity and progression in the vital transition period between Foundation Stage and Year 1 can be mediated by pedagogies commonly adopted in contexts outside the classroom.

Two major reviews of the English national curriculum have recently taken place (Alexander, 2009; Rose, 2009). Both reviews advocate greater continuity between Foundation Stage and primary education to encourage children's engagement with learning and less attention to testing and more to the development of positive attitudes towards learning dispositions. In fact, the Foundation Stage has been extended to age 6 and play-based learning is promoted as most suitable for children up to this age already in Wales. Such moves are not isolated to the UK. Rose cites the INCA study in 2008 of primary curriculum change in 10 countries and the rationales given for using areas of learning rather than subject-based curriculum in the primary phase, which included:

▪ the cognitive development of learners;

▪ easing the transition from pre-primary modes of learning;

▣ curriculum integration to optimise learning;

▣ a new importance attached to cross-curricular skills/competences; and

▣ a need to simplify the curriculum and its assessment, or a need to make the curriculum more manageable. (Rose, 2009: 115)

One of the first actions by the coalition government in May 2010 was to invite primary schools to apply to become academies (fast tracked for those with 'outstanding' Ofsted assessments). This status is purported to bring greater self-determination for schools regarding the curriculum and its delivery. However, a continuing emphasis on attainment and judgement of schools through pupil testing may constrain this supposed 'freedom' somewhat.

In this chapter we focus on the transition from the Foundation Stage to KS1 and the ways in which opportunities for outdoor provision may change and diminish as children move into statutory schooling. As in other chapters in this book, we argue that outdoor learning is important for all children, wherever they are. But our particular interest here is in how outdoor learning opportunities might serve to ease transition between settings and curricular frameworks. We begin, however, by sharing teachers' stories of outdoor learning from Foundation Stage and Year 1 classes in our current ESRC project, highlighting some of the theoretical issues and points for practice in them. We then describe some children's perspectives on their play drawing also on Rogers and Evans' study (2007) and reflect on the practice that this implies. We close with a summary of the main messages from our research on this key period in children's schooling and suggest some possible ideas for you to try in your own setting.

Case Study 📁

Foundation Stage and Year 1 teachers' understanding and use of spaces outside the classroom

Sam and Chloe, Foundation Stage teachers at Brock Valley School, love the opportunity to provide free flow of play inside and outside. During the day, the children drift in and out of their classroom through the conservatory, sharing that space and a safe enclosed outside area with the other Foundation Class and therefore mixing with children from both classes, extending their social sphere. There are boxes of resources linked to different Areas of Learning and a teaching assistant helps the children

(Continues)

(Continued)

to pursue their own interests. These often arise through serendipitous encounters with wildlife or mud rather than planned resourcing. The teachers strongly praise the experienced TAs who build contingently on children's interests. They also value the space available in their dedicated outside area which allows the children to make bigger movements and louder noises, the physical activity which helps develop their gross motor skills, fitness and health. They express their view that outside the classroom represents a greater freedom for the children, compensating not only for the more crowded conditions in the classroom but also for many home situations where no safe outdoor space is available. Sam and Chloe think the child-led and playful nature of the outdoor activities help to motivate the children. Outside the classroom is also a place where holistic observation is possible; seeing *the child* 'what kind of character they are', rather than *whether they can do* a specific thing. Yet local contexts can place some constraints on entirely child-led approaches advocated in the EYFS, planning and topic work is expected and there is sometimes a tension between this and following the children's interests.

While Chloe and Sam have a similar approach, Rowan and Karen, Year 1 teachers at Brock Valley, have rather different practice from each other, although their belief in the value of learning outside the classroom is also strong. Their classrooms don't have open access so they have to plan supervision for learning outside the classroom. When there are fewer adults working with the children in Year 1, having sufficient adult supervision can become a major barrier. Yet they would love to provide that feeling of space, and find it challenging to be in a small space with children who are still used to pursuing their own interests. There seems more conflict with a planned adult agenda when in a confined space. But Karen also has some concerns about sending groups out with teaching assistants who, she fears, may not know how best to support learning. There is also the ever-present pressure of SATs and 'getting things down on paper'. With all the other pressing priorities Rowan is frustrated that there just isn't time to put into developing many ideas to 'embellish the curriculum' outside the classroom. It is a sobering thought that Karen witnesses children experiencing going out of the classroom to other parts of the school as a big adventure, which suggests the pressure to 'get on' dominates the desire to 'get out'. She tells us:

> If you're moving around and you're outside and you're not sitting down as a passive learner – things being fed to you that you've got to learn – you're taking knowledge out and extending that with things that you're seeing. So, you're, I suppose, being more of an active learner … It might stimulate things for the children that they're interested in and want to find out more about so they're being more of a learner rather than just having everything spoonfed to them.

If we consider Karen's tale of the tensions she feels in getting children to *acquire* the required set of knowledge from a psychological standpoint, we might conclude that the needs of children are not being met. The expectation that they should sit still and be spoon-fed in order to learn the things they have to learn does not take account of the social, emotional or indeed cognitive readiness of the children. Yet, once they enter the years of the National Curriculum, it would seem that getting the children ready for Year 2 is one of the principal aims of Year 1 and so on throughout their schooling. Foundation Stage pedagogy, therefore, where contingency to children's interests and needs is paramount, seems to have minimal upward influence at present. Indeed, some would suggest that the National Curriculum rather reaches down into the Foundation Stage (Fisher, 2009). Nutbrown also comments, 'The best way to help children to get ready to be 5-year-olds is to allow them to be 3 when they are 3 and 4 when they are 4' (2006: 124). Dickson (2005) and Humberstone and Stan (2009b) draw attention to how well-designed processes do not necessarily result in participants achieving the intended outcomes, recognising the gap between what is offered and what is received, as Waite and Pratt comment in Chapter 1. Structure imposed at the outset is bent by unpredictability in responses by children and the environment. However, meaningful talk, using open-ended questions that the child genuinely needs to think through, can support and extend child-initiated learning. Such speculative conversations open rather than close down the possibilities for learning; the child and adult learn much on the way to a shared end goal, not least ways of thinking about and considering possibilities. Yet often the pressure for required outcomes makes the end more important than the means and many learning opportunities may thus be lost. Optimum Education's argument is that:

> The curriculum offers up strange knowledge, not knowledge that would extend or interact with children's everyday experience. Indeed, if school knowledge drifts towards children's everyday understandings then children's power is increased, [which is] not something organisations interested in control and induction are looking for. (cited in Alexander, 2009: 20)

We have seen in Chapter 3 how embracing aspects of children's home lives can increase both the children's and their parent's involvement in their education. This involvement tends to decline as children progress through school, but it is always worthwhile looking for such opportunities.

Thoughts on theory

- How do the tales told by Chloe, Sam, Rowan and Karen resonate with your own experience in school?
- Are the tensions represented here about psychological factors or might a socio-cultural way of looking at this movement between stages offer some useful insights? Refer back to Chapter 1 to remind yourself of what these perspectives might bring to an understanding of these stories.
- Thinking especially about transition between play-based and curriculum-led learning, what theoretical positions might help you to adjust your practice? Is this something that needs to be undertaken as a whole school?

The reduction in opportunities to spend learning time outside the classroom is marked. In our observations, we found about one-third of time was spent outside the classroom in Foundation Stage compared to about 10 per cent in Year 1. In addition, these figures represent an inflated estimation of the total proportion of time for outdoor learning as the two schools make efforts to invite us when more outdoor activity is taking place. So, it is keenly indicative of the fall in opportunities to learn in the outdoors for children over this transitional period, corroborating earlier findings of a decline in the use of the outdoors between preschool and primary school (Waite, 2011). Yet, planning to minimise any contrast in children's experience of teaching and learning is a deliberate aim:

> ... in the first term we need to try and keep it varied and play-based and not so structured being conscious of the big jump, and we're kind of trying to do that now from Foundation to Year 1 with that intervention programme in the Summer term. We bring the Foundation children in because it is a big change to have that structured session ... whereas before perhaps I would have just gone into Year 1 and thought well it's Year 1, knuckle down and lessons all the way. (Y1 Teacher 1, School A)

If 'care is taken to see that they have ample opportunities for active learning, such as outdoor play' (Rose, 2009: 93), maintaining play-based learning in developmentally appropriate groups helps summer-born children to settle and learn at school. One of the teachers mentioned the age of the children but felt the need for greater play-based pedagogy into Year 1 was individual and sometimes unpredictable:

> It surprised me that perhaps some that I thought might be more kind of play oriented and not quite ready have actually really jumped and it's suited them

and vice versa, so you can never quite tell really. Some of them have made brilliant progress. I do think some of the younger ones still need that bit of free option. (Y1 Teacher 1, School A)

However, the spontaneity offered by less 'managed' outdoor contexts is also valued and can reverse the usual flow of information from adult to child:

> Sometimes things do happen when you are outside and they just want to find out about it. Or they might tell me things, I have a little boy in my class who is really, really intelligent with knowing lots and lots of different facts and sometimes he tells me things and I learn from him almost. (FS Teacher 2, School A)

In comparison with our observations inside the classroom, being outdoors seems to interrupt the usual power relationships to encourage less adult-directed activity.

Drawing on data from an earlier study (Rogers and Evans, 2007) about how the children use the spaces available for learning around their school, different play episodes seem to be prompted amongst girls and boys in outdoor environments compared with the indoors. At times children's play, especially boys' play, exceeded the boundaries of what would be deemed acceptable behaviour in the classroom, a tendency also noted by others. For example, Patricia, a practitioner, comments: 'I know what you mean. I have boys like that every year I've decided it's pointless trying to change nature' (MacNaughton, 2000: 11). Teachers found the difficulties the children experienced in working in constrained indoor spaces were exacerbated in mixed age-group classes. Children in these were often engaged in National Curriculum activities in close proximity to play-based activities, leading to conflict in providing appropriate space for their activities, due to

> [the] smallness of the environment and they're involved in some noisy play and they're working beside a group of children who are trying to do some writing or whatever it's got to be restricted because you know they're going to be disturbing the children who are doing the writing activity and that's just the nature of the mixed year group. (Teacher, mixed FS/Y1 class, in Rogers and Evans, 2008)

Clearly, dual aims in mixed-age classes to meet National Curriculum standards for Year 1 and the EYFS guidelines for Reception children cause tensions, which are replicated for children and teachers in the transition between Foundation Stage and Year 1 classes. As we have seen, our teachers are aware that many children are too immature to settle immediately to the demands of Year 1 but how can play-based pedagogies sit alongside the quiet concentration and focus required for more directed teacher-led activities in the narrow confines of the classroom? We suggest the spaces outside the classroom may offer a means to release some of this tension.

Case Study 📁

Expanding opportunities for learning

Billy, Joe and Gareth were busily playing outdoors in the sandpit for the whole session. Occasionally Myra, the teacher, would ask them to stop doing certain things, but for the most part they played completely unsupervised, entirely focused on the task at hand. Rain water got into the sandpit through a little hole in the cover and this stimulated some fantasy play. Tom prompted this with the remark 'Look the tide's come in', and all three cooperated in digging tunnels to make the tide go 'in and out'. Soon they began to build a dam, learning all the while about how the properties of dry sand have changed with the water leaking into the pit, negotiating and cooperating with each other to sustain the play narrative. Inside the classroom, such 'cooperation' often led to arguments with each other and adults about sharing tools, and making noise and mess, but outside their play could follow its own course relatively uninterrupted by adults and their peers allowing them to create a sustained learning opportunity. Girls too often adopted far more active and expansive leadership roles in the open spaces outside the classroom while generally conforming to more stereotypically gendered quiet and caring play inside. Outdoor areas can also influence other pedagogical issues. For example, Joe, a large-framed boy with additional learning needs, often ended up in conflict situations in indoor play settings, but outdoors he integrated well and played for extended periods of time without interruption or the need for adult intervention.

Play-based and playful pedagogies

While the culture of Early Years pedagogy encourages more playful approaches to learning, in Year 1 as one teacher told us, 'they need to have so much structure in lessons or they're not going to achieve'. 'Free play' has been criticised (Hutt et al.,1989) as mundane, repetitive and lacking adult involvement, not recognising that repetition may support consolidation of learning and offer a source of security for children, and that lack of adult intervention may be valuable in promoting self-regulated learning. Such views, reinforced by early work by Sylva et al. (1980), have diminished the cultural value of free play in schooling. Indeed, more recently, settings often refer to 'structured', 'directed' and 'purposeful play' (Tovey, 2007: 114) as if planning per se adds value. The distinctions between these planned forms are not unambiguous, however, and run somewhat counter to understandings of play as flowing and lacking imposed structure (Bruce, 1991). The structure we have observed thus far in our study includes substantial amounts of monitorial pedagogy, where the children's playful exploration is arrested either because it differs from the planned intentions of the adult or through an exaggerated perception of risk in the outdoors. Yet structure does not just reside in the plans of adults; children structure play through negotiation within their own social and cultural norms (Garvey, 1991; Trawick-Smith, 1998), as we see in the following case study.

Case Study 🗁

Privileging the child's perspective outdoors: a change of view?

In the following exchange in the Foundation Stage garden, we see how children develop a theme suggested by a remark by the adult and how the repetition serves to reinforce common experience and sharing cultural currency for play.

Becky [Teaching Assistant]: Wow. These kind of look like hamster cages to me, you know when you have a hamster and you put them in a little ball and they run around.

The adult offers some of her own experience.

Charlie: I don't have a hamster, I only have a kitten.

One child builds from this that she has experience of a kitten but not a hamster.

Becky: Oh, you've not seen a hamster cage then and they go in and they've got all bits they can play in? Like a hamster thing.

Charlie: I used to have. This is so funny! When I had a hamster and it had a long tail and it went in and my dad held it upside down with its tail.

Another child joins in, recalling how her dad also used to play with their hamster.

Becky: Did it like it? I don't think I'd like to be held up by my tail.

Cultural norms of kindness to animals are introduced subtly, using putting oneself in another's situation to develop empathy.

Charlie: I'm a cat so I curl up in a ball.

Child returns to own interest and offers more information about animal behaviour through role-play.

Becky: What kind of cat are you? Are you a small cat we can cuddle or a really ferocious big cat like a tiger or a lion?

(Continues)

(Continued)

Adult tries to build upon the game by questioning. Another approach might have been to enter the role-play.

Charlie: Small cat.

Becky: We thought a puma because he's got lovely black hair, hasn't he?

Charlie: Small cat! Small cat!

Insistent. The adult doesn't take up the child's response – the sort of cat was 'obvious' through the behaviour of the 'cat' so the child is puzzled by adult's insistence on misinterpreting the role.

(Audio-recording and observation, Foundation Stage, School B, *our commentary in italics*)

The pedagogy we see here imports some of the teacher-direction from inside this classroom but the adult is also trying to understand the child's point of view and the child is steering the interaction.

 Points for practice

- Remember that motivation is vital to support learning, therefore accommodating opportunities for children to follow their own lines of enquiry/direction is important (see Chapter 3).

- The majority of children will welcome the opportunity that the bigger outdoor spaces afford to be louder and move more. Think especially of summer-born children and their readiness to sit still and listen.

- Be ready to listen carefully yourself; blossoming inquiry skills can be nipped in the bud by not picking up sensitively on the child's meaning-making (Clark et al., 2005)

- Find ways to use children's interests to build activities that will also meet necessary learning points. Being flexible and creative will help construct a respectful learning community.

Spaces: intentions and tensions

As we noted in Chapter 1, space is converted to 'place' by the meanings attributed to it (Tuan, 1977). In our studies, we have noticed how 'place' as a concept in the schools in our study has fine distinctions related to the cultural meaning that different areas have for individuals. There are different affordances in different areas through their functional meaning for children (Fjørtoft, 2001) but also through the mediation of different roles taken by facilitators. The play park in Chapter 1, for example, had very different connotations for children from the teacher, who was aiming to illustrate scientific work on forces. From our observations and interviews, we perceived a distinction between the outdoor areas close to the classroom which are largely for extension of activities that could equally be carried out indoors, at least if space allowed. Yet the pedagogies here are not necessarily closely related to those just over the threshold of the classroom door. There is an expectation that bigger movements, louder noises and greater independence will be possible here and that adults' roles will be principally monitorial rather than facilitative. It seems that, ideally for teachers, this would be an area for 'free choice' for children once what 'has to be done' is finished, thus distracting less from the prevailing 'work' culture of the classroom and allowing opportunities to observe without being drawn into direct teaching. However, from our observations outdoor spaces are often facilitated by teaching assistants and in some cases are more directly integrated with stimulating and extending curriculum-related activities. Clarity about what pedagogical role teaching assistants are expected to take would be valuable.

An even more ambiguous area, the playground is more often regarded, by both children and adults, as somewhere for children to play (and learn) independently; yet this cultural expectation can cause confusion when it is appropriated for teacher-directed learning, as we saw in Chapter 1. The cultural symbol for 'work' was a pencil; when the children didn't have a pencil, they felt free to play. The distinction between 'work' and 'play' appeared less marked for the Foundation Stage children and they moved in and out of play and adult-directed activities more smoothly. It is worth considering whether this demarcation should also be blurred by maintaining playful pedagogies in Year 1. It should depend on what learning is intended and what the unintended outcomes might be (see also Chapter 6).

For some children and teachers certain outdoor space is valued for not having to sit still in it and being able to use gross motor skills, but a diversity of space is important (Fjørtoft, 2001).

> And not necessarily just in the outdoor area but in other areas like in the playground, we could do numeracy out there and all sorts of things. I've taken them out to the playground, we've got a big 100 square out there and I've taken them out a few times and I've done circle time outside quite a bit when we've stood up and played games and sang songs and particularly because

we've open plan, it's nicer because you've got a bit more room, you haven't got tables in the way, you can all stand there in the circle playing. (Foundation Stage Teacher, School A)

Bilton (2010) suggests that zoning helps support different types of play. Waite et al. (2006) also noted how zoning with children's input to how space is demarcated can help to decrease social tensions in a small playground and can also lead to imaginative games for the educational markings if children feel ownership of these through their involvement in the playground's design (Armitage, 1999).

Other teachers have spoken of the importance of 'standing back' to allow children to be independent. Yet our initial observations and those of Tovey (2006) suggest that the reduction of risk and control of behaviour is uppermost in interactions between children and adults. Taking risks is important for emotional health and the development of resilience (Mental Health Foundation, 1999; Play Safety Forum, 2002). This is discussed more fully in Chapter 2. Rather than curtailing activities, adult interventions can support children in assessing their own competence to take on different personally appropriate levels of challenge. Children in our latest study have few areas out of adult monitorial control but actively seek them out at times. Private spaces have been deemed to be important for the imagination (Kylin, 2003; Moore, 1986). Outdoor spaces should give children time away from the adult gaze and provide children with greater opportunities for independence than in indoor adult-defined and regulated spaces (Baldock, 2001 in Garrick, 2004). Rose also notes how many schools have 'transformed their grounds, sometimes from very unpromising conditions, into excellent areas for cross-curricular studies, offering exciting opportunities for children to learn out of doors about horticulture, energy conservation and recycling technology from first-hand experience' (2009: 49) (see Chapters 12 and 14 for more detail on these). However, while wilder areas may be seen as messy by adults, they are rich in possibilities for children.

Although linked to a topic and planned, the school trips we have observed seemed to be viewed as 'an occasion' by children and adults. They were usually to more distant places requiring a trip by coach, involved parent helpers and principally appeared to provide an opportunity for social bonding between the children and adults. The 'delivery' of the educational content was devolved to the place visited and adults were often also in a learning role which perhaps enabled the children to see them in a different light. However, maintenance of the external reputation of the school also created a pressure which, coupled with high levels of pupil excitement, made some of the adult–child interactions even more weighted to behavioural control than within school sites.

Evidence from our studies indicates that outdoor spaces enable children to create learning spaces for themselves and to exercise greater choice over materials, location and social groupings. Such choice fosters independent learning, a valuable lifelong skill, but is at risk when pedagogy becomes predominately teacher-directed. As we noted in Chapter 1, place plays an active part in this process. We need to consider carefully how different places outside the classroom will impact on the cultural and psychosocial expectations of children and adults. They may have a potential advantage in not being classrooms with the weight of established norms for how we should teach and learn, but they are not neutral spaces. We need to reflect on what the adults and children will bring to that place in terms of past experience and social norms and what that place has to offer in terms of learning opportunities with its cultural associations and functional features. The mutual influence of place, child and others offers a powerful mediation arena for innovative pedagogical approaches (see Figure 1.2) and is able to accommodate contingent responses to assist transition for children between Foundation Stage and Year 1 (see Figure 2.1) and to maintain and develop their independent learning capacities throughout primary school and beyond.

 Points for practice

Supporting transition from the Foundation Stage to Key Stage 1 is vital so that children build on good practice in Nursery and Reception and maintain their motivation and independent learning. It is often through their outdoor child-initiated play that children show how they are making sense of new situations and relationships with others, so it can also be a useful window for assessment. With this in mind, key points to consider include:

- Maintain friendship groups as children move from Reception to Year 1.
- Continue to offer opportunities for outdoor exploration and play in Year 1 to help children form and re-form friendships and social groupings; extend their imaginative and physical capacities; support growing independence and skill.
- Identify key people who are familiar to children as they move from Reception to Year 1 and who are adept at facilitative responses to children's curiosity.
- Find out what the children in transition know by building on familiar Reception class topics in Year 1.

(Continues)

(Continued)

- Offer children open-ended resources in the outdoors so that they can create their own play contexts and themes.
- Ensure children have weather protection in terms of clothing and Wellies etc. so they are able to use outdoor spaces even when wet, cold, muddy.
- Engage parents in the curriculum, pedagogy and assessment processes, including learning and playing outdoors.
- Observe children outdoors as well as indoors to build a full picture of how they are managing transition.
- If access to the outdoor play spaces is limited, make time to take children to nearby outside spaces including visiting the Foundation Stage, 'zoning' playground areas, parks, woodland and other public spaces.
- Ensure that the interests of all children are reflected in the curriculum and pedagogy adopted at the point of transition to help overcome gender stereotyping and avoid cultural bias (see Chapter 3).
- Photograph and document children's achievements outdoors to encourage children to reflect on their learning and share experiences with family members.

Summary

In this chapter you will have considered examples of ways teachers and children in Foundation Stage and Year 1 approach their outdoor spaces as contexts for learning and have some pointers about how this might support children in the transition from Foundation Stage to Year 1. The differences highlighted in Foundation Stage play-based and child-initiated learning and Year 1 practices should help you to consider how your own teaching and learning intentions may be received by the children and how you might smooth transition through pedagogies more commonly associated with the outdoors.

Further reading

Bilton, H. (1997) *Outdoor Play: Management and Innovation.* London: David Fulton.
Broda, H. (2007) *Schoolyard-Enhanced Learning.* New York: Stenhouse Publishers.
Fabian, H. and Dunlop, A.W. (eds) (2002) *Transitions in the Early Years: Debating Continuity and Progression for Children in Early Education.* London: RoutledgeFalmer.
Rogers, S. and Evans, J. (2008) *Inside Role Play in Early Childhood Education: Researching Children's Perspectives.* London: Routledge.

Section 2

Learning Outside the Classroom Across the Curriculum for Primary Aged Children

The next six chapters address learning in the primary phases of KS1 and KS2 and adopt a cross-curricular approach (between the Early Years Foundation Stage and the Primary Curriculum), which potentially supports greater continuity in pedagogy. The six chapters focus on:

- English and language
- mathematics
- science and technology with environmental awareness
- history, geography and understanding of places
- the Arts
- physical development, health and well-being.

Each chapter offers case studies and interesting ideas about how being outside the classroom can support learning across the curriculum.

5

English and language outside the classroom

Howard Cotton

Chapter objectives

- An awareness of children's language use in and out of school
- An appreciation of how schools promote language use in children's play
- Understanding environmental print
- Knowing how these map onto your own intentions for children's learning

English and language occupy uniquely central positions in the curriculum as the communication tools through which other areas are accessed; they are fundamental to successful participation in other learning and a vital life skill.

English as a medium for learning in and out of school

English is the language that is used across schools in the British Isles, alongside the national languages of Welsh, Scottish Gaelic, and Irish. Although there are no monolingual speakers of these languages, there are schools that teach through the medium of Welsh, Scottish Gaelic and Irish. These children also speak English as a first or second language. There are many community languages as well, such as

Polish, Urdu, Punjabi and Hindi. Children may speak these as either a first or home language but they principally access their school education via the medium of English.

English as a subject comprises the skills of reading, writing, speaking and listening and so permeates the whole of the curriculum. Children as infants learn to listen and then to speak. Most children naturally learn to speak at home before they come to school and are taught to read and write at school using their talking and listening skills. They access areas of learning at school through their own and others' talk and eventually though reading and writing independently. Language, as noted in Chapter 1, is the means through which children are acculturated, first within their family and then into community and school cultures, and is a medium for learning. Their reading, writing, listening and speaking skills allow their language and learning to function. They learn *about* their language and they learn *through* their language. This is true of any child in any literate culture and the same applies to Chilean or Gambian, Finnish or Japanese children.

Through language, children learn how to think, socialise and communicate. Children who are proficient at reading, writing, speaking and listening in their own language have the power to think thoughts, to express ideas and feelings and to share them with others, aspects perhaps more fully explained by psychological theory (Jarvis, 2009). They can engage people and influence their ideas and actions. And children who have English as their language have a strong position in the world community for English also functions as a major world language used in film, television, music, on the Internet and in global business (Medwell et al., 2007).

Our children are surrounded by language both within and out of school – nursery staff, teachers and TAs talk and listen and surround children with writing, in the form of books and posters, signs and name labels. Outside school, parents talk to them and to other adults, take them shopping where signs and labels abound and they encounter notes, labels, books, papers and magazines at home. Other media such as the TV, games consoles and computers provide an endless source of speech and interactive or ambient reading both in school and out of school. The skills of reading, writing, speaking and listening are modelled and reinforced within and outside of school. Children carry these worlds with them and can be seen playing schools at home or role-playing the outside world of the doctors, the vets or the farm shop within school. Thus learning outside the school informs learning within it and vice versa, as we also saw in Chapter 3.

The role-play area

Role-play is a useful focus for reflection as it is used to help model and produce language from other contexts in its spoken and written form. It will not have escaped your notice how children naturally immerse themselves in the world of play, where they reflect the outside world in their imagination. Indeed the word 'play' is there within role-play as well as the play you would see performed on stage. Here adults have shaped play to an art form in order to do what children are doing – exploring and making sense of their world. Thinking back to Chapter 1, its 'performance' can be related to a socio-cultural understanding of learning, whereby it allows children to rehearse participation in a particular community of practice. From a psychological perspective, it also affords children opportunities to 'try out' identities and attitudes. What we do as educators with our role-play areas and use of drama across the primary years is to facilitate, direct and model the process of making sense of the world.

> It's when we do this foolish, time-consuming, romantic, quixotic, childlike thing called play that we are most practical, most useful, and most firmly grounded in reality, because the world itself is the most unlikely of places, and it works in the oddest of ways, and we don't make any sense of it by doing what everyone else has done before us. It's when we fool around with the stuff the world is made of that we make the most valuable discoveries, we create the most lasting beauty, we discover the most profound truths. (Pullman, 2005)

Children explore speech patterns when they play shops – 'That'll be 64p, please' – and written patterns – reading and filling in a vet's appointment form and noting down the animal's name, age and illness. Role-play areas are set up to encourage the use of language: the adult will leave different types of pens for the children and papers to fill in, signs that the children can use – 'Open', 'Shut', 'Estate Agent' and signs around the area indicating what to do – 'Big envelopes need a large stamp' – and special equipment – 'weighing scales', 'till' and 'stethoscope'. Often the adult will enter in role as a customer or as a pirate and model the tasks to be done and the language to be used for that context. Specialist equipment and clothes to dress up in are part of this role-play, in much the same way as we use costume and props within a play for performance. So, the role-play area may be set up as a series of microcosms of the world beyond the classroom or may be more open and commandeered with ambiguous props for the children to bring in their own 'outside worlds'. Open-ended props are frequently used in outdoor areas, where a twig may become a sword or a wand to support role-play (Waite and Davis, 2007).

The role-play area is intended for children to 'become' the persona of the roles they take on. Role-play areas exist both in and outside the classroom but are within the school culture, reflecting and encouraging reflection on what is known about the world outside school. This relationship is important to note for if they have little or no experience of this outside world, children will find it hard to model the spoken and written language; and the ways of being that pertain to that area. Settings and schools acknowledge the need for direct experience of place and a visit to an estate agents or farm shop is often an integral part of the subsequent role-play area. In such a case it allows the children a chance to see and experience what it is to be an estate agent, an authenticity discussed in Chapter 1. But equally the role-play area is essential to the re-enactment of direct experience that allows children to reflect on and make sense of these experiences; such rehearsal may be an important element in memorising and making meaning from experience. As Sue Waite and Nick Pratt establish in Chapter 1, children in the Western world live their lives and learn both in and outside of formal education; their learning in both contexts may be more easily linked and developed if the boundaries between the two are blurred. A good teacher and a good parent will encourage their migration of learning.

It is worth noting that even children outside formal education need this personal space to play at the real world (Smith, 2010). The difference is that within school this is a formally set up time for play and interaction with language and it is worth reflecting on how this situation varies in quality from the informal re-enactments that take place in the playground, the street or at home.

Case Study

A moving experience: role-play in Key Stage 1

Mahmoud was moving house and a discussion ensued as to who had moved house and what it involved. Some children knew about estate agents but others not, so the children's teacher arranged a visit from one of the mothers who worked in an estate agent office. She wore her uniform and brought in brochures of houses, flats and shops for sale. There were the photos to look at and text to read about the property. In addition the estate agents kindly donated some 'For Sale' and 'Sold' signs which the children used in their large outside play area to advertise and sell various areas of the playground (climbing frames, play areas and Wendy houses representing houses and shops) to each other. There was some parental consternation when the whole school went up for sale for a day from a sign left on the playground railings but, although tempted, the Head refused all offers.

The five staff used child-initiated ideas and adult-directed activities to encourage their children to talk, listen, read and write about houses and homes and constantly supported the children in making associations with their class, out of class and out of school activities. Table 5.1 summarises some of the activities, situations, language and other skills involved in this topic.

Table 5.1: Activities and language opportunities

Type of activity	Situation	Language opportunities	Links
Story of 3 Little Pigs	In class, staff-directed	Reading, listening	Comprehension, discussion of house types and materials
Discussion of children's homes, rooms and their uses	In class, staff-guided	Listening and speaking	Discussion, understanding of what a home is
Moving house using the dolls' house to create rooms	Role-play area, children-led	Speaking and listening	Role-play and negotiation. Reflection
Models of children's houses	At home with parent(s) and carers, conversational	Speaking and listening	Discussion, model building with carer. Shared time
Visit around school vicinity	Local area, within walking distance, staff directed	Speaking, listening and reading	Reading shop and road signs. Understanding amenities
Re-creation of estate agents office	Within class, staff-guided and children-led	Writing on forms and on computer, reading, speaking and listening to clients	Role-play, spoken and written language modelling by adults
Discussion of journeys to school	Within class, staff-led	Speaking and listening	Reflecting on world outside. Use of Google Earth
Planning and drawing your house	Class area, children-led	Drawing, writing, speaking and listening	Use of clipboards to list materials. Reflecting and decisions
The construction site – role-play	Outside play area, children-led	Reading construction site signs, speaking, listening	Use of construction tools and dumper trucks. Negotiating

This topic actively promoted the use of the four language skills in contexts that reflected their use in the worlds outside the school. Not only was language being acquired and practised but ideas were being discussed and new understandings forged through a careful blurring of the areas of learning within and outside the class, out of school and at home. A judicious mix of teacher-directed and child-initiated learning allowed language to be created by the children, supported by adult interaction and modelled by adult input.

Thoughts on theory

- Role-play can be understood here on a socio-cultural plane as about learning how it is *to be* an estate agent rather than being told what an estate agent does. It also bridges the gap between Mahmoud's home and school life and builds on his experience to give a purpose to speaking, reading and writing.

- And from a psychological point of view, we can also see that affective benefits for learning might accrue through enabling Mahmoud to role play the excitement and disruption in his home life.

- In England the role-play area tends to be prevalent in nursery settings and in Y1 but often disappears altogether once children are in Y2 and above. Why do you think this is?

- A school may use an initial class visit to a place like a farm or supermarket before incorporating it into the role-play area. Could a role-play area function as effectively without the visit?

- What then is the 'authenticity' and 'relevance', referred to in Chapter 1, within these learning experiences in your view?

Points for practice

- What key linguistic elements would you hope to incorporate in the visit and the linked role-play area?

- Consider the need for child-initiated talk and writing as well as models of language from an adult. These are useful windows on their interests and prior learning.

- Use peers as models too. Children with strong social and linguistic skills and certain experiences outside of school may be able to stimulate, support and act as models for other children.

- The skills of reading and writing, speaking and listening are mutually supportive. Ensure the role-play area encourages children to play with them all.

ICT ideas

- Role-play is an excellent way to introduce everyday technology in this area of learning. Consider using non-working mobile phones. They enable children to practise conversations on the move.

- Awareness and criticality of the media can be encouraged by use of a TV box, made out of cardboard, in outdoor learning areas.

- Digital still and video cameras, such as Tuff cams, can be a window to understand children's interests through their narration of images and can be made available all the time. They can also add value in 'bringing the outside in' again after a visit.

- Consider setting up an outdoor private space with a camcorder for a while. But be alert to the potential ethical considerations in this invitation to share thoughts. Children should be made aware of the limits of privacy and of duties under child protection.

- A mini audio recorder can be a very useful tool to record the immediacy of experience on learning outside the classroom to reflect on when back inside.

Environmental print

Have you noticed how the written word insinuates itself into your thoughts as you go about your daily activities? Walking down the street you may start thinking about poverty because a bus advert on poverty has just passed you. Street names can catch your eye or the name of a new shop or café that has opened. Or for those of us partial to retail therapy a '50% off' sign or 'buy one, get one free' supersedes whatever we are thinking or talking about at the time. As you are reading this, let your eyes wander round the space you are in. Writing is everywhere from labels on your clothes and on your mobile phone to the make of car that has just gone by. You may be drinking from a mug that has writing on (mine, a present from my daughter, has three handles and the warning 'Dad! Handle with care!'). Perhaps there are cards from friends, sticky notes you have left or 'to do' lists you have written yourself. A quick trip to your kitchen will reveal packets of cereals, tins of beans, milk containers with labels that are carefully designed in text that catches your eye and informs you about the product. Our lives involve us in print from the moment we wake (what time is my clock reading?) to the moment we squeeze on our preferred brand of toothpaste (mine apparently is 'multi-action, whitening') before going to sleep.

And all this because we can read. The reason the black marks that you have in front of you at the moment are speaking to you is because you can decode and make meaning. This section of the chapter examines how children notice the print that surrounds them – environmental print – well before they can decode it and begin to try such decoding before they can fully understand it. Let me give you an example: a child named Amy is likely to notice any word that begins with *A* and claim it says Amy. She will have seen it written for her and may even have begun practising forming the letter herself in order to write her name. It is her letter and she will notice and claim it as hers when she sees it on a cereal packet, shop sign or car registration plate.

Environmental print – print found at home and outside it as well as in school – is a tremendous stimulus to the young child to learn to read. Someone has created these marks for a purpose and the adults around her constantly refer to them – 'I see England beat the All Blacks', 'There's a parcel addressed to you here' and 'Hang your coat up here where it says Amy'. They also make the marks too – on shopping lists, emails and texts, notes to Dad to feed the dog. Children naturally imitate and want initiation into this adult world. They want to understand by making the meanings the adults are making:

> because they are born sociable and curious and observant, babies and young children are eager to understand and be able to use the power of print. They want to be powerful members of their community and to engage with familiar others in ways they have come to recognise as meaningful. (Goouch and Lambirth, 2007: 15)

The same symbols are repeated enough times for a child to start understanding that these marks refer to sounds and these sounds refer to their world. Hence Amy will probably claim *A* as hers but not *a*, which is formed totally differently. Only later will she understand that they say the same thing. And later still that writing HELLO sounds different from 'hello' and that dear mr. smith might not get you a job whereas Dear Mr. Smith might.

Environmental print is socially situated: it has a writer, a reader and a context. The writer has a purpose – to convey specific information to an identified audience through a variety of choices over the medium he or she uses. Years ago, milestones were common when people travelled mostly by foot. They both informed and encouraged the traveller that he or she had covered another mile and was heading in the correct direction. Missed by the motorist today, who drives by too fast to notice them or does not need them with a SatNav and milometer within the car, they remain embedded by the side of the road, their print small but legible enough to the passing walker or rider. It is, like old Roman letters and runes, carved in capitals, as straight lines are easier to form in stone than curves. The writing on the stone was placed to face the traveller, to indicate where the traveller should head, and the information is terse – To London 55 miles – for the carver was paid by the letter. The audience brings their understanding of the world to the print not only to decode but also to situate it and give it meaning. The traveller knew only too well how far a mile was and what 55 to go meant – several days' walk, places to stay overnight, food and water to carry for the journey.

Behind print, there is a writer making choices and a study of environmental print involves children noticing print and wondering about the person behind it, their purpose for writing it, the choices they made with the design and materials used. The children can examine the effect the writing has on them, and they can analyse how effectively it does this. Older children will pursue this in greater depth, looking at letters – the choice of size and colour and capitals and font in signs has a purpose. That purpose is created by a writer and that writer has made a choice.

They will look at how the writer has made a choice about the information he or she wants to convey. Advertisements are often succinct, persuasive, informative, entertaining. They also involve complementary graphics. The choice of information and how it is laid out depends on the purpose the writer has and the intended audience. A moving bus needs a different approach to advertising from a brochure to be found in a travel agent.

How was the print physically created? What material was used for the print and what material was it printed on and why? Several children were involved in delivering a flyer for the local Fish and Chip shop, which was printed on A5 size paper using a photocopier. It was in black and white, cheap and easy to produce, transport and pop through letter boxes. This was in contrast to the glossy school handbook which had just arrived from the printers to go out to parents. The paper was a far better quality, it was printed in colour, full of photos and was expected to be durable and impressive as well as informative – a celebration of the school community.

The table below illustrates the variety of environmental print there is to be found and some of the aspects that can be brought out with children. The purposes and affordances of print in a real context are those which we, as teachers, strive to recreate within our classrooms, with greater or lesser success. It therefore makes sense to return our children's thinking to the authentic (with purpose beyond school learning) situations they encounter outside the classroom.

Table 5.2: Environmental print

Text location	Purpose of writer	Aspects of print
Bus, van, taxi and lorry sides	To inform and persuade	Often accompanied by graphics. Use of colour, different print sizes, capitals, interesting fonts
Cars	To inform	Mixture of numbers and letters, interior and exterior, for make and type, registration, dials, warnings for airbags, fuel, oil and so on
Road signs including speed limits, stop or give way, directions and parking, road and street names	Warnings and limits Information and directions	Often within a shaped and coloured symbol and often in capitals. Large for visibility and small for specific locations like car parks
Shop exteriors, shop interiors	To inform, persuade and direct	Outside – shop name, window displays with goods, descriptions, offers and prices. Inside – very varied according to shop but often labels and prices, leaflets and brochures, text to explain and persuade and direct.
Supermarket	To inform, persuade and direct	Large signs within supermarket for toilets, tills, goods within an aisle. On shelves smaller signs for prices, weights, quantities and name of goods. On goods themselves description often accompanied by graphics and mix of fonts, print size and colour
Doctor's or dentist's surgery or hospital	To direct and inform. To entertain	Large signage outside and in to direct customer. Smaller signs to direct and inform. Brochures and leaflets about services. Magazines, newspapers and comics to entertain. On screen text for checking in patients
Home – different rooms tend to contain different print: kitchens – food labels; sitting room – magazines, books, text on TV; bedroom – books, posters, toys, perhaps computer. Telephone directories, calendars, phone books, diaries	To inform, persuade, give instructions and entertain	Print that is produced by a member of the family is often hand-written. Food and packaging labels persuade, inform and give cooking instructions. A computer allows on-screen print and graphics: emails, Internet sites, games and DVDs. Mobile phones to receive and send texts. Clothes, mugs, electrical goods are generally labelled
School – office, corridors, classrooms, hall, specific areas for work such as library and IT suite, canteen, caretaker's office	To inform, instruct, direct, share, persuade or advise	Few examples of teachers' written work for display – mainly children's. A variety of hand-written and printed work, often accompanied by graphics, by children of different ages and stages stages. Signage for classrooms and other areas. Posters and brochures for parents. Many examples of on-screen text

Case Study

Culture capture: discovering purpose through environmental print

Mrs Watkin's class of Y6 children in Cardiff were looking at environmental print within school, beyond school and at home. She had chosen to focus on print from both the Welsh and English language, for the children to examine a number of issues relating to the print. Their task was to use a prompt sheet to make notes during their walk round the city in school time and, as homework, sheets to complete about their journey to and from school, about their home and for trips to town at the weekend. The prompt sheet covered the following areas:

Choice of language

- Where have you seen Welsh and where have you seen English used? Is environmental print more common in one or other language?
- How often are both languages used alongside each other?

Purpose of writer

- When you have noticed Welsh or English environmental print, why has the writer chosen to use one or other or both languages?
- What effect does this language choice have on the reader?

Your opinions

- What do you feel about the writer using Welsh and English?
- Are there times when you would disagree with the writer's choice of language? Why?

Although Cardiff is in an English-speaking area, Welsh is spoken in many shops, especially the larger supermarkets, which also produce signage in both English and Welsh. Street and road signs are often in both languages and some of the newspapers are printed in both Welsh and English. Government offices of course produce documents written in Welsh and English. The children automatically learn Welsh at school from age 3 upwards and may attend a Welsh-medium school.

During their study of environmental print, the children were involved in discussions about their own language preferences and their cultural identity. A rugby match between Wales and England was a simple test of cultural allegiance! However the children were conscious that all of them were English-speaking and that Welsh, to many, was a second language. They could understand why their Cornflakes packet was written in English and why vans and lorries mostly carried English-only advertising. However, the children showed a keen appreciation of how a language and cultural identity are closely linked, mostly accepting that fluency in English was necessary for them to understand and be understood but that learning Welsh was an entry into a culture they saw as theirs. This view of bilingualism can be seen in other native language communities within Britain, and the many communities that have settled in Britain with their own languages, such as Mandarin, Bengali, Gujarati or Polish, represented in their homes, local shops, community centres and places of worship and in local amenities such as medical surgeries and, of course, schools.

A study of environmental print begins by drawing children's attention to aspects of print in their environment that many will already not even notice as it is so familiar. This stimulates new learning about something taken for granted (Jarvis, 2009). It looks at the intention of the writer and the expected effect on the reader; there is a purpose (what is it for?) and an audience (who are they?) in this writing. The choice of physical message-carrying medium is important to get right and can vary from stone, wood, metal, plastic and paper. What are the reasons for these choices? Similarly the appearance of the words influences the reader and their colour, the type font, the letter size and graphics can all be pressed into service to make an intended effect. The effect of print on the reader can be examined: a street name can merely supply information or provoke a feeling of comfort or fear or strangeness depending on the reader and the situation. These could be examined through role-play or fiction writing. Other messages intend to provoke: '1 in 3 children live in poverty'. Print can be looked at from its absence: remove it all from our environment and what effect will that have? Why is print needed now and how did an illiterate population manage in the past? And finally, in what way does environmental print reflect the prevailing language and culture of the place? What assumptions does it make about the reader?

Thoughts on theory

- Over the last 150 years we have become a print-dependent society in the UK. What are the reasons for this?
- Because print is culturally situated, children from language-poor backgrounds or with English as a second language will have less cultural capital (Bourdieu, 1991) than that of their peers and are likely to be disadvantaged as a result.
- A socio-cultural plane of focus may help our understanding of purpose in environmental print.

Points for practice

- Environmental print initially fascinates young children and then becomes part of their everyday lives. Sensitise them to their growing and unconscious reliance on print.

- Society's use of environmental print is purposeful and situated. Involve children in the creation of environmental print for the school to provide a meaningful context and outcome to their writing.

- Children's cultures are often reflected in environmental print at home. Consider how to use these to explore language, cultures and community with the class. In what ways does environmental print in the UK reflect the multi-national society that is Britain?

In support of equity

The subject English could be narrowly defined as learning and then practising the skills of reading, writing, speaking and listening. However these skills are all modelled and provided for children long before they begin formal schooling. Each skill is socially situated and purposeful. A literate society will value and build on the experience of language that children already have before they come to school. Naturally this provision varies from child to child. Professor Maryanne Wolf (2008) refers to a gap of 32 million more words heard by a middle-class child from a language-rich environment compared to an underprivileged child by age 5.

And this is just the spoken word. How much then might separate those children's experience of read or written words? However, it remains a fact that children are surrounded by printed and spoken words even if they are not directly addressed towards them. The teacher can use the pervasiveness of language and the child's instinct as a social learner to want to acquire language to enrich the quality of learning taking place. Over a quarter of a century ago, in his inquiry into English Sir Alan Bullock (1975) referred to a *language across the curriculum* to give coherence to curriculum planning within schools but he also alluded to how language threads through a child's life both in and beyond the school. Using role-play and studying environmental print are ways of using the language that supports the community of which the child is part and which comprises school, home and beyond both. Language is taken from outside of school and reflected within the school curriculum. There is reflection of language and reflection about language. How much does the child talk outside of school and with whom? Who and what does she listen to and how well? How much does she read and how much is read to her? Does she see reading and writing taking place and how much can she talk about it in an informed and reflective way? A well-informed teacher is in a position to ensure that each child has a broad and rich language experience, for as Wolf points out:

> Many factors that children bring to the table in the early years cannot be changed. Language development is not one of them. (2008, cited in Rose, 2009: 3.17)

Summary

Two case studies of children's experiential use of language in their environment have been presented to illustrate the inter-relationship of language within and beyond the classroom. They focused on how attention to the uses of language for life beyond the classroom setting can increase criticality and acknowledge how cultural factors affect learning. 'Outside the classroom' is sometimes simply seen as a stimulant for writing in English; here its fundamental importance as a medium for the entire curriculum is recognised.

Further reading

Bearne, E. and Wolstencroft, H. (2007) *Visual Approaches to Teaching Writing*. London: Sage.

Eyres, I. (2007) *English for Primary and Early Years*. London: Sage.

Mallett, M. (1999) *Young Researchers*. London: Routledge.

Winston, J. (2004) *Drama and English at the Heart of the Curriculum*. London: David Fulton.

6

Mathematics outside the classroom

Nick Pratt

Chapter objectives

- Understanding the challenges associated with taking maths outdoors and developing mathematical thinking through experience and context

- Understanding the nature of mathematical work and its implications for these challenges

- Providing models to support the coherent development of mathematics through the use of the outdoors

During the 20 or so years I have spent working in primary education I have heard constant reference to the idea of making mathematics 'more practical' and 'based in the real world'. I am also frequently told that maths is 'useful', justifying its place as one of the core curriculum subjects. In this chapter I want to explore why, therefore, these claims seem so hard to realise in practice. To do so, I first begin by considering the nature of maths and suggest that the challenge of taking it outside is perhaps greater than we give credit for. I also offer some ideas for addressing this and hope that they might provide some starting points for you to develop mathematical thinking in new and interesting ways.

What mathematics is – and isn't

My experience is that most people find it very difficult to describe what maths actually *is* and that their schooling has done little to help them make sense of this question. Indeed, more worryingly, many people appear to dislike the subject or even take pride in doing so! Let me begin then with some thoughts about the nature of maths.

Think of some 'ways to make 10' – a very common task in the first years of schooling. Write down a few now, or at least think of them … I would guess you had something like 3+7=10, 8+2=10, 5+5=10 etc. and in thinking and writing these we have begun to use a mathematical idea, addition. My 5-year-old son, Sam, brought home a sheet of these sums this week, however, the act of working them out, or of recalling them if they were already known, only scratches the surface of mathematical activity. A useful analogy here is with music. Imagine that I had asked you to work out how to play a few notes on a recorder. Would this be music? Well, of a sort, in the sense that it asked you to use the musical skill of playing notes, but not in the sense of actually engaging in *musical activity* or of *being musical*. Similarly, when Sam worked out his ways to make 10 he did not engage in any *mathematical activity* or any sense of *being mathematical*. To do so he would have had to make use of these mathematical 'notes' and do something with them.

What might the business of doing maths look like in practice? My son might have been encouraged to lay out his problems in some kind of reasoned pattern, perhaps like this …

$$1+9=10$$
$$2+8=10$$
$$3+7=10$$
$$4+6=10$$
$$5+5=10$$
$$6+4=10$$
$$7+3=10$$
$$8+2=10$$
$$9+1=10$$

Already he would be likely to have made an important mathematical step, *generalising* the pattern so that he could note, perhaps, that the 0+10=10 and 10+0=10 were missing at each end.

Other generalisations might include the idea that even numbers pair up, as do odd numbers, to make 10 (you cannot make 10 with an odd and an even). On his own this might have been it, but with some intervention from me he might be able to join in with another mathematical process: *conjecture*. What happens if we want to extend the table up and down? If he does not know about negative numbers, he soon will because this list of 10s provides a lovely opportunity to discuss them … after 0+10=10 the pattern suggests □+11=10, so what could the □ be?

What about if we extend it sideways; indeed, what might this mean? Sam decided this meant the following …

1+9=10	2+8=10	3+7=10	4+6=10	… etc.
2+8=10	3+7=10	4+6=10	5+5=10	… etc.
3+7=10	4+6=10	5+5=10	6+4=10	… etc.
… etc.				

Had he known about place value he might have got into …

$$1+9=10 \quad 10+90=100 \quad 100+900=1000 \quad 1000+9000=10000$$
$$10000+90000=100000 \ … \ \text{etc.}$$

Finally, I might have asked Sam to convince me that what he had written was accurate and to *justify* his decisions. This would have been a young person's version of a third important mathematical principle, the idea of *proof*; which for young children starts with the idea of trying to convince others about one's thinking.

These three mathematical ideas – conjecture, generalisation and proof – are central to mathematical thinking, just as elements like rhythm, timbre, intonation etc. are central to music. What is more, we would want youngsters to develop personal qualities through actually doing maths. Koshy (2001) suggests that pupils should develop curiosity, creativity, fluency (i.e. the ability to carry out mathematical tasks fluently), skills and facts (tables knowledge etc.).

I would add to this list the idea of developing a 'mathematical dis-position', or the ability and desire to notice mathematical relationships and to use mathematical thinking in one's activity. This can be understood from the socio-cultural perspective outlined in Chapter 1 as coming to know maths as a particular *form* of activity – investigative, conjecturing, curious, creative etc. – rather than as a body of knowledge to be learnt. Indeed, this is perhaps the most important thing of all since without the capability and willingness (even better the desire) to do so, learning maths serves little purpose. There is considerable evidence (e.g. Boaler, 2002a, 2002b; Lampert, 1990; Schoenfeld, 1996) that the best, perhaps only, way to do this is to engage regularly in activity that is mathematical (as opposed to just 'learning' mathematical knowledge).

Finally, in thinking about what makes things mathematical, one more important idea remains. This is the notion that mathematical ideas, such as addition, are just that: ideas. Any mathematical object, such as a right-angled triangle, exists as an idea, although of course you can represent that idea with a physical object – a plastic triangle perhaps. What is crucial here is the very special way in which these ideas 'exist' in the mind, because they are not just created randomly at the whim of the inventor. Rather, ideas follow on from each other logically so that if you have the idea of counting then addition is, in a sense, out there waiting for you. Similarly, the idea of a rectangle (any four-sided polygon with all its angles right) immediately implies the idea of a square, that special rectangle where the sides happen to be equal too (for a fuller discussion, see chapter 2 of Pratt, 2006).

Crucially then, maths is actually a process of *abstracting* ideas and generalising them. If I want pupils to learn to count by using their fingers then I want them to abstract the idea of counting from their fingers, not get stuck using fingers for counting. Being able to do this unlocks the power of maths for pupils because it allows them to work on more complex ideas (in the abstract) and then reapply this to the concrete situation. It is well documented that, in practice, pupils are often held back by not making abstractions from the practical materials (Gray, 1997; Thompson, 1997).

Representations in the physical world will therefore be useful in as far as they help pupils make abstractions and work with these. One place where they have developed this idea is in the Netherlands where the use of Realistic Mathematics Education (RME) is well established for pupils of primary age (Treffers and Beishuizen, 1999). In RME, pupils are taught to 'mathematise' the situation; that is, to see the mathematics involved, and its structure, and to articulate this through symbols and/or representations of one sort or another. However, this mathematisation takes place in two directions. First, pupils are helped to mathematise 'horizontally' by representing (abstracting) the physical world in some kind of structured mathematical way, and vice versa. Then they are taught to mathematise 'vertically', developing the mathematical structures into more sophisticated ones. It is worth noting that the word 'realistic' is used by the Dutch in both senses – the use of a 'real' world, but also the development of calculating strategies and mathematical procedures that are 'real' (i.e. personal and meaningful) to the individual child, a further elaboration of 'reality' referred to in Chapter 1.

A model for mathematical thinking

Pointing to mathematical ideas as being mental constructions in the abstract does not imply that there is no role for the outdoors. As well as wanting pupils to acquire mathematical knowledge, mathematics is something that one *does*. Pupils therefore need to engage in *mathematical activity* – by which I mean activity that is *implicitly mathematical*; not just the activity of learning mathematical knowledge. Part of this engagement will be the use and application of mathematics they know in their everyday world and the learning of new mathematics from doing so. Furthermore, the fact that mathematics consists of abstract, mental objects does not mean that physical objects are not important in *making* these abstractions. Seeing, touching and hearing in the physical world will be crucial to children in making sense of these ideas.

The relationships between different aspects of mathematical learning are shown in the model in Figure 6.1.

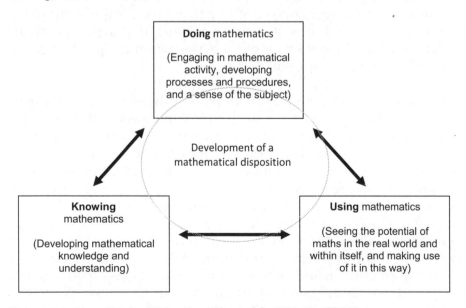

Figure 6.1 Learning mathematics (adapted from Pratt, 2006)

Having introduced several frameworks for thinking about maths, and before we turn to the role of the outdoors, you might like to think about some of the general implications for developing mathematical topics with pupils.

 Points for practice

- Imagine developing pupils' mathematical thinking in relation to even numbers. What are the (many) things that you might aim to do?
- How do these things interact with each other – how do these create opportunities and/or tensions for you as a teacher?

In responding to the points above, you might have considered the following:

- Knowing:
  - Knowing some even numbers.
  - Generalising the pattern for all even numbers.
  - Understanding how to check that a number is even or not.
- Doing:
  - Being curious and asking questions and conjecturing about properties of even numbers. (Do all evens give another even when halved? Which do; which don't? What is the longest chain of even halvings?)
  - Justifying and convincing others about things. (How to demonstrate *why* 6, say, is even, or why adding two even numbers always gives another one.)
  - Developing a mathematical disposition towards even numbers. (That is, being on the look out for of them and seeing/taking opportunities to make use of them.)
- Using:
  - Using even numbers in other 'mathematical' contexts, such as tables facts (such as seeing relationships between evens and the 2x table, 4x table etc.)
  - Using even numbers in real world situations (such as in sharing situations, geometrical patterns etc.).

One obvious tension in all this is the sheer number of things that might be going on at once. There is a big difference between this complex view of mathematical development including elements that are most easily noticed through the socio-cultural lens (Chapter 1), and the much narrower view (unfortunately reinforced by an objectives-driven curriculum) of simply learning the pattern of even numbers.

A second tension exists in the last bullet above – the use of even numbers in the real world. Perhaps you quickly thought of several relevant situations in which even numbers would figure in everyday activity in ways that would motivate pupils. I have to say I found this hard, hence my vague references to 'sharing situations and geometrical patterns'. It is significant that it is actually quite difficult to find genuinely interesting, and accessible, applications for much of the maths that we have in the curriculum. Ironically, it is easier to start with a situation and to draw out mathematical ideas from it, but this may be problematic for teachers following a curriculum based on conceptual content in which 'we are doing evens today'.

The role of the outdoors

Let us turn then to the outdoors and start by considering the roles that it might play in developing mathematical thinking. I make no apologies for delaying this introduction until after a discussion of the nature of mathematical thinking. The history of mathematics education is littered with the corpses of those who have tried to make mathematics 'relevant' to pupils through recourse to the 'real' world.

However, the outdoors might support mathematical development in the following ways. First, the stimulation provided by *being* outdoors – understood through the psychosocial plane in Chapter 1 – might be harnessed in learning about mathematics (or anything else) and the opportunity to touch, manipulate, see etc. might support learning. Secondly, engaging in everyday situations might help pupils to develop a *mathematical disposition* towards the world – a feeling that they are always on the lookout for mathematics and ways to use it (socio-cultural plane). Thirdly, the outdoors may provide opportunities for pupils to find mathematical solutions to problems that might be solved less effectively in other ways. Finally, everyday materials and experiences might serve as starting points for developing mathematical ideas – though the point of using them will be to abstract the mathematical ideas from the experience, not leave them rooted there.

On the other hand, each of these things also has a corresponding danger associated with it – the 'dark side' of mathematics teaching. The stimulation provided by *being* outdoors might well distract from the mathematical nature of the experience and make it difficult for pupils to focus on the mathematics itself (balanced of course by the value of other, more tacit, learning). Repeated recourse to the use of pseudo-real problems can easily persuade pupils that it is simply a 'book subject', as well as often being boring. Problems in the outdoors can often be solved by non-mathematical means just as effectively and can therefore often feel forced and false. Lastly, every-day materials and experiences might well provide short-term success for pupils but discourage them from moving to more abstract, more efficient approaches which are vital to continued success.

 Points for practice

- Consider the alternative viewpoints above and reflect on how these relate to your teaching experiences.
- In what ways do you engage in the positive aspects of working outdoors in maths?
- Do you recognise any of the dangers I describe, and if so, are there ways in which you might lessen their impact?

In order better to understand these ideas about the use of the out-doors, let me provide a simple case study (actually, a composite 'case' taken from a range of experiences). The context is a visit to an old Abbey, built in the 12th century and sold off by Henry VIII in the 16th century as part of the Dissolution of the Monasteries. Despite a turbulent history, much of the Abbey remains and the buildings and surrounding landscape provide a rich opportunity for work in all sorts of areas for children.

Case Study

Maths at the Abbey – take 1

The visit is a one-off – not ideal since the best experiences often result when pupils can explore the site over a number of visits (see Chapter 14). Nonetheless, on arriving at the Abbey some Year 4 pupils are given a printed sheet (there are similar sheets for different ages, 'differentiated appropriately') and asked to 'explore' the buildings by following the 'maths trail'. On the first side, decorated with pictures of parts of the buildings, pupils follow directions to various parts of the Abbey and are asked to:

1. estimate the height of the church tower;
2. sketch tile patterns from the floors and mark on lines of symmetry;
3. find out the height of a dead abbot by looking at his grave;
4. decide if he was taller or shorter than the pupils;
5. measure the length of a stone seat in the chapter house;
6. work out how many monks could have sat on it.

It seems to me that even leaving aside the obvious question that pupils might ask (i.e. 'why?'), these questions, and the similar ones that fill the second side of the sheet, only ask pupils to mathematise horizontally. Pupils are required simply to use bits of mathematical knowledge to answer the question – not asked to do anything with this either in terms of developing new mathematics or in terms of understanding the historical/social context more fully as a result of their mathematising. Furthermore, note the jumble of mathematical ideas involved: linear length, as height and width; tessellation; symmetry; and a brief reference to either addition, multiplication or division depending on how you work out the number of monks. This jumble of historical context and maths – all too familiar if one looks at similar trails created by learning professionals in a range of situations – serves to ensure that, at best, pupils would be confused by what, mathematically, this was all about and, at worst, convinced still further that maths is not really about anything much.

It all seems like a poor use of the opportunity presented by the context; so what might one have done instead? Taking the frameworks provided in the earlier sections, one might begin to look differently at the opportunity, considering the opportunities for *using* maths by mathematising the situation horizontally to relate mathematical ideas and the physical context; how these might be developed vertically so that pupils develop opportunities for *knowing* new mathematical ideas; and in doing so, what opportunities there are for *doing* maths, acting in a mathematical manner through conjecture, generalisation and proof.

What is more, rather than mixing a jumble of mathematical ideas seemingly at random, the context presents the opportunity to focus on the relationships between a few connected ideas, and hence to have the opportunity to develop some mathematical ideas from the context. Potential foci here include:

1. Linear length
   – working with different units and the conversion between them
   – using practical measuring equipment
   – estimating and approximating
2. Area
   – the idea of area as a measure of surface space
   – practical ways to measure areas
3. Money
   – calculating prices and costs of things
   – working in medieval, pre-decimal coinage [12 pennies to a

shilling and 20 shillings to a pound weight of silver]

4. Directions
   – recording and creating directions to different parts of the Abbey, or from the Abbey to different places around it

 Thoughts on theory
The planned curriculum

One objection to this case study might be that some of these topics are not in the prescribed curriculum document for the age of the pupils (Year 4). This is important to consider for a moment. Following the curriculum across a year has a great deal of merit, not least because it is one way to ensure the pupils experience a good range of mathematical ideas. The ideas build on each other too – counting coming before addition etc. However, there are also good reasons for breaking free of this curriculum.

First, though it is easy to be taken in by it, the curriculum does *not* illustrate the *way* pupils learn. Indeed, there is a good argument to say that it can inhibit learning by focusing too strongly on particular ideas and not on the way that they relate to each other. As we noted in Chapter 1, learning is all too easily appropriated by adults so that it always becomes mediated through the adults' (cultural) position.

Secondly, and relevant to outdoors, the practical contexts involved can strongly affect the outcomes both in terms of the way they structure the mathematical meaning of the ideas involved and in terms of the social context through which learning can be understood. To take my son as an example again, at age 5 he was quite able to read and write numbers in the tens or hundreds of thousands, yet still could not manage all the numbers in the teens. This was simply because we played Dinosaur Top Trumps (a card game based on data about dinosaurs), read dinosaur books at length and visited museums. The big numbers involved here allowed him to make connections that otherwise his teachers might have said he was 'not ready' for. I hope you can see the relevance to the outdoors here and how it exemplifies what we meant by the roles of 'place' and 'others' in Figure 1.2.

Having established potential mathematical foci – not a random jumble of mathematical ideas – how did maths at the Abbey actually develop?

Case Study

Maths at the Abbey – take 2

First, linear measurement was chosen as the key idea to work on. As well as a mathematical focus though, it made sense to have an historical focus too. Henry's dissolution of the monasteries offered a coherent case – a nice tale of power, politics and manipulation – and the pupils were asked to imagine being sent as envoys by Henry to evaluate the worth of the Abbey and its grounds so that it could be sold off to the laity. (See Chapter 8 for how cross-disciplinary work can enhance understanding through engagement.) Opportunities for lots of other aspects of the curriculum were present here, but mathematically this created the opportunity to consider issues of measurement and money. Importantly, the teacher did not define the idea of 'worth' in advance. This became the focal point for pupils to start their investigation prior to arrival, deciding on the size of buildings and grounds as being important, as well as the value of anything that might have been in the Abbey. Some preparatory research on the Internet had revealed the latter and a list of items and their values had resulted in considerable work calculating the totals, with the need to work with multiplication and division by 12 and 20 as pennies and shillings were converted to and from pounds. Horizontal mathematising, as pupils worked with representations of money on these issues, then led to opportunities for vertical mathematising as relationships in multiplication tables between the 10 and 6 and the 20 and 12 respectively were identified and practised. The teacher tried to work on the conversion from old pounds to decimal currency, but this proved too difficult for pupils and a tactical withdrawal ensued; a battle to be fought another day.

Other opportunities for mathematising in both directions came as pupils discussed how best to measure the 'size' of the grounds. This provided the chance to talk about area (a difficult concept because of its two-dimensional properties) and the relationship between calculating area and array-models of multiplication. More research was done about measures of length in the 16th century. This proved complicated since standard definitions of some lengths (the yard for example) changed considerably during this period, but cubits, yards, chains, rods, poles and furlongs were all discussed, created using string and related to modern metric units – providing the opportunity to work on the relationships between metres, centimetres and millimetres. Finally, it was decided that the main activity on the day should be for groups to measure different parts of the Abbey carefully so as to bring this information back to add to an aerial view that had been created using mapping software. This would then provide the stimulus for future work on calculating the value of the site and for writing and creating posters about this in suitably authentic Tudor style. Despite being focused on just one visit, the preparatory work provided plenty of opportunity to practise using these measures in the school grounds.

One thing to note here is how much mathematical thinking happened even before pupils had got on the bus! On the day, focusing on the practical task of measuring meant that pupils were active and working towards a goal together. There was also plenty of time to engage in other activity, both formally organised in other curriculum areas and simply experiencing being in the old Abbey. The teacher therefore avoided using this precious time doing the calculating; this would be done back at school. (See Chapter 14 for how sandwiching learning outside the classroom with good preparation and follow-up enhances its usefulness.)

> ## ICT ideas
>
> Another alternative to doing the research and calculations before and after back in school is to use the increasingly mobile technology of netbooks and laptops to record on the hoof with digital photos to contextualise the measurements.

As an example, pupils' construction of equipment for old measures first involved finding out about how these measures were gauged – the cubit being the length from elbow to fingertip etc. – and this led to horizontal mathematising as pupils developed their own representations for these units and their relationships to one another and practised using them in the playground. However, as pupils then tried to relate these to metric measures, they needed the teacher to initiate vertical mathematising in terms of learning about relationships in a decimal system and seeing the generalisations involved. This was dealt with by having some lessons focused on specific learning developments, in which pupils worked in the mathematical arena rather than the real world arena. Not only did this arm the pupils with the more generalised and powerful ideas that they could reuse in their project work but it also allowed the teacher to control the direction of the learning to some extent. This presents us with a useful model for the business of mathematising, as shown in Figure 6.2 overleaf.

The outcome of this kind of approach was both the use and application of mathematical ideas in order to solve a complex problem relating to Tudor life, but also the development of mathematical ideas themselves in order to be able to solve this problem, and as an end in itself.

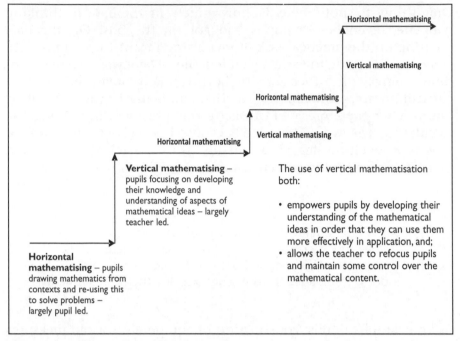

Horizontal mathematising

Vertical mathematising

Horizontal mathematising

Vertical mathematising

Horizontal mathematising

Vertical mathematising – pupils focusing on developing their knowledge and understanding of aspects of mathematical ideas – largely teacher led.

The use of vertical mathematisation both:

• empowers pupils by developing their understanding of the mathematical ideas in order that they can use them more effectively in application, and;

• allows the teacher to refocus pupils and maintain some control over the mathematical content.

Horizontal mathematising – pupils drawing mathematics from contexts and re-using this to solve problems – largely pupil led.

Figure 6.2 A model for mathematising

 Points for practice

In planning and carrying out this activity, the teacher had to let go of her usual way of teaching maths and work in a more holistic, but therefore potentially risky, manner (see Pratt and Berry, 2007). You might like to consider some of the issues involved in doing this, including the following:

■ To what extent did the planned work provide opportunities for doing, knowing and using maths? How did 'Place', 'Child' and 'Others' (Chapter 1, Figure 1.2) interact to create activity?

■ In particular, what opportunities are there in the work for conjecturing, generalising and proving/justifying, as well as for developing skills, fluency, facts, curiosity and creativity (Koshy, 2001)?

■ How would you feel about planning and carrying out this kind of work? What effect would it have on planning procedures and how would this fit in with what you are required/choose/would like to do?

■ This approach demanded a fairly strong mathematical understanding of the teacher because the emphasis was on seeing and working with connections as they arose.

The more one does this, the less can be planned in advance. How confident are you and your colleagues (including teaching assistants) in doing this, and what implications are there for you here?

Summary

I hope that it is clear from the foregoing discussion that taking maths outdoors has great potential, but also raises a number of dilemmas, both practical and in terms of the nature and purpose of the subject itself. In conclusion, therefore, I summarise *key principles*, taken from the case studies, for guiding this kind of work.

Mathematical ideas were identified in advance and used to create a coherent *mathematical* 'pathway' for the pupils. We want children to travel through the mathematical world, but this should be a reasonably organised walk, not a random mystery tour.

Preparation also included identifying opportunities for *doing*, *knowing* and *using* mathematics, as well as for the mathematical principles identified by Koshy. But note that these opportunities did not need planning as *separate* objectives in a sterile way. Experiential, outdoor work simply provides these opportunities naturally.

Preparation was crucial so that pupils arrived at the Abbey ready to start thinking mathematically and knowing what the task was. However, there was enough 'openness' to ensure that pupils had to think independently (see Fielker, 1997).

Time on site was used for practical engagement. Calculations etc. were held back for their return to school.

Finally, the way in which mathematising can take place in both directions (horizontally and vertically) overcomes the tension that can arise in work emerging from experiences – namely that the inherent freedom for pupils to control the direction of things makes it harder for a teacher who is accountable for covering a particular curriculum.

Further reading

Fielker, D. (1997) *Extending Mathematical Ability through Whole Class Teaching.* London: Hodder & Stoughton.

Pratt, N. (2006) *Interactive Maths Teaching in the Primary School.* London: Paul Chapman Publishing.

Skinner, C. (2005) *Maths Outdoors.* London: Beam Education.

7

Science and technology outside the classroom

Beth Gompertz, Julia Hincks and Rachael Hincks Knight

Chapter objectives

- To give an appreciation of the distinct contributions that science and technology can make to children's learning
- To consider the outdoors as a resource and as a context for scientific and technological understanding
- To explore children's potential relationships with the outdoors

It is important first of all to consider the relationship between science and technology and how approaching these two curriculum areas together in the outdoors might aid learning. Are science and technology the same, do they overlap or are they separate and distinct subjects? The Science Council has defined science as 'the pursuit of knowledge and understanding of the natural and social world following a systematic methodology based on evidence' (2009). Science then appears to focus on the practical and measurable and on knowledge acquisition and disciplined skills; what then is technology? Lane defines technology as concerned 'with understanding how knowledge is creatively *applied* to organised tasks involving people and machines that meet sustainable goals' (2005: our emphasis). Technology appears to have several elements within it; process, objects or products, creative design, and the way these elements interplay.

Science and technology then certainly overlap, but have distinctly separate aims; science is concerned with understanding the world around us, whereas technology is often concerned with the design of products to make the world around us 'better'. An example of overlap might be the Apple iPod: science has allowed the development of a device which is small but holds a large volume of music, whereas it is technology that has created an accessory everyone wants to own (Lane, 2005). Both disciplines encourage creative thought, interpretation and questioning, and combining them together inside and outside the classroom can allow for extended activities that can develop a more holistic understanding, taking account of both these perspectives as argued in Chapter 1.

Also, given the inherent application of scientific ideas in technology, it is likely that authentic experiences and examples of practice beyond the classroom will be particularly important aspects of this combined area of learning. In this chapter, we consider how children can develop a sense of belonging in the outdoors, how they can begin to understand the world around them and how they can start to reduce their negative impact on the environment. Activities give practical examples of how theory may be put into practice, utilising the outdoors as both a context and a resource, and employing scientific and technological understanding. This practical engagement also has implications for environmental awareness and action, as suggested by Palmer's 'emergent environmentalism' (1998).

In many instances, the outdoors will provide a suitable context; in this chapter we discuss an activity involving a wind turbine, something that clearly is best suited to the outdoors with natural access to windy weather. But the outdoors need not only provide the context; it can be a resource itself. In this chapter we will also look at the outdoors as a habitat for studying familiar species, as a source of energy and, crucially, as a place to *enjoy* science and technology.

Developing a sense of belonging – Earthwalks

Earthwalks were initially intended to engage children with the natural world and develop empathy with nature. Within the primary school years they are also seen to be of potential benefit in providing welcome variation from more traditional approaches to nature study. As such they are useful tools for motivating and enthusing children in engaging with science work, developing observational skills and developing understanding of underlying ecological concepts such as the connectedness of life and similarities between living things. This emphasis on enjoyment of the experience in the outdoors is a recurrent theme in Earthwalk approaches and links with the observed impact that 'positive emotions contribute to enduring memories' (Waite, 2007: 335) helping to enable a wider observation and perhaps more vivid recall (Bixler et al., 2002; Carver, 2003). Psychosocial perspectives provide the theoretical basis for this work, but the following comment by Van Matre, a pioneer of this approach, shows that it can also be understood in socio-cultural terms:

> I wanted to convey a feeling of at-homeness with the earth, a feeling similar to what you have in your own house ... I wanted the kids to have that same feeling of security and comfortability that they have in their own homes, but with the planet itself – our pre-eminent home – the earth and its communities of life. (Van Matre, 1999: 33)

The Earthwalk activities used with student teachers at the University of Plymouth incorporate the concept of flow learning, which offers a rationale for sequencing the activities in order to raise enthusiasm, focus attention, offer deeper experiences and share inspiration. Cornell suggests that working this way can offer an 'inside view of the way nature works', help children to 'tune feelings to special qualities of nature', 'experience a profound sense of joy, serenity and belonging to the natural world' and that it gives opportunities to 'teach ecology creatively' (1998: 10–11). He claims that this approach 'brings us into harmony with our natural surroundings both physically and emotionally' (Cornell, 1998: 9). Since most of the activities involve using particular senses in an enhanced or deliberate way, they also seem to be effective in developing observational skills.

There are lots of activities like these – many of which are adapted from Cornell (1998). They collectively encourage children to develop the use of all senses, increase awareness of the pattern, complexity and detail of the natural world and contribute to an appreciation of observation skills.

Berryman considers a child's relationship with nature as a crucial aspect of their development, drawing on the concept of matrices (Pearce, 1992, cited in Berryman, 2000) as centres of security that the child operates from as each phase of their development unfolds. He identifies the years between 7 and 11 as a very important time in this development when a child moves towards becoming secure in the environment:

> by seven the child feels comfortable and confident enough in the natural and social worlds to begin to differentiate himself from the mother and from his family unit and he thus moves towards the earth matrix. (Berryman, 2000: 5)

Table 7.1 Earthwalk activities – developing scientific skills *and* a relationship with nature (developed from Cornell, 1998)

Activity/group	What to do	Purposes
Bats and moths Whole group Any outdoor space	Children form circle to protect active participants. Some children are chosen to be blindfolded bats or moths in the circle. They call out 'bat' or 'moth' and the bats have to locate their prey by the sound. Vary the number of bats and moths and size of circle to illustrate the effects on rates of capture.	*Raise enthusiasm and energy Enhance listening skills Understand predator confusion and prey/predator ratios Appreciate what it is like to be prey or predator Trust in others when blindfolded*
Sound sensitivity Whole group Any outdoor space	This can be done in a circle, sitting on carpet tiles for comfort or scattered around a bigger natural area. Children are asked to sit still and quiet with their eyes closed for 3 minutes, listening carefully. Each time they hear a new sound they raise another finger, until on average about 6 fingers each are raised. In a circle, all share what they heard. Reflect on the process and the sounds. What do they tell us? Could be extended by asking them to draw a sound map.	*Focus attention Enhance listening skills and ability to be quiet Understand listening is a form of observation useful in scientific study Appreciate how rare silence is even in 'tranquil' settings Share experiences*
Sky eyes Small or whole group Area with trees Woodland	Children are given a secret sign (the branching pattern of lines on their palm) and sky eyes (safety mirror held across bridge of nose facing upwards). A crocodile is formed behind adult or trusted peer to wander under trees so they see the canopy in the mirror 'as if they were in it'. Can search for their secret sign in the branching patterns above and experience a link with a particular tree.	*Focus attention Awareness of patterns in nature Development of observational skills, using different perspectives Observation of tree canopies Connecting with nature Trust of others in guiding when blindfolded*
Hug a tree Pairs Area with trees Woodland	One child of each pair is blindfolded and led by partner by a roundabout route to certain tree. They are encouraged by peer to feel the trunk high, low and all around, drawing attention to distinguishing features. They are led back to start and then asked to find the tree again. Often children have to hug the tree again with their eyes closed to make sure!	*Focus attention Share experiences Trust of others in guiding when blindfolded Development of observational skills, using different perspectives Understand feeling materials is a form of observation useful in scientific study Connecting with nature*
Film show Whole group Area with trees Woodland	Ask children to find a 'ticket' in the form of leaves from different tree species. Place the leaf in a slide mount and return to the children, who form a circle. Everyone closes their eyes. When the teacher says 'open', they look at their slide, then pass it with closed eyes to the person on their left. At each 'open' they see a different leaf until all have been viewed. The 'tickets' can be displayed back in the classroom window.	*Focus attention Share experiences Development of observational skills, using different perspectives*

However, he warns that this is also a delicate process that may take time. He further contends that the responsibilities that come with our relationship with the natural environment should only be considered after that relationship is established and the transition to 'earth matrix' is complete. Sobel (2004) calls this tendency in education to address generalised issues before background understanding and confidence is established 'premature abstraction' and warns that consideration of abstract theorising can develop a phobia of the subject as children struggle to master concepts that they are not ready for. This idea is worth considering too in connection with mathematical abstraction (see Chapter 6). In the case of the environment, connection and security in the environment is seen as fundamental to our own personal development during middle childhood for

> if the curriculum gives the message that the earth is in danger, that it is bat-tered, that it is abused and that it is poisonous, it can discourage the children from exploring the earth and bonding to it. (Berryman, 2000: 8)

This is a consideration for all educators, as is the need for real con-texts. Opportunities to reinforce and practice learning, challenge appropriate for the learner and scaffolding are established ideas. Sobel (1995) proposes three phases that are relevant here:

> *Empathy* between the child and the natural world should be a main objective for children ages four through seven. (p. 3)

> *Exploring* the nearby world and knowing your place should be a primary objec-tive for the 'bonding with the Earth' stage, from ages eight to eleven. (p. 5)

> *Social action* appropriately begins around age 12 and certainly extends beyond age 15. (p. 6) [emphasis added]

The emphasis on empathy in Key Stage 1 and exploration in Key Stage 2 resonates with our own experience of children and has implications for the use of different types of activity that engage children in belonging to and understanding their own 'backyard'.

This is particularly relevant in the context of recent government promises for increased freedom for schools in adhering to the National Curriculum through the opportunity for academies at primary level to determine locally determined curricula.

Finding out about the world around us

Case Study 📁

Birds' business: technology and observation skills

As part of a whole-school gardening project, Year 4 children were tasked with designing an area to encourage birds and tested out ways in which they might observe birds and record their behaviour. Ms Beasley took the class outside so they could begin to look around the school grounds and develop ideas that might make their garden attractive to birds. The children decided that the most important features were:

1. places for birds to live (it was agreed that the bird area would be near trees but that they could also make bird boxes for them to live in)

2. somewhere warm

3. food (suggestions included 'bird food', 'worms', 'snakes').

Over the course of the next few weeks, the children made bird feeders (see Table 7.2 below), designed bird boxes (made by Year 6) and made periscopes in order that they could hide away (the notion of not scaring the birds was a priority for the children) but still observe the birds.

Table 7.2   Feeding the birds and recycling: making knitted bird feeders

Stages	Instructions
A. Preparation of plastic 'yarn' from carrier bags	1. Lay bag flat and cut off the bottom 2. Cut across width of bag to form narrow rings of plastic 3. Join by looping over one another and pulling tight into knot
B. Option 1. Use circular knitting looms (see Photo 7.1)	Sew one end closed using plastic yarn
C. Option 2. Use large knitting needles	For those able to knit using needles: 1. Knit a strip till about 18 cm wide by 20 cm long using large needles for loose-knit effect 2. Knit stitches two together when 20 cm until only one stitch remains and bind this off 3. Sew together sides using a large sewing needle and plastic yarn
D. Filling and attaching	1. Fill the tubes with seeds, nuts, etc. large enough not to fall through. You could try different sorts of foods in different feeders 2. Attach to a suitable branch using plastic yarn (see Photo 7.2)
E. Experiments and observation	Watch and record what birds are attracted to which feeders Predict, observe and collect evidence to support your ideas

(Continues)

(Continued)

Photo 7.1   Using the circular knitting loom

Photo 7.2   The finished bird feeder

The ICT technician also set up a video camera next to the bird feeders and another in a bird box so the children could review footage to begin to see how birds behaved.

ICT ideas

- Rather than purely using ICT to create a remote and 'virtual' environment, for example, by viewing websites, virtual tours or CD/DVD (Harlen and Qualter, 2009), ICT can be used as a means for deeper investigation into the experiences taking place outdoors and to bring those first-hand realities back into the classroom. For example, children can use portable devices such as handheld gaming consoles, smartphones and netbook computers to record video and audio, and to give commentary to their observations. Their work can then be shared within the classroom, or can be used in conjunction with a wiki or a blog as part of an interactive resource to be accessed anywhere. An interesting video exploring mobile technology can be found on Teachers TV at www.teachers.tv/video/30878.

- Children are no longer restricted by space as technology can be taken with them; it can also allow them to do things that might not be achieved by traditional means. In the case study above, the video footage of birds nesting or feeding could be edited to focus on specific behaviours and considered along with the children's real-time first-hand recordings. In addition, children could take advantage of geo-technology by uploading photos and videos to interactive maps such as Google Earth. This would enable people around the world to see the behaviour of birds in this specific school, but also allow the children to make comparisons with what is happening elsewhere.

Learning outdoors need not be about wide open spaces or far-flung destinations but about utilising what is outside your door or window. In the previous case study, the school grounds are used as a rich resource for studying the behaviour of birds and allowing children to experience this first hand.

Studies by Rickinson et al. (2004) and Dyment (2008) identify that three barriers to the use of school grounds persist: teacher confidence, teacher expertise and the requirements of school curricula. Teachers and schools need to work together in order to overcome these barriers and utilise the potential of the outdoor classroom, something that could be embedded in the curriculum and viewed in the same way as any other 'learning space'. In urban areas where school grounds may not be green spaces, observations of animals common to these habitats could be observed; for example, foxes via video overnight. However, this is not to say that comparison cannot be drawn by visiting another area and that outdoor education off-site is not a good thing.

Identifying ways to reduce impact on the environment

Case Study

Alternative energy sources and wind speed

A group of Year 5 children are exploring the use of wind power to make electricity and Mr Green has brought in a wind-powered mobile phone charger to demonstrate this in practice. The children are particularly fascinated that a small turbine can make enough power for a phone to work and made comments such as 'but the energy is kept in a battery so the windmill isn't doing anything'.

The teacher decides to explore their ideas and misconceptions by looking closely at how a wind-up toy boat works. Each child has a toy boat to look at, to find out how it works and then to take part in a race to see whose boat is the fastest. The children spend time winding the paddle until the elastic is wound tightly; the teacher interrupts once all children have done this and asks them questions about what they are doing and what they think is happening. A number of children respond that 'when we let the turbine go it spins around so the boat moves forward'. The children test their boats in the water and the race takes place; the teacher asks the owner of the winning boat to give an idea as to why their boat was the fastest. Becky replies, 'I think I wound it up the most.' The teacher then introduces the children to 'stored' and 'movement' energy and the class consider the energy changes taking place, relating it to the movement of the turbine in the wind-powered phone charger as well.

The second activity relates to how much wind is needed to generate electricity and how windy it is in their school grounds; the children make a ping-pong ball anemometer (a wind speed measuring device) and on a rota basis measure wind speed at various times of the day over a few weeks. (Comprehensive instructions along with pictures of how to make an anemometer can be found courtesy of the Royal Meteorological Society at www.rmets.org/activities/schools/make-anemometer.php). This activity was then used as a lead in to considering whether wind turbines could be used to generate some of the school's electricity, with children putting forward ideas, plans and designs to the school council.

It is important that children are given opportunities to develop first-hand experiences that will support the development of their understanding. Children are naturally inquisitive and will test out ideas and repeat actions in order to make sense of what is happening around them, asking questions along the way. It is the job of the teacher and teaching assistant to encourage children and to further their enquiry (Hincks, 2007) by asking relevant questions.

Thoughts on theory

- Place and pedagogy interact in learning (see Chapter 1, Figure 1.2).

- Elstgeest (2001) describes a distinction between *'unproductive questions'*, those with a 'correct' answer, and *'productive questions'*, those that encourage investigation. In the Alternative Energy Sources case study above the teacher could have used productive questions that start with 'what happens if …' This could lead to 'what do you think is happening …?' Children can consider what they have seen or experienced and begin to attach meaning, to which they will then be able to attach scientific terminology – a constructivist approach. It is important that so-called 'scientific language' does not become a barrier to understanding scientific concepts.

- Harris (2006), however, questioned whether this constructivist interpretation is entirely appropriate pointing out that in her research a high proportion of children were unable to answer an open question. She suggests rather that the whole situation in which the learning takes place affects the likely response patterns, not just how a question is phrased and that there is therefore a need for a practical, observable situation for the children to understand the nature of the question in order to begin to answer it.

In the Alternative Energy Sources case study the teacher encouraged the children to look at the wind-up boats, to consider how they work by playing with them, giving the children a demonstrable context within which they could then ask and answer questions. In the second part of the case study, making and using an anemometer, the outdoors is the most appropriate context; this cannot be adequately explained by using any other means such as video or second-hand accounts. In this example, children are able to actually observe and quantify wind speed, allowing them to begin to understand why we would want to use wind power, moving to how we might harness it.

The government's sustainability agenda (DfES, 2006b) included a 2020 target that all school buildings and grounds are seen as learning spaces and that children's involvement with these spaces will lead them to develop a sustainable lifestyle. By using activities such as those in the Birds' Business case study, children are given opportunities to engage with the school environment and to consider ways in which it can be improved; by concentrating on familiar surroundings and familiar species young children can develop an awareness and appreciation of the environment and consider these issues of sustainability without feeling under pressure.

Once they have become familiar with the concept of being responsible for their own school grounds children will come up with their own ideas to take these forward and should be allowed increasing autonomy in caring for their surroundings and local area.

 Points for practice

Bloom (2006: 10) discusses the need for children to be actively involved in 'doing science' in order to understand the nature of science and that children should be 'producers of knowledge' rather than rote-learning facts and being 'consumers':

- Strengthen scientific skills by children designing and carrying out their own scientific investigations.

- Give children an opportunity to lead their own learning and find things out for themselves, discussing ideas with their peers and being able to argue their case for a certain way of proceeding.

- Let children decide in groups what they are going to investigate, what equipment (from a wide selection) they will use and which materials they will test.

Some ideas for scientific investigations:

- Let children determine which might be the 'best' materials to use for their bird feeders (other than carrier bags) by considering weather-proof properties or strength.

- Let the children choose items to bury for half a term to see what rots and what doesn't. They can then speculate about how this relate to composting.

- Reuse plastic bottles with the tops cut off for plant growers. If you replace the top (with lid on) you have a mini greenhouse or terrarium. Let children compare plants grown with and without this.

The notion of child-led activities can be quite difficult for teachers to engage with; to be able to hand over control of a lesson or an activity to a class of pupils. However, with careful consideration, this approach can be of benefit to both children and teacher as children are motivated by independence and the teacher can gain a better understanding of how the children in their class learn and their understanding in terms of scientific concepts.

Summary

Using school grounds to explore observations and scientific investigations gives children a real context for their learning. They are also a rich source of children's ideas for designing products to improve and use our environment. We hope that this chapter has given you some exciting ideas to adapt and use in your own school – we certainly enjoyed them all first time around!

Further reading

Bourne, B. (ed.) (2000) *Taking Inquiry Outdoors: Reading, Writing, and Science Beyond the Classroom*. Portland, ME: Stenhouse Publishers.

Braund, M. and Reiss, M. (2004) *Learning Science Outside the Classroom*. London: RoutledgeFalmer.

Buchanan-Dunlop, J. (2008) *School Grounds Projects Using Google Tools*. [Online] Available at: www.google.co.uk/schools/files/schoolgrounds.pdf.

'Nature Detectives' is a Woodland Trust project designed to engage children in learning about nature through the seasons. It has ideas to try and activity packs to download for Science, Technology, Citizenship and ICT: www.naturedetectives.org.uk/

Understanding places and society through history and geography outside the classroom

Orla Kelly and Roger Cutting

Chapter objectives

■ An awareness of the potential learning opportunities in urban and rural landscapes

■ An appreciation of drama as a teaching medium in the outdoors

■ An appreciation that an integrated approach to learning is necessarily the only way that the social, geographical and historical landscape can be understood

---

In this chapter we will examine the potential of outdoor settings to learn history and geography and develop an understanding of place. It considers some of the obstacles to outdoor learning in this topic area and describes an approach that has been adopted to try to provide an outdoor learning experience that engages the children's imagination and sense of creativity but that still provides valuable learning about the geography and history of a local area as well as providing opportunities to explore people's impact on the landscape.

However, let's start with a joke. In a classroom a teacher says to a child, 'Give me a sentence that starts with the letter I.' The child thinks for a moment and then hesitantly begins, 'Err ... I is ...' 'No, no,' says the teacher, quickly jumping in and adding helpfully 'I am'. 'Oh,' says the child. 'I am the ninth letter of the alphabet.'

OK, so it's a poor joke, but it illustrates how as teachers we are quick to provide assistance as well as to help guide responses. It also demonstrates how, on occasion, such rapidity (and control) can actually be counterproductive to learning. This sort of response is quite understandable, as teachers rightly want to help, after all it is what we do and it is well intentioned. However, it can be inappropriate in supporting independent learning.

Standing back and letting children get on with the business of learning can be a difficult proposition as teachers may be reticent to give up their control of the process for a number of reasons including the need to meet outcomes and the pressures and confinement of a packed curriculum (Maynard and Waters, 2007). When time is in short supply, the emphasis inexorably shifts to levels of achievement, competency and other predetermined objectives (Braund and Reiss, 2004: 7). With such a pressure to 'get through' things combined with the seemingly constant addition of more content, is it any wonder that teachers feel they should control and guide learning so proactively? Furthermore, there may be reluctance to organise an outdoor learning session as it is perceived as time-consuming. (See also Chapter 3). A further contributing factor may be the anxiety that teachers themselves may face in unfamiliar territory. Even the vagaries of weather can put staff off (Waite et al., 2006).

Yet, despite the crowded curriculum, the emphasis on outcomes and the shortage of time, there is undoubtedly growing support for outdoor learning and an increasing body of work that suggests that it can afford a range of positive learning experiences (Nundy, 1999; Rickinson et al., 2004). These include learning to deal with risk (Furedi, 2001; Greenfield, 2004; Little, 2006; Stephenson, 2003; Waters and Begley, 2007), the value of physical exercise and related health issues (The Children's Society, 2009) and an increasing interest in countering the disassociation of many children from the natural environment (Dyer, 2004; Thomas and Thompson, 2004). Indeed, given the weight of such evidence, there has been growing support for outdoor learning with a recent all-party Parliamentary inquiry producing a manifesto for outside learning (Learning Outside the Classroom, 2006). It seems that most agree, even if we don't quite know why, (Rea and Waite, 2009) that teaching outdoors provides a number of benefits.

It is difficult to envisage at this time how the apparent contradiction of curriculum constraints and the growing support and recognition of the benefits for outdoor learning will be reconciled without a significant change in the curriculum focus. There are already signs of such changes in Scotland where learning outside the classroom is more established. Under the initiative 'Curriculum for Excellence', much less emphasis is placed on academic 'subjects' but rather on skills and attitudes (Nicol et al., 2007). In Wales, too, the value of learning outdoors has been more widely recognised. However, whether implied greater independence for heads to determine their curriculum in England, through participation in the extended Academy initiative, translates into more use of the outdoors remains to be seen. However, the varied distinct types of outdoor education exacerbate the problem: one type involves play, adventure and promotes engagement of the imagination; another involves more cognitive learning in ecological or geographical field studies. Both approaches have much to offer, but the latter is certainly the more easy to evaluate in terms of testable outcomes; the promotion of imagination and engagement with the natural environment, while attractive propositions, remain elusive in this respect. However, these are the very outcomes that many would want to promote. The loss and even suppression of imagination has been commented on by many, including the poet Ted Hughes:

> What's happened to imagination? It has been discouraged by literalism, by complacency, by technical rationality and by obsession with predictable results. (1988: 43)

Subject disciplines bring their own traditions in terms of pedagogies; a community of practice is constructed within them (see Chapter 1 and the discussion about mathematics in Chapter 4). Geography has a long tradition of fieldwork, while history often uses drama and role-play to meet learning objectives. Cross-disciplinary study outside the classroom opens up possibilities for shifts in pedagogical practice. There is more material available about fieldwork practice in geography (e.g. Rickinson et al., 2004), so the example we have chosen combines different disciplines in a holistic approach that sits firmly in the imaginative, creative and adventure type of outdoor learning.

Learning *for* a landscape

Any area beyond the classroom, whether it is a field, a woodland or public park, is a product of its history, its geography and of people. Any cultural landscape is a complex interplay of forces and any attempt at understanding needs to appreciate this complex relationship. The history of a landscape is not a single history of a place: changes over time reveal the subtle influences of different values, attitudes, and societal impacts. Indeed, without a consideration of the history of a place and its people, the landscape becomes a simple backdrop that we never learn to 'read' and even less appreciate beyond the aesthetic (Stewart, 2008). Landscapes (urban and rural) lend themselves to integrative approaches and story telling is part of an oral tradition of history that not only helps us appreciate the dynamism of landscapes but is a way in which we can encourage both imagination and cognitive development. Educating *in* a landscape, the simple transfer of the classroom outdoors, is one thing; however, learning *for* a landscape is a very different approach. Joy Palmer talks of learning *about* the environment *in* the environment *for* the environment in her discussion of 'emergent environmentalism' (Palmer, 1998).

What value do we place on a landscape? This is problematic in that we imbue value in different ways. Is the value economic, cultural or aesthetic? We can try to teach each by categorising them into subject areas. Geography may consider land use and economic utilisation through farming or tourism. History would look at the cultural development, past major events that have perhaps physical manifestations etched on the land. The Arts would perhaps be most at home with exploring the aesthetics of the landscape. Yet with a full curriculum and the pressures on delivery, is the artificiality of such division desirable? A change in focus would see the complexity of the landscape as its defining feature. To teach and learn in such environments requires an approach that accepts this complexity and a cross-curricular approach supports this. To subdivide such learning into subject areas is to miss the point. An integrative approach to such learning is necessarily the only way that the landscape (in its broadest sense) can be understood. In outdoor learning environments, history, geography and social understanding can be brought together and placed into a local context. This provides a deeper appreciation of the locality (its people, geography and history) which could be interpreted as a more emotionally informed understanding and from a socio-cultural perspective, as engaging with what it would be like to *live* in that landscape. This promotes reflection on the impact of people's action on the landscape. Howes (2005) speaks of 'emplacement' as the identification and embodiment of the social being in a place. It is through such engagement that we promote our environmental and social responsibilities, indeed;

> they exult in a new sense of freedom and wonder in the face of the beauty and mystery of the natural world. And, given the opportunity, they return again and again. (Dyer, 2004: 31)

the ideal would be an integrative approach that can provide both recognised cognitive learning outcomes, but at the same time promotes imagination and a sense of adventure. Drama, role-play, narrative and adventure play offer possible avenues for this integration to be achieved.

Drama as a pedagogy for outdoor integrated humanities

Student teachers asked 'what is drama in the primary classroom?' often respond 'the Nativity play' or 'role-play'. These represent the two faces of drama in the primary school – product and process-oriented drama. Taking part in product-oriented drama, such as the Nativity play, is an important social event in the school year, but process-oriented drama represents an opportunity to support all children's learning and development across curriculum boundaries.

One way that process-oriented drama promotes learning is through the adoption of teacher-in-role. In teacher-in-role, the teacher takes on the role of a character in a story to facilitate learning and understanding. It enables critical dialogue and exploration of emotions, morals, attitudes and factual data to broaden the learning experience in everyday life situations and historical or environmental contexts. While teacher-in-role allows teachers to maintain control, it can encourage creativity and freedom and a positive shift in the typical dynamic of the teacher–pupil relationship as they have adopted the persona of whomever is the protagonist.

On some occasions teachers may fear losing control of the groups that they may have struggled to achieve and in outdoor settings this can be frequently compounded by genuine concerns over health and safety. It is little wonder that teachers may be reticent about combining drama and the outdoors.

The student teachers' examples of drama all took place in school, but drama can happen anywhere: in the school playground, playing fields, local woods, parks or historic buildings and ancient ruins. These environments can spark interest, stir-up emotions, evoke previous experiences, challenge our values and attitudes and allow for greater creativity. We consider these benefits can be interpreted from a psychosocial perspective in the effect that the new situation and new pedagogy can have on learning. Most of all, since these environments are outside the traditional realm of the classroom, they may enable everyone to wear a new metaphorical 'hat'; the shy child to become more confident; the controlling teacher to become more relaxed; the typically disruptive child to feel less troubled. So how can outdoor environments, be they on our doorstep or further afield, be enhanced to allow for learning to develop?

Props, costumes, puppets and teacher-in-role are some of the ways to do this. Props and costumes give children something tangible to support their imagination, which enables them to get into character more easily. For example, Powderham Castle, in Devon, invites school children to take on the role of potential servants in their Victorian Educational Visit (Powderham Castle, 2010). Children come dressed as Victorians; scrubbing brushes and chimney brushes add to their ability to get into role.

Puppets can be used in role and they have also distinct advantages for social development. 'Young children have long been entertained and charmed by puppets. The brilliant colours, assorted textures, and exaggerated physical characteristics of puppets may help to promote higher interest and attention levels' (Salmon and Sainato, 2005: 12). Puppets also enable children to communicate using their own words, pacing and needs (Dillen et al., 2009); they encourage increased participation in learning (Salmon and Sainato, 2005; Simon et al., 2008) and foster an environment where children feel more comfortable talking about sensitive issues compared to talking directly with adults (Hall et al., 2002; Turner, 2003; Webster-Stratton and Reid, 2003). Combined with the apparent positive emotional affect of many outdoor experiences (Waite, 2007), substantial benefits for children's social and emotional development might be observed.

 Points for practice

- Consider using other process-drama conventions such as conscience alley, freeze-frame, hot-seating and flashbacks/flash-forwards to develop ideas about geography and history and to further explore issues and characters:

  - Conscience alley is a means of exploring a character's mind at a moment of crisis and of investigating the complexity of the decision they are facing.

  - Freeze-frames are still images or tableaux used to illustrate an incident or event.

  - Hot-seating focuses closely on a character and enables motivation to be explored.

(Continued)

(Continued)

- Flashbacks and flash-forwards are effective for getting children to focus on the consequences of action rather than on the action itself. (DfES, 2003b: 2)

All these are effective tools to foster critical thinking skills across these curriculum areas. For more information and for further dramatic techniques, see DfES (2003b).

The benefits of flashbacks and flash-forwards would be particularly valuable in exploring the impact of people and communities on others and the environment, encouraging children's social understanding development. An outstanding example of citizenship teaching in a recent Ofsted report involved a Year 6 class working on current world affairs within a cross-curricular geography lesson which used a variety of drama techniques, including children-in-role and hot-seating (Ofsted, 2010).

To transform familiar places, it can be helpful to provide a 'gateway' to signal the different use of the space. In a recent drama session with a group of student teachers, they produced a lesson around the story 'Where the Wild Things Are' by Maurice Sendak. The traditional classroom space was transformed into the wild forest by everyone wearing simple monster ears and travelling through a magic door (a foil door curtain). This breaks the moulds and perceptions of the traditional classroom practice; it is discussed in Chapter 1 how this comes with a set of ingrained expectations of the way things will be managed. Such 'magic doors' can also help transport the children to a different time and/or place in an outdoor context, particularly if it is also imbued with school expectations. This is best done improvised and described by the children. What does the door look like? Is it big or small? What is it made of? Is there a password to get through the door? And more importantly, what is behind the magic door? Of course actually being in a wild forest might be even better!

These elements combine to enable more effective narrative and story telling as a useful pedagogy for cross-disciplinary subjects. What follows is an illustrative case example of drama-based activities for geographical, historical and social understanding, which has been developed by initial teacher training students for primary school children.

Case Study 🗁

Discovering and telling the story of a place

The Harnham Water Meadows sit adjacent to the mediaeval cathedral in the city of Salisbury, Wiltshire, UK. The location provides an interesting, but by no means unique, opportunity for learning as it is an ancient landscape with a rich social history and its field archaeology of aqueducts, bridges and mills also provides the basis for historical studies. It has a significant environmental value, both in terms of providing a 'green space' in an urban centre, and for its rich ecology. The site provides a secure environment and rich resource for history and geography. Indeed, the site is clearly recognised as an important educational resource and is the subject of many visiting parties at a variety of academic levels. In this activity we attempt to combine imagination with history and geography through a combination of activities that are carried out across the day.

There is a general consensus that all successful fieldwork begins long before the visit with good preparation (Braund and Reiss, 2004: 15, see also Chapter 14). Here we begin several months beforehand with a dedicated workshop led by a professional storyteller. The workshop begins with a story, which the students then look at in terms of its component parts (particularly the beginning, middle and end), characterisation, plot development and associated metaphors and messages of the story. Having gone through the workshop (which includes elements of drama and acting) the students then begin to develop an agreed story line through a co-operative learning process. Often stories involve legends and magic and the characters in the stories are those most normally associated with children's 'magical' adventures. Throughout the story the characters are set a number of challenges at which they must succeed.

A story developed by the 2008 Early Adventures module students

> Long ago, a great dragon called Salis had terrorised southern England. So bad had the dragon's attacks become that the King had commanded his champion to fight and destroy it. Unfortunately, due to a clash with a dentist's appointment, he declines. The King then asks his knights, who one by one decline due to a variety of reasons (sports injuries, bit of a head cold, have to pick up the kids from school). No adult is brave enough to fight the dragon and when the King in exasperation declares 'Will anybody fight it?' a young girl steps forward and volunteers. Not really believing the girl will ever really fight the dragon, but to shame his knights, the King sends her off. Her journey begins when she meets an old wizard who tells her that she will need a map to find the dragon and that

(Continues)

(Continued)

pirates draw the best maps. Luckily further along the road she meets some pirates (who worryingly are rather lost) but help her to learn to draw and read maps. The pirates suggest that she should visit the witches who will show her how to make potions that put dragons to sleep. On meeting the witches she is set another task (involving finding specific plants) [scientific botanical identification] and on completion she moves on and meets other fantastical characters, each time completing a task. Eventually she completes all the tasks and is ready to meet the dragon. When she gets to the dragon's den, despite the fire and smoke she actually finds that there is no dragon. On return the wizard tells her that all problems are like that. No matter how scary or worrying, if you talk to people about and take advice, problems just turn to smoke.

On the day, the children are led to the 'wizard's house' decorated with throws, old books and candles (in reality the Harnham Meadows Education Centre – Harnham Water Meadows Trust, 2010). There the children are introduced to the 'old wizards' (the staff members) who explain they are there to provide help and advice. After this the students' in-role tell the children the agreed story. The story remains incomplete, however, and the children are encouraged to embark on a similar journey to that of the lead character in the story. Small groups of three or four are then led down to the meadow gates. Once the gates are open the children are invited to wander (but in reality, run) around the open landscape of the ancient water meadows. Across the site and as much as possible hidden from each other's view, the students are dressed as characters from the stories. Fences and hedges border the meadows and there is no public access, providing an extensive but secure area. This freedom to roam is an important part of the day.

Although it is recognised that outdoor education affords an opportunity to stand back and let broader and perhaps less well-defined learning emerge (and these undoubtedly are part of the day), nevertheless the student characters also carefully develop specific learning activities. Each of these has an explicit risk assessment and clearly identified learning outcomes. The 'lost pirates', for example, had organised a session around drawing maps, with emphasis on scale and orientation [geographical skills]. The children drew a map of a small area around the pirate camp, before being given a map that would lead them to a buried treasure, a mix of a representation of local historical artefacts [the use of historical evidence]. Each group of characters had activities based around the geography and/or history of the site which also combined co-operative learning and teamwork [social skills]. These could be adapted to emphasise different aspects of the curriculum and each year the nature of the stimulus story has led to a different stress, for example, environmental education, or the historical nature of the setting.

An example dealing with history involved a group of 'Ents' (students dressed as trees) who told the children about the history of the 'bumps in the ground' (the ancient carriers and bedworks of the water meadow system). The children, role-playing the water that once ran across the meadow, carry oxygen and plant 'food' to help the Ents to grow. This helps them to appreciate the reasons for such ancient irrigation systems and their significance to the lives of the people of that time.

The characters are important not only for the plot development, but also because the students act the various characters throughout the day, placing the children within the narrative of the story, actually meeting and talking with the characters. The children also have the freedom of the meadow environment to explore as the narrative unfolds. Engagement with such environments through such exploration may encourage an appreciation of such sites and promote them as something worthy of conservation and social value.

 Thoughts on theory

- Using psychological and socio-cultural planes of focus (see Chapter 1), what do you think the learning is in this case study and how is it being supported? What are the roles of others and place? What is the particular contribution of this outdoor context?

- Integrating historical, geographical and social aspects may contribute to more meaningful learning. As described earlier, landscapes and life are not subject-compartmentalised.

 Points for practice

- Can you recognise the times when staff and students were using the technique of 'teacher-in-role' to support the children's learning? Would you be confident to take on these roles?

- Can you suggest ways to extend the narrative using further drama conventions?

(Continues)

(Continued)

- Can you suggest appropriate learning objectives for the case study?
- What would assessment for learning look like in the case study?
- Are there sites local to your school where you could carry out a similar activity on a smaller scale?

ICT ideas

Another approach to a landscape study could be to use digital mapping techniques. Before the visit, you could examine the area through maps, aerial photographs and historical overlays. Then, during the visit, handheld devices (Geographical Positioning System-enabled) could be used to show the actual locations on a map. GPS trackers could record the journey around the site and be uploaded to a PC. You could also employ geotagging, taking photographs and recording their location via GPS on maps. After the visit, you could carry on the research by looking at Google Earth for changes in the location over time and extend Geographical Information Systems with additional data collected in the field. The children could create their own multimedia stories or reports based around the visit with this rich background data to hand.

Research in drama education

Heathcote (1980: 37) describes the process of drama as a way of drawing children to an awareness of 'universals', essential truths and structures that reveal the world as it is and it has been. This clearly links with the objectives described in this chapter and in the case study. Research has shown the following benefits of drama in the primary phase:

- Improved attainment for literacy and mathematics (Fleming et al., 2004)

- Cognitive, affective and technical objectives supported in science (Dorian, 2009)

- Discussion between teacher and pupil positively influenced (Simon et al., 2008)

■ High motivation among students, attributed to perceptions of ownership and empowerment (Ødegaard, 2003).

Frequently outside agencies work with school groups in drama and outdoor education. However, a major limitation of using outside agencies is that the long-term outcomes are rarely measured or measurable. In contrast, if the teacher takes the initiative with drama and outdoor learning, there is more opportunity to build relationships, develop knowledge and understanding and measure the long-term effects. Therefore, teachers need to feel empowered to engage in the outdoors using novel pedagogies, where many traditional barriers to creativity and imagination are broken down. Furthermore, Ofsted recognised that 'a lack of independent learning and creativity characterised the weaker lessons' (2010: 43) in citizenship. Additionally, they identified that 'particularly strong contributions to the citizenship curriculum came from cross-curricular work and themed weeks. Overall, however, the schools visited made too little use of local opportunities for pupils to participate in real activities beyond the school' (2010: 44).

Although our example relied on external resources (in relation to people, props, transport etc.), similar activities could be conducted with the assistance of other local organisations. Local museums and field study centres offer an exciting and imaginative addition to any existing portfolio of provision. Comparable benefits could also be obtained from a project using the school's own locality and may also have the advantage of having extant meaning for children.

Enjoyment of learning, of achievement and confidence and the promotion of social responsibility are important aspects of learning that can be addressed in contexts outside the classroom, building on children's interests. Certainly drama, narrative and designing 'adventures' provide enjoyable learning experiences, and throughout the events described in the case study, the emphasis has always been on group achievement. Social responsibility is harder to evaluate, however, but developing familiarity with your environment and appreciating it for its aesthetic, or its history or ecology, may be important aspects in encouraging responsibility (Davis et al., 2006).

Furthermore, learning that stimulates interest and engages children in the world around them and that promotes understanding of the impact of human actions on the environment is crucial for sustainable education. History and geography are disciplines that support a social understanding of the world, but also promote an understanding that our future can be shaped by understanding the present through the past. These intentions are laudable and relate to the dynamic epithets such as engagement, enjoyment and exploration mentioned in Chapter 1. The new coalition government in England is equally effusive in their aims for children to become successful learners, confident individuals and responsible citizens. It is difficult to be critical of such worthy, if ambitious aims for education, but if we are to achieve them, then new dynamic approaches are required; approaches that engage the imagination, that promote learning as an adventure and that help children (of all ages) engage more closely with their locality.

In a chapter about adventure, narrative and drama, it is perhaps appropriate to conclude by considering the words of a fictional character. In *The Wind in the Willows* by Kenneth Grahame, Badger explains to Mole that he didn't build his house in the Wild Wood, but rather where he lived had once been part of a human city. The city had become abandoned and the woodland re-established. He concludes that people and cities come and go but badgers (like nature) are patient, and eventually return. This lyrical passage reminds us of how landscapes tell such stories. Any landscape, be it urban or rural, planned or wilderness, has a story to tell, from its form, its ecology, the people and buildings and we can tell these tales in a number of ways. They can be through visits, worksheets and observation, but perhaps more effectively through drama, adventure and problem-solving.

Summary

This chapter shared, through a case study, the use of drama-based activities to engage children in a landscape. It showed how the history and geography of this landscape could be explored using simple narrative and drama techniques. The barriers to outdoor learning are discussed but contrasted with the benefits that emerge from the freedom to explore, imagine and be creative. This pedagogical approach and outdoor context appear well suited to cross-curricular methods of learning. We finish with a challenge to use your own imaginations and have confidence to tell the stories of landscapes.

Further reading

Nabhan, G.P. and Trimble, S. (1994) *The Geography of Childhood*. Boston: Beacon Press.

Thomas, G. and Thompson, G. (2004) *A Child's Place: Why Environment Matters to Children*. London: Green Alliance.

The Arts outside the classroom

Jeff Adams, Martin Ashley and Ian Shirley

Chapter objectives

■ An awareness of how performance art in the outdoors contributes to children's aesthetic sense across the curriculum

■ An awareness of how heightened sensitivity to sound creates multi-sensory awareness of the outdoors

■ An understanding of how visual art is created in the outdoor environment

---

What picture is conjured in your mind when it is suggested that an outdoor art lesson takes place? Perhaps your first reaction is to imagine children with sketch pads, recording what they see outdoors. This might be through simple media such as pencil sketching, or it might involve messier materials. Perhaps you see the archetypical artist at his easel capturing the landscape through water colour? This may have its place, but this chapter is going to alert you to other possibilities. Perhaps surprisingly, we begin, not with drawing or painting, not even with the sculpting of found objects, but with music. You will see that music is not something to be feared, something to be avoided because you can't sing or read crotchets and quavers. Music, in the sense we describe it here, is part of children's perception and personal reconstruction of the world. Through the activities we shall introduce, children will see, hear, feel and experience the world outside the classroom in new and vivid ways using multiple senses (Porteous, 1990). The second part of the chapter describes the creation of outdoor artefacts that connect almost seamlessly with the musical sense.

Taking music outside

Like many homes, our home is filled with noise: the noise we make ourselves in conversation, discussion and argument. The noise of pots and dishes, of doors and cupboards, of bells and chimes. All kinds of jingles, and jangles, whizzers and gadgets, mobile phones, computer games, and domestic devices. In truth, we don't notice most of these, despite their incessancy. Almost spirit-like, they have an eternal presence in our home but, save for the unexpected or particular, they infiltrate every moment of waking existence to the point where we hardly notice that they are happening at all.

The Canadian composer and music educationalist Murray Schafer (1975) has suggested that this response is serving to reduce sensitivity to all forms of sound. He argues that the truly sensitive person is always alert and aware of noise. He states, rather wittily, 'There are no ear-lids' (Schafer, 1975: 13). No doubt, the murmur of dissent concerning our lack of sensitivity to the sensorial world has been ticking over for some time. Dewey suggests, 'Recognition is perception arrested before it has had the chance to develop freely' (1934: 52). Perhaps one of the great strengths of the outdoors, then, is awakening children's senses and helping them to become alert to the sensory world around them.

In many ways, children are naturally open and inquisitive. For young children, touch is the first and most important means of knowing. For the young child, to look without touching is an experience of sensory deprivation. Neither is *listening* simply a matter of hearing. To listen properly, children need to see, and have a sense of the sound in relation to themselves. As they listen and as they see, they are naturally taken by their curiosity to discover more about that which has taken their attention. While we take concern for the macro-image of the grand vista, children are often far more concerned with the minutiae of the micro-image. Nabhan and Trimble point out the difference between the adult and the child perspective, 'We would position ourselves to peer out over a precipice, trying to count how many ridgelines there were between us and the far horizon. Whenever we arrived at such a promontory ... [the author's children] would approach it with me, then abruptly release their hands from mine, to scour the ground for bones, pine cones, sparkly sandstone, feathers, or wildflowers' (1994: 6). In our work with children we should recognise that they will see the world in a child-like fashion, and not through adult eyes. The point is not to show them the error of their ways, but to begin by seeing the world through their eyes. This, then, is the realm of the aesthetic experience.

Becoming sensitive to spaces – engaging the aesthetic

In providing opportunities for the Arts outdoors we allow for both children's artistic development and their awareness of spaces: these spaces provide a stimulus for artistic activity, and the Arts provide a way of coming to know the space anew. At first, children will need time to explore the space and to become sensitised to the aesthetic features: to the smells, the textures, the objects and the sounds.

 Points for practice

- Encourage the children to map the territory. Ask them to notice sounds around them, but to listen very carefully and make detailed comments about the sounds they map. Notice the timbre of the sounds, changes in dynamics. Notice rises in pitch. Ask them to consider how the sounds could be recreated.

- Invite them to create a map of the sounds in relation to themselves. Notice how sounds move around them and show direction of travel across a map. It may help to include an image of themselves at the centre.

- Ask them to explore the area and find the closest thing to silence. Encourage them to notice all the sounds that are preventing silence from occurring. Invite them to fill pockets of silence with sounds, each sound getting progressively louder. Such pieces of music should begin and end with silence.

- Next encourage the children to notice the visual features of the landscape – especially the micro-scale. Notice where different materials meet, or where there are contrasts in terms of light and shade. Allow opportunity to make miniature sketches with a view-finder and encourage them to represent the light, the shade, the textures and the shadows. Take one special photograph of a tiny fragment of the space, or make up stories about the *spirit* that resides there.

- Collect a few interesting objects from the space. Make the children trace their hands over and offer words to describe, as accurately as possible, that which they feel. Collect these words, and use them to inform their art-making.

Such multi-sensory exploration has the potential to impact on all aspects of children's artistic activity. In the context of music children can create pieces that build on the essence of these objects: textures, timbres, dynamic contrasts, structures and sequences. The objects become a graphic score – the stimulus for musical composition.

Making up music

Let's begin by considering the immediate environment: the school grounds, the street, or a local park. Many experiences such as viewing the location at dusk, or in frosty weather, focusing specifically on a small, verdant area, or a particular tree, studying the sky or mapping possible journeys, offer suitable composing experiences. By allowing the children to explore the space as described earlier, they will begin to gather ideas for a musical composition that features some of these aesthetic aspects. For dusk, fading light, shadows, variations of light and shade; vast expanses of sky or the chill of a late autumn evening are powerful images to capture in music and children could be encouraged to choose two or three ideas to capture in a piece of music.

In small groups of four or five they can collaborate to develop musical responses to their ideas. This can be supported by providing opportunities for the children to share their ideas in progress and encouraging the class to appraise the musical ideas that emerge. They may find it helpful to develop a graphic representation of their work, which captures the elements of loud and quiet, of length of note, of pitch change, and of timbre to consider the structure of their composition. By recording the work in progress, they have the opportunity to revise and restructure the work.

In the following case study an example is given of how one school explored the concept of 'night' through composition. Of importance, was the direct experience of 'night' that the children gained in preparation for the composition.

Case Study 📁

Night notes

Over the week the Year 4 children had been asked to collect impressions of the night, which they had gathered through their senses. Some children had tried to draw the night sky with buildings silhouetted in the moonlight. One had been exploring in the garden with a torch to see if

(Continues)

(Continued)

insects go to sleep in the dark. Another had found a poem about the Night Mail on Google and brought it in to read to the class.

We used the ideas gathered through all our senses to begin to make night music. One group opened with a gentle rhythm on a woodblock. A rain-maker entered next with a long sound that accompanied the tap-tap, tap-tap already established. The metallophone entered with a rather beautiful ostinato (repeated) figure: legato and situated at the high end of the instrument, twinkling like stars. Soon the rain-maker and the metallophone dropped out to leave the woodblock alone again. The rain-maker entered again, as did the metallophone; no louder than before. Then gradually, one by one, the metallophone ended, the rain-maker ended, and finally, the woodblock gave way to silence.

This was the group's first draft – their presentation of work in progress. The structure, the instrumentation, the layering of textures, and the control of dynamics were effects they had decided on entirely for themselves. Not perhaps a piece ever likely to extend beyond this particular classroom, but a recognition that three children had engaged in musical invention. They had found a way of representing their impression of a night time piece. Furthermore, they now had some idea of what other composers may be trying to achieve in their music about the night – or the sea, or the dawn, or space, or winter, or the landscape.

To regard them, as some do, as 'plinky-plonky' sound pictures is to misunderstand the nature of children's creative play, and the ability children have to structure highly effective musical miniatures. To dismiss children's musical creations in this way is as irresponsible as dismissing their artwork or sport.

On a recent visit to a local city centre I noticed a crowd had gathered around a central cordon in a pedestrianised area. Within the cordon sat three workmen, apparently on a tea break. One grunted, another grunted back. One stirred her tea, and tapped her spoon rhythmically on the side of a tin cup. Another flicked his newspaper, which created a satisfying rhythmic effect. Soon the layers began to build and a very dynamic and rhythmic (not to mention dramatic) composition ensued. All around me feet were tapping, hands were patting, and children were rocking from side to side, as the event transformed from a simple per-formance to (almost) a piece of community stomping. This approach to composition is readily available to all schools and children of all ages find it engaging. Older children particularly respond well and it is absolutely right to engage drama as part of the performance.

It is interesting to reflect on commonalities and differences between this experience and the Night Notes case study; applying a socio-cultural plane of focus may help unpick how children are learning in these contexts. Yet aesthetics and creativity might be argued to have more psychological aspects (see Chapter 1).

 Points for practice

- Begin by asking the children to explore the sound potential of objects around the school grounds (alert your colleagues, of course).

- When they have selected four or five sounds they should begin to explore the rhythmic potential of the sounds. Simply begin by layering the rhythms. Begin with one, perhaps feet in gravel. Add a second, tapping on a fence with a stick. Add a third, perhaps a tube or pipe drumming the ground, or tapping on some wooden decking.

- Encourage the group to begin making important decisions about the composition: who will start? How many times will the pattern be played? What is the dynamic at this point? Who comes in next? Where will the piece go from here? What surprises could there be? How will it develop? What could the combinations of sounds be? How could you include variations or repetition?

- Allow rhythmic pieces to emerge and be careful to share good work as a model to other groups.

 Thoughts on theory

- Consider the challenges that musical exploration offers children: think about their cognitive development, social development; cultural, physical and spiritual development. How does music require children to think, to solve problems, to explore, to be brave, to examine and assess, and to become resilient?

- Consider too what is good about taking part in musical activity with other people. You may have something here of the essence of what music education is all about.

- How do the learning theories in Chapter 1 help to make sense of the activities you might offer to foster these aspects?

For the youngest children, in Key Stage 1 and Early Years settings, musical play should be a daily part of provision. Opportunities need to be offered to explore sounds inside and outside the classroom.

Children should go on sound walks, but here their listening needs to be focused, in small groups. They need the opportunity to listen in silence, to draw what they hear; to map what they hear, and to try to recreate what they hear. (This develops some of the listening activities in Chapter 8.) Sounds should be recorded, both by live recording, or on paper using signs and squiggles that capture the elements of what they hear: the quality of the sound (we could call it timbre); the loudness or energy of the sound (we could call it dynamics); the movement of the sound from high to low (pitch); the length of the sound (duration); and the effect created by the layering of sound (we could call this texture). Children can invent symbols using squiggles, or spiky shapes, or circles of differing sizes. Just ask them; they'll have an idea of how to record what they hear.

There should be opportunity to explore a variety of sounds by filling containers, and tapping, scraping, shaking and strumming a variety of home-made and purchased musical instruments. Children can use these instruments as they march in the playground, singing a favourite song, or as they go on a bear-hunt, chanting the familiar rhyme as they make their way across the school field. The music corner could be set up in a den and where the children make up some music about a mummy bear, a baby bear and a daddy bear, focusing on how they use pitches or dynamics to represent the different bears.

 Thoughts on theory

- The Early Years Foundation Stage guidance (DfES, 2007) identifies six areas of learning: Personal, Social and Emotional Development; Communication, Language and Literacy; Problem Solving, Reasoning and Numeracy; Knowledge and Understanding of the World; Physical Development; and Creative Development. Consider how children's engagement in music and the Arts might enhance their learning across these areas of learning, both within early years and across the curriculum in primary school. Look at chapters in Sections 2 and 3 of this book and consider how a musical or artistic approach might add value to some activities by engaging more of the senses (Howes, 2005; Porteous, 1990). Think also how using multiple senses might be beneficial for children with significant learning difficulties.

Teachers need to be alert to children's developing musical schemas and there should be the opportunity to respond to these as and when they arise (a useful account of schemas is provided by Nutbrown, 2006; see also Chapter 3). In a recent article, Helen Tomlinson and Mary Arthur (2009) report on the activities of very young children in improvised sound gardens. The gardens included improvised instruments and beautifully manufactured pieces designed specifically for musical exploration: aluminium tubes, wooden panelled marimbas, large springs, cans and frying pans. Such gardens arise out of the observation of children's desire to explore sounds in the environment. A few words of encouragement from the teacher, or a brief suggestion that they could explore both quiet and loud sounds in their piece, result in some highly musical products from very young children. Good practitioners will know how to enhance such opportunities (see, for example, Young, 2003 for a detailed examination of music with very young children): to add instruments, to limit choice, to create opportunities, to join in, to keep out, and to value the children's work as musicians, doing musical things. Such activities emerge out of children's natural drive to explore sound materials and their developing schemas involving tapping and shaking.

Musical development

Clearly such composition requires a degree of understanding that only emerges from regular opportunity to compose. Perhaps controversially, we argue here against the atomised and didactic approach to the teaching of musical elements. While we advocate the building of skills and knowledge, we, like Swanwick, would argue that such skills emerge best through necessity, brought about by musical invention and 'within the context of a practical activity' (1999: 58). This requires some knowledge and skill on the part of the teacher, in order to respond to children's developing ability (well described by Glover and Young, 1999; Mills, 2009; Young and Glover, 1998), and on a 'need to know' basis. In some ways, this runs counter to Ofsted's guidance, which suggests that music learning develops through 'clear stages of progression' (2009: 3). Music learning often progresses in leaps and in non-linear routes, and such a simplistic notion of musical development may serve to hinder progress.

Through music, children come to a new understanding of natural phenomena such as light, or night and day; such as the movement of water, or of animals. They come to understand more sensitively the characteristics of different forms of weather, perhaps, and they begin to view the world through the multiplicity of their senses and forms of intelligence. The children may first sketch, or paint; they may map, or write poetry. They could photograph, or simply observe and feel, by engaging directly with the world outdoors. If they are to write music about a river, they need to draw on various forms of knowledge about rivers: geographical knowledge about what rivers are and experiential knowledge about how rivers feel, sound and appear. Through writing a piece of music they create a multi-dimensional representation of the river that involves a number of forms of intelligence: certainly natural and musical, but others too.

In conclusion, it has been interesting how, in preparing for this chapter, we have turned to many texts of the 1970s. Such texts provide a child-centred approach to Arts education which favour the needs of the individual over the needs of subject heritage. In recent years the teaching of music has become atomised as children learn about pitch, or pulse, and about timbre or rhythm (see, for example, QCA, 2000b – schemes of work for music). Csikszentmihalyi and Schiefele had noted this issue with regard to the arts in general as far back as 1992, making the comment, 'It seems obvious that an atomistic and reductionist approach is far from being helpful to instructors who seek to increase feeling-based, intuitive, and holistic thought processes in their students' (2009: 3). The intention here, then, has been to rekindle something of the artist in the child as explorer, and to reconsider the possibility of children being awakened to a rich sensory world that exists more fully in the great outdoors – beyond the classroom.

 Thoughts on theory

- The way of 'becoming a musician' suggested here appears rather different from the process of 'becoming a mathematician' described in Chapter 6. Here we see music as intimately connected with awareness through all the senses of the wider world; that holistic and child-centred approaches are necessary to connect with affective aspects and exploratory learning is key. These are pedagogies frequently associated with the outdoors (see Chapter 1). Yet there is also a sense that this is then supported by sensitive contingent teaching to develop children's ideas and skills (see also Figure 2.1 in Chapter 2).

In the next section, we move to a consideration of how the outdoors also provides the resources as well as the inspiration for the Arts.

Land and environmental art

The emergence of contemporary outdoor, land or environmental art is usually marked in art history narratives with works like Ana Mendieta's figure pieces made from stones, tree remains, mud or fabric (e.g. The Silueta series, 1976) or Spiral Jetty (1970) by Robert Smithson. The significance of these works is that the sculptural form is constructed on location from indigenous materials, rather than the sculptor relocating a sculpture made in a studio or elsewhere; in this sense the works are 'site-specific' – they are unique to the place of their construction and are dependent upon their site for meaning to be generated. The land art movement encouraged many artists across the Western world of art to work in this direct way with the landscape. Such practices are now common, and young people in the UK can see and work in landscape settings that are essentially outdoor galleries for art, for example Grizedale in the Lake District, or the Yorkshire Sculpture Park at Bretton Hall; these are spaces for art that arose out of the increasing interest in outdoor site-specific artworks.

On one hand the land art movement can be seen as arising directly from the profound changes in the art world in the 1960s and 1970s that saw the establishment of performance and conceptual art, and its breaks with the traditional features of the artwork; evidenced by land artists' insistence on sculptural works being produced and then remaining in the landscape. On the other hand, land art can be seen as having a provenance that would link it directly with the European Romantic art movements of the late 18th and early 19th centuries that gave rise to the canonical landscape art of J.M.W. Turner or Caspar David Friedrich: the idea of encapsulating the sublime, the overwhelming and intimidating power of nature.

Rural environmental artists have been affected by the greater public interest and concern for ecology – the interest in the fragility of the eco environment and the effects that industry is having on the world. These artists have also been affected by the debates and issues surrounding public sculpture and its societal place, and this has had a fundamental effect on their practices in relation to the permanence of the artwork, which has resulted in a tendency to insist on a transience or a temporal curtailment of their art. This can be seen in the work of Andy Goldsworthy (e.g. Stick Throw, 1991) or Cecilia Vicuña (e.g. Antivero, 1981), where their works have been rendered deliberately fragile, ephemeral and transient. Works such as these can be thought of as events as well as objects, in which people manipulate the landscape for a limited period or time and use material of the landscape itself, thus ensuring that the work will disintegrate or decay naturally, thereby having minimal environmental impact.

This transience of the artwork is compensated by the recording of the construction and completion of the work. Artists like Richard Long have for many years regarded the landscape itself as the primary object, and the artist's intervention leaves little trace in the landscape. When an outdoor work has to reoccur as an artwork in the gallery it is not always in photographic form. In the case of Long the pieces often make use of text, sometimes in conjunction with images, typically in very large letters on a gallery wall, rather like a poem (e.g. Walking Music, 2004). These texts are often accounts of ephemeral moments on a walk and resemble Japanese Haiku with an economy of words. Common to all Long's works is the importance of date and time; this insistence on temporal and topographic specificity has a lineage that can be directly traced to the French Impressionist painters like Morisot, Sisley and Pissarro and English painters like Constable. This has a genealogy in 19th century scientific natural science procedures of meticulous observation and recording of the natural world and also relates to concerns for the centrality of situated practice and cultural historical authenticity.

Context and subjectivity

This historical context is important to bear in mind as it provides the cultural environment within which the artworks that young people produce will be located, and fundamentally affects their subjectivity, their identification with the work and their place in it (Atkinson, 2002; Page et al., 2006). Children working outdoors directly from nature in the Lake District, for instance, by painting a landscape, are firmly in the European *plein air* tradition developed a century and half earlier, and this will have an effect on the teacher's direction as well as the learners' responses, consciously or otherwise. The countless reproductions of Impressionist work cannot help but inform the images that are produced, and even the means by which their production occurs.

The social and cultural politics of the landscape (Mitchell, 2002) are evident in artists' responses to it, as Ingrid Pollard demonstrated in her work exploring colonialism, Wordsworth Heritage (1992), in which black walkers were photographed in the Lake District in juxtaposition to more typical 'heritage' icons. Similarly, when young people create sculptural works in the vein of land art they inevitably find themselves making responses that are profoundly influenced by cultural and identity factors.

The collaborative features of a project are, for many theorists and teachers, especially significant (Adams, 2008; Cazden, 2001; Heath, 1983). Collaboration is often essential for the gathering of materials and the construction of many works, as they often involve considerable volumes of the former and complex multiple tasks for the latter. As Goldsworthy's work illustrates, it is necessary to have large numbers of people involved in order for the production of the work (although when it comes to the attribution of the works these other makers are often neglected). Pedagogically, collaboration has much to commend it for supported learning (Cazden, 2001), and it figured prominently in an interesting example of a school-initiated environmental art project, the Dressing Room.

Case Study 🗂

The Dressing Room project – performance art

This project, derived from environmental art and the social forces that shaped it, occurred when a group of children aged 10 embarked on an installation piece called the Dressing Room, which comprised: 'workshops, performances and events, designed around a withy structure (resembling a yurt) with woven fabrics (recycled clothes), with auditory and other sensory inputs' (Adams et al., 2008: 43).

Right from the inception of the project many of the principles that had informed the environmental movement as well as land art were present in this contemporary school manifestation: concern for sustainability, recycling, the value of life 'outdoors', an emphasis on nature, and contextualised by equity and social justice, especially global homelessness. This loose coalition found a focus in the Dressing Room project and captured a constellation of young people's concerns and interests at a particular moment in the cultural life of their city. The form of the sculptural form of the project – the yurt – encapsulated the older land art movement's interest in natural materials, using technologies from older or marginalised communities. The project took a contemporary turn when it was transformed into a mobile installation and performance site. The woven sculptural form of the yurt was then overlain with recycled clothes garnered from local charity shops or provided by the group themselves, representing the displaced and homeless, as the covered yurt now became an adaptable and mobile 'home'.

The covering of the yurt added to the performance aspect of the piece – hands could protrude through the walls of the yurt through the arms of the jumpers and shirts. The young people carried the work from site to site, where other people could enter and interact with the makers and with the work itself, and sound pieces were created which furthered the

(Continues)

(Continued)

audience's participation. The yurt could act as a gallery itself, with items hung on the inside and the outside, and also as a theatre, as the makers or others could perform their works.

The continual transformation of the piece into a multiplicity of works with its nebulous group of collaborative makers located the work firmly in the dynamics of contemporary art, with all of its interest and excitement: relevance, social engagement and exploration of identity. It also revealed the many strictures of current educational policies: the emphasis on collaborative work, the absence of an overt skill base upon which to base judgements, the lack of competition amongst the young people, and the dominance of ideas and effects over received knowledge. All of these run counter to the prevailing culture of competitive individualism, and made the attribution of individual assessments for recording and auditing purposes very difficult (Lindstrom, 2006). Yet the project represented an exploration of the forms of a socially engaged environmental art that provided a platform for many of the social and political concerns of the wider community.

As Thompson explained (quoted in Adams et al., 2008: 50), particular artists' work proved important in the conception and development of the project: Lucy Orta's and Michael Landy's in particular. Orta builds temporary dwellings in extreme environments (e.g. Lucy and Jorge Orta's Antarctic Village – No Borders, 2007) that are representative of the insecurity of refugees and immigrants in their search for secure and stable environments. Landy's work Break Down (2001), in which he systematically destroyed (after documenting) all of his possessions in a department store in London, raises questions about ownership, which the Dressing Room children developed in their project.

 Thoughts on theory
Similarities and differences

- We hope you will agree that there are some surprising similarities between the two case studies. Both involved children in *exploring, forming, presenting, performing* and *responding*. Both developed aesthetic concepts such as *balance, contrast, symmetry, harmony, unity, surprise* and *structure*.

- What theories of learning might help to explain these commonalities?

- What do you consider the key differences and how might these fit into your developing theory?

Summary

A good knowledge of music and art as separate disciplines is likely to underpin the best work, but we must not ignore the equal significance that attaches to knowledge of aesthetic principles more generally. Most of the ones mentioned in the Thoughts on Theory box above would also apply in other aesthetic areas such as dance and the real skill of the more experienced primary teacher lies in her or his ability to interweave such aesthetic knowledge with the equally important knowledge bases relating to children, their development, their relationships and their ways of seeing the world.

The two case studies described drew on children's experience beyond the classroom in order to highlight personal meaning. It suggests that effective education relies on acknowledging and building upon children's lives outside the classroom to encourage them to engage their intuitive and creative faculties.

Further reading

Adams, J., Worwood, K., Atkinson, D., Dash, P., Herne, S. and Page, T. (2008) *Teaching through Contemporary Art: A Report on Innovative Practices in the Classroom*. London: Tate Publishing.

McNicol, R. (1992) *Sound Inventions: 32 Creative Music Projects for the Junior Classroom*. Oxford: Oxford University Press.

Painter, J. and Aston, P. (1970) *Sound and Silence: Classroom Projects in Creative Music*. Cambridge: Cambridge University Press.

Tillman, J. (1976) *Exploring Sound: Creative Musical Projects for Teachers*. London: Stainer & Bell.

10

Physical development, health and well-being: the role of physical education 'outside'

Emma Sime and Liz Taplin

Chapter objectives

- An understanding of the concept of physical literacy and the contribution that learning outdoors makes in the physical literacy journey

- An awareness of the additional challenge and learning opportunities offered in the outdoors in the context of outdoor and adventurous activities (OAA)

- An appreciation of the need to scaffold children's learning moving from indoors to outdoors contexts so that learning is scaffolded and success likely

In this chapter, we intend to explore the vital role physical education plays in a child's physical development, health and well-being and highlight how taking the subject 'outside the classroom' contributes an additional, very desirable, layer to a child's education. Having discussed the aims of physical education and defining terminology, we will draw on two case studies (scenarios based on actual events) to illustrate the importance of scaffolding children's learning experiences by progressing from indoor to outdoor environments. This process of scaffolding can be demonstrated across all areas of physical education, but we have selected outdoor and adventurous activities (OAA) as a vehicle for our discussion.

Learning 'outdoors' and 'outside the classroom'

Before we embark on a further exploration of the learning opportunities offered in the outdoors in the context of outdoor and adventurous activities (OAA), it is important at this point to clarify how we intend to use the terms 'outdoor' and 'outside the classroom' in respect of our discussion. As highlighted in Chapter 1, different subjects bring particular cultural expectations, and as physical educationists we have always seen the school hall, the sports hall, the swimming pool, the playground, and/or the grass pitches as our classroom. The muddy pitch in the darkening gloom of a December afternoon is as much 'a classroom' as the well-lit, centrally heated hall, for this is where high-quality teaching and learning regularly takes place in physical education.

Indeed, one of the authors recalls the start of a games lesson when an excited Year 1 group were finding it hard to focus on the short teacher-introduction. Understandably the children wanted to get moving; but they needed to receive brief instructions first! The teacher explained that the football pitch was an outdoor classroom and the same rules regarding listening, cooperating and respect applied as in the indoor classroom. It was a message the children understood and as a consequence the children's behaviour changed and opportunities for learning increased. Here we found the power of socio-cultural norms for schooling beneficial!

If contexts such as the playground and the pitches are considered as the physical education teacher's classroom, then 'outside' the classroom must be understood as a context beyond these everyday facilities. There is then a sound case for defining 'outside' the classroom in physical education as being 'off the school site' either in the immediate outdoors of the local community, or further afield.

However, we recognise that 'outside' may be understood as equivalent to 'outdoor' and that there are important messages to be communicated about learning in physical education in any outdoor context. Thus, in this chapter, we will attempt to examine both learning 'outdoors' through the use of the school grounds and learning 'outside the physical education classroom' through the use of the local environment and residential centres.

Physical education and the concept of physical literacy

As teachers of physical education we find ourselves in a fortunate and unique position. As previously mentioned, unlike other areas of the curriculum, there has always been an expectation that physical education should take place in a variety of contexts, both inside, outside and 'outside the classroom'. Consider this statement and its implications in terms of communities of practice (see Chapter 1). Historically, however, it has been found that some teachers see the value of physical education as being merely an opportunity to provide children with a change of scenery and the chance to 'let off steam' in a large outside space and therefore evaluate the effectiveness of their teaching on the 'busy, happy, and good' principle (Placek, 1983). Whilst this view has no place in today's understanding of the value of physical education (for where is the learning if the children are merely 'letting off steam?'), it could perhaps support the idea that physical education was the first curriculum area to realise the value of learning 'outdoors' and/or 'outside the classroom'.

In order to understand the important role of physical education, it is necessary to consider its aim and to develop a rationale for it being an essential and central aspect of the primary school curriculum. The Association for Physical Education states that,

> the aim of physical education is to develop physical competence so that children are able to move efficiently, effectively and safely and understand what they are doing. (2008: 32)

Physical education, then, is the principal subject in the curriculum where the focus is on developing the child's physical competence and confidence and whose core purpose is to provide opportunities for every child to learn through their physical embodiment. Whilst the 'physical' plays a central role in physical education, it should also be recognised that high-quality physical education is a holistic experience, helping the child to develop intertwined and inseparable physical, cognitive, social and emotional capacities.

During the Early Years Foundation Stage and Key Stage 1, physical education plays a crucial role in helping children to develop their fundamental movement skills. By the age of 7, children have the capacity to have reached the mature stage of Gallahue and Ozmun's (2006) fundamental phase (a developmental term relating to an approximate age span of 2 through to 7). Doherty and Bailey (2003) highlight research that indicates an appropriate level of physical skill enhances self-esteem, which creates a feeling of well-being and confidence. Clearly, lifelong health and personal well-being, brought about by active and healthy lifestyles, are important outcomes of physical education, which are more attainable if the core purposes of physical education (e.g. developing physical competence and contributing to one's physical literacy) are achieved.

Conversely, however, a child may not develop efficient and effective fundamental movement skills and whilst this may be the result of a movement difficulty, it is just as likely to be the result of a lack of appropriate instruction, opportunity to practise and encouragement by the teacher (and/or the parents). This can inevitably result in a lack of enthusiasm on the part of the child which can further perpetuate, and contribute to, the child's movement difficulty, negative self-perception and unwillingness to participate in physical activity (Gallahue and Ozmun, 2006). It is the teacher's responsibility therefore, to ensure the physical education programme provides success orientated, developmentally appropriate instruction; opportunities for the children to practise their developing skills; and plenty of encouragement. In doing so, teachers will be able to identify children who require further support through the implementation of movement intervention programmes in order to avoid the continuation of this negative cycle, which could potentially lead to inactivity and health problems in later life.

As children enter Key Stage 2 they should be entering a period of their development in which they can begin to specialise (Gallahue and Ozmun, 2006). That is, they have become fluent in the fundamental movement skills and are ready to begin using these skills in increasingly complex situations. It is during Key Stage 2 that the children should further develop their ability to use their physical capacities in changing contexts; to be able to read the environment and adapt and respond accordingly.

An understanding, and acceptance, of the concept of physical literacy is very helpful in supporting primary school teachers to appreciate the aims of physical education. Whitehead defines physical literacy as:

> Appropriate to each individual's endowment ... the motivation, confidence, physical competence, knowledge and understanding to maintain physical activity throughout life. (2010: 11)

Over recent years it has become increasingly accepted that high-quality physical education plays a major role in an individual's journey towards developing their physical literacy, as well as providing children with an opportunity to be active and contributing to the health and personal well-being of the children through the physical learning context that it provides (afPE, 2008).

Learning 'outdoors' and 'outside the classroom' through outdoor and adventurous activities (OAA)

Prior to the inclusion of outdoor and adventurous activities (OAA) in the Physical Education National Curriculum (DfEE, 2000) and the findings of the House of Commons Education and Skills Committee in 2005 which led to the Learning Outside the Classroom Manifesto (DfES, 2006a), children through the decades have taken part in both school-based outdoor and adventurous activities (involving problem-solving, cooperation, trust, challenge and creativity in the school grounds), and experiences 'outside the classroom', usually in the form of a residential experience, or excursion to outdoor activity centres (for more specialised activities such as orienteering, abseiling, caving, canoeing and rock climbing).

The prevalence of outdoor adventure education suggests that policy-makers, outdoor educators, teachers, parents and indeed children believe these activities to be of value (Gair, 1997). Evidence of the potential benefits of learning in the outdoors, and more particularly experiences that involve adventure, challenge and risk, has been provided by Rickinson et al. (2004), who suggest that well-managed outdoor and adventurous activities can have a positive impact on self-esteem and self-confidence. There is also evidence that these activities can have a lasting impact on participants. During her research, Waite (2007) asked practitioners in primary schools, early years settings, nurseries, preschools and play groups to describe a memory from childhood of a significant experience in the outdoors. Responses were grouped into four emergent themes, with 'adventure, risk and challenge' having 135 incidences of reported memories. Some of the sub-themes that emerged included exploration, tree climbing, camping and lighting fires. Waite concluded that 'challenge and overcoming difficulty ... appear important factors for the design of memorable outdoor learning experiences' (2007: 344).

Indeed many researchers attribute positive outcomes to the inclusion of 'challenge' in the form of actual or perceived risk and the outdoors (Boniface, 2006; Ewart, 1983; McKenzie, 2000). Boyes and O'Hare believe that the 'interrelationships of perceived risk and competence is one of the key aspects that define outdoor adventurous activities' (2003: 64) and the juxtaposition of the two elements are evident in Martin and Priest's (1986; Priest, 1990) Adventure Experience Paradigm. They suggest that optimum benefits are evident at the 'peak adventure' stage, or the 'risk threshold' (Gair, 1997: 48) when an individual's competence is equal to the risks involved and the experience is generally viewed as 'positive and educational' (Boyes and

O'Hare, 2003: 64). This argument is furthered by Whitehead, who surmises that when an individual reads their outer world (i.e. the environment) and responds to it appropriately, they are further developing their physical literacy, as the interaction is effective, and ultimately 'the interaction will have added to the individual's knowledge, self-confidence and self-esteem' (2010: 3).

Conversely however, if an individual's competence level exceeds the level of risk, it is likely that boredom will result as the individual will be under-challenged. More concerning, however, would be where risk levels exceed competence levels, as this may result in unacceptably high levels of anxiety or when facing real, rather than perceived, risk lead to 'devastation or disaster' (Martin and Priest, 1986). Mortlock (1984) claims four stages, which can be seen as a continuum, ranging from 'play' through to 'misadventure', are apparent in any outdoor journey. He highlights the role that real and perceived risk play in the development of 'frontier adventures' whereby,

> the person has fear of physical harm, or physical or psychological stress ... If he succeeds, he has experienced what I term 'frontier adventure' ... He has feelings of satisfaction, if not elation, about the result. (Mortlock, 1984: 23)

Brown suggests the 'comfort zone model', which is widespread within adventure education literature, 'is based on the belief that when placed in a stressful or challenging situation people will respond, rise to the occasion and overcome' (2008: 3).

 Thoughts on theory

- What sorts of learning theory perspectives appear to be operating here? On the one hand, there seems to be a community of practice in adventure education that suggests pushing beyond the comfort zone is important as a psychological breakthrough in terms of character development. Yet, the awareness of the individual's competence levels suggests that this is a personal point. How also does this optimum challenge square with Forest School pedagogy (see Chapter 12) where success is assured through breaking down tasks into achievable steps? Where too is the 'place' in this internalised experiential model?

This clearly raises a number of pedagogical issues. It is imperative that an individual's previous experiences are taken into account when planning outdoor and adventurous experiences. Whilst differentiation in any area of the curriculum is vital, Woodhouse believes that unfortunately when planning OAA activities for children there is a 'tendency to think first that "the blindfold trust walk is a good activity, I'll do that with the pupils next week"' (2003: 114). The idiosyncrasies of each participant and the subjective nature of risk and challenge demands that there should be a variety of developmentally appropriate, success-orientated activities and approaches, as without careful scaffolding the increase in perceived risk may prove too much for some children. Teachers of primary school children know their pupils well and will have developed an understanding of each child's strengths and weaknesses (see Figure 2.1 in Chapter 2 which illustrates how the contingent facilitator manages differentiated response). It might also be pertinent to mention that where physical education is taught by outside sports coaches during planning, preparation and assessment time, the teacher's knowledge of the children's physical capacities may not be as sound as it should be. The outcomes we would be looking to achieve through OAA activities (e.g. skills, leadership, teamwork, problem-solving, creativity, trust) can be scaffolded in physical education from Early Years throughout Key Stage 1, Key Stage 2 and beyond. As with all learning, challenge and success in increasingly complex situations are the essential ingredients as this causes the pupil to re-evaluate the taken-for-granted.

Notwithstanding the level of adventure present in the activities themselves we should also acknowledge that the perceived risk brought about by an unfamiliar outdoor environment may in itself provide a high level of challenge for some, often younger, participants. Mortlock suggests, in relation to his four-stage model, that 'a cow in a field, or climbing over a gate, can be stage III [frontier adventure] for some youngsters' (1984: 25).

The Physical Education National Curriculum dictates that challenges should take place in 'familiar and unfamiliar environments' (DfEE, 2000: 133), therefore it might be appropriate to begin teaching and learning in the place the children are most familiar, the classroom. Kimball and Bacon support this view, recommending that adventure education activities should be 'structured so that success and mastery are not only possible, but probable' if the development of self-esteem is to be achieved (1993, cited in McKenzie, 2000: 21). We suggest therefore that careful planning and effective teaching will ensure that success is probable as children's learning can be scaffolded by progressing from inside, to outdoors, to 'outside the classroom', as this presents further appropriate challenge, and will extend and enhance learning. However, we should also bear in mind that children in Foundation Stage are more used to managing their indoor and outdoor learning themselves than children in later stages of primary education (Waite, 2011).

Orienteering activities could begin in the classroom during a geography lesson with the children being taught to orientate a simple map in order to find a range of hidden objects or clues. The progression of this learning to the context of a physical education lesson, in a larger, slightly less familiar, indoor space such as the school hall and then to the school grounds, increases the difficulty and the level of perceived (because all the necessary risk assessments are in place) risk and therefore the level of challenge. This process of scaffolding allows the children to gain the skills, knowledge and understanding required to build confidence, which will develop motivated learners equipped to meet further challenges. The process also allows the teacher to monitor each child's progress so that teaching can be differentiated and learning personalised. Although at first sight this might appear an essentially psychological process, the scaffolding can clearly also be understood on a socio-cultural plane of focus, in that children are gradually accustomed to 'what we do here' (see Chapter 1 and the following case study.)

Case Study

Scaffolding outdoor and adventurous activities – playground to residential

Chloe (age 11) is participating in an OAA residential with her year group. The obstacle in front of her is a granite tor on Dartmoor; and she is halfway through her first climb. She is stuck, unable to climb higher; she is ready to give up and wants to come down. She freezes and begins to panic. The instructor begins to coax Chloe and points out where the next foothold is. The teacher accompanying the group repeats and reinforces the instructor's words. Chloe doesn't move, she has reached her 'panic zone' and is unable to think coherently.

The other children watch intently, waiting quietly because the instructor and teacher are talking. One by one, the children begin calling out words of encouragement. 'Go on Chloe!' 'You can do it Chloe!' The children become more and more persuasive and Chloe takes a deep breath and starts climbing again. She reaches the top, abseils down and receives cheers and 'high fives' from her peers.

The trust Chloe showed in her peers and the support they gave her was not a chance occurrence. It was a moment that the children had been guided towards. Throughout Key Stage 1 teachers used Sherborne Devel-

(Continues)

(Continued)

opmental Movement (Sherborne, 2001) as a platform for activities designed to help children understand 'caring, sharing and against' relationships and to develop an understanding and appreciation of their physical capacities. In Year 3, the children had worked on team-building in OAA lessons in the playground and on the playing field. They also had an over-night stay at a residential centre just a few miles from the school. In Year 4, their OAA lessons took place in a local park, with the children working in small groups building on their orienteering skills which sometimes took them out of view of the teacher, thus developing a sense of group responsibility. In Year 5 and 6, the children accessed outdoor pursuit opportunities provided by the local school sport partnership. By the time the Year 6 week-long residential arrived, a whole school approach, a knowledgeable subject leader, receptive class teachers and well-prepared children had resulted in a common understanding that each individual would be travelling their own journey and might need support along the way. As a result of participating in high-quality physical education, the children already had respect for each other and understood that they all have personal strengths and areas for development. They were supportive of their peers as they challenged themselves to achieve their individual potential.

 Thoughts on theory

- Consider what aspects of the case study throw light on how learning might be taking place in this series of outdoor experiences.
- What is the learning that is happening and who is doing it?
- How is it being facilitated?
- What theoretical planes of focus are helpful in understanding the pedagogy employed here?

 Points for practice

- How might you scaffold the children's learning so that activities are developmentally appropriate and success is not only possible, but probable?
- How could you balance the competence of the children with the risk of the task and involve the children in the assessment of risk, so that they begin to learn how to keep themselves safe?
- How might you utilise the resources that are available to you in your school, its grounds and the local area?

Overcoming the barriers to learning in the outdoors

If the benefits of learning outdoors in both familiar and unfamiliar environments are so widely accepted, why are we not exploiting the opportunities available to us? Perhaps some teachers are not as ready and willing to commit to the outdoors as their pupils are. Waite et al. suggest that some adults may 'be averse to getting cold or wet in the name of learning' and that these attitudes are barriers to learning beyond the confines of the classroom walls (2006: 52). Paradoxically, as highlighted in Chapter 1, this may be as a result of their own childhood and schooling, as children who had not had access to the outdoors in their childhood were far less likely to choose to spend time in the outdoors as adults. In addition to this it could be argued that a lack of appropriate hours spent on physical education during initial teacher training may also contribute. If trainees are not convinced of the special nature of physical education, if they feel they lack the expertise to organise (and manage) children in the outdoors, or if they feel being outdoors is outside their comfort zone, then it is little wonder some teachers use avoidance strategies.

This makes it even more important that practitioners break this negative cycle and venture outside, avoiding excuses that it is too hot, too cold, too wet or too windy. Children want to move; they need to move. They need the relative freedom that the outdoors provides. They are remarkably resilient and can cope with the changing environment as long as they are appropriately prepared and appropriately dressed, as we see below.

Case Study 🗁

The challenge of a changing environment

Jonny, age 10, is participating in an OAA residential with his year group. The fourth day is a 4-hour trek on Dartmoor. Accompanied by a suitably qualified instructor from the activity centre, and a class teacher, the group of 12 pupils are responsible for map reading and guiding themselves around a course. During the trek, the group experiences four changes of weather – it begins as a clear sunny day, rain falls after 30 minutes and by the hour mark, heavy mist has descended. By the time the pupils stop for lunch, snow is falling and continues to do so as children eventually find their way back to the mini-bus. Jonny finds the trek exhausting. It is the farthest he has ever walked; he was late to sleep the previous night, and the terrain was difficult. By the end of the trek he is tired and wet, but happy. The instructor comments on how well the children took the changes in weather in their stride.

(Continues)

(Continued)

However, the children were used to working outside in all weathers, because of actions taken during a unit of work using invasion games, when they were in Year 4. The first lesson, focusing on practising dribbling skills, took place during the first week after the summer break. It was a hot sunny afternoon and Mrs Bell, the class teacher, ensured the children had applied sun screen, that they were appropriately dressed and had access to drinking water. Two weeks later it was raining and whilst the children had basic kit, they did not have a full change of clothes, nor did they have track suits or towels, so Mrs Bell reluctantly stayed in the classroom. Whilst she was quite happy to stay dry, she was uneasy about the loss of physical education time. In consultation with the head teacher and the physical education subject leader, Mrs Bell discussed the effect of the inclement weather on outside games with the children in her class. They discussed reasons for and against going outside whatever the weather and created a list of things they needed to address if they were to play in the rain. Guided by Mrs Bell the children wrote a letter to their parents, which resulted in everyone bringing in a kit bag with a complete change of clothes and a towel.

Next time it rained, the lesson went ahead as planned. Everyone got soaked and to begin with several of the children were not happy (they later explained they were anxious because they felt they were doing something wrong). By the end of the lesson, which was shortened so no one became too cold, everyone was laughing and jumping in puddles. The original learning objective was achieved, but more importantly, the children understood the need for them to dress appropriately in order to cope with the unpredictable British weather.

It was of no surprise to anyone therefore that when it snowed in the spring term Mrs Bell and the children once again 'dared' to go ahead with their outside lesson. Despite 3 inches of snow, Wellington boots, hats, gloves and coats were donned and Mrs Bell endeavoured to teach the planned lesson. Within minutes, the footballs began to 'grow' and became heavy as the snow stuck to them. Instead of the planned 'three versus three' games of football, a snowball fight became the vehicle through which the learning objective of how to outwit opponents was achieved. The lesson ended and everyone returned to the classroom to change into dry, warm clothes. It was a lesson the children would never forget and one that would serve them well on their OAA trek a few years later.

This case study highlights the quandary that exists for practitioners as they gaze out the window at the ever-changing UK weather conditions. Some, like Mrs Bell, will see the value of learning outdoors despite (or because of) the weather and choose to think creatively and see the potential difficulties presented by the elements as opportunities to develop the children's learning (Waite et al., 2006). Unfortunately, however, other practitioners will cancel their physical education lessons, choosing instead to stay warm and dry inside. The English government set a target that all children (aged 5–16) should have 2 hours of curriculum physical education and the opportunity to access a further 3 hours of sport or physical activity beyond the curriculum per week. These targets (often referred to as the 'Five Hour Offer') are designed to lead children into lifelong participation in physical activity and, with the expertise of the teacher and significant others, can support each child on their physical literacy journey. They reinforce the importance of taking physical education 'outside the classroom' in the broadest sense so that it becomes 'what we do' for children throughout their lives. As previously mentioned adults are more likely to spend time in the outdoors if they were encouraged to do so as children. Activities that don't involve any equipment, such as walking and running, can be enjoyed throughout life, especially when the demands of work and family impinge upon an adult's time.

Waite and Rea highlight the important role that outdoor adventure centres play in developing this love of the outdoors and respect for the elements that come with it, stating that 'overcoming difficulties presented by the weather is embedded in the principles espoused by outdoor centres' (2007: 57). Children who are away from home on residential experiences are given the responsibility of packing their own 'kit' for the day's activities and have to live with the very real consequences of forgetting anything. Davis et al. believe that such responsibility offers 'powerful learning opportunities … about learning to live with their mistakes' (2006: 8) (see also Chapter 11).

Reading the environment

A changing outdoor environment, brought about by the weather that typifies each of the UK's seasons, provides a further challenge for children. Life indoors is more regulated, while outdoors is unpredictable. Skills and learning developed in an indoor 'closed' context can be transferred to an outdoor 'open' context and further refined and developed. For example, running on wet grass requires additional and different skills to those required for running on dry grass – increased awareness, balance and an understanding of how to control the body (perhaps by slowing down and/or anticipating changes in direction). Likewise, on rock hard ground in the summer, when the grass may become rutted, the runner will need to make adjustments. Trying to run with, or against, a powerful wind is a unique experience (a following wind helps children experience pure speed, whilst running into the wind requires strength and determination). Fascinating discussions will result, as children begin to analyse what happens to their body and to their performance. Understanding and reading the environment are an important part of developing one's physical literacy, but the skills required need to be learned, experienced and practised. We should not deny children an opportunity to develop an appreciation of the natural environment; a wet, cold or windy day should be seized on by the teacher as a special learning opportunity for their pupils.

 Points for practice

- Avoid cancelling lessons when weather conditions are inclement.
- Encourage children to become accustomed to the wonderful variety of weather and make the right choices in terms of clothing and equipment.
- Encourage children to take responsibility for their own kit at school and ensure they understand that having the correct clothing and equipment is an essential precursor to the residential experience and to being physically active in the outdoors.
- Ensure that the children you teach are receiving 2 hours of high-quality physical education; plus one hour of extra-curricular school sport; plus access to 2 hours of community-based sport and/or physical activity, in order for them to continue on their journey towards becoming physically literate.

Summary

This chapter has outlined a number of factors that need to be taken into account during a child's physical education in the early years and primary setting. Physical education is important if we are truly concerned about children's holistic development. Physical education will often be a child's only regular experience of learning 'outdoors' and provides numerous opportunities for the experience to be scaffolded. Learning can begin in a closed familiar indoor environment and can ultimately be transferred to an open unfamiliar outdoor environment. Challenges can be enhanced by working outdoors and ultimately 'outside the classroom' – these challenges

(Continued)

(Continued)

> encourage children to move outside their comfort zones, where they utilise skills such as reading the environment and personal risk assessment.
>
> Physical activity in the outdoors should be an essential element when planning a curriculum that addresses physical development, health and well-being, as it encourages children to develop an appreciation for our environment and provides an opportunity for them to develop physical competence and confidence in their physical literacy journey.

Further reading

afPE (Association for Physical Education) (2008) Manifesto for a World Class System of Physical Education. *Physical Education Matters*, 3 (4).

Gallahue, D.L. and Ozmun, J.C. (2006) *Understanding Motor Development*. Madison, WI: Brown & Benchmark.

Physical Literacy website. www.physical-literacy.org.uk

Sherborne, V. (2001) *Developmental Movement for Children*. London: Worth Publishing.

Whitehead, M. (2010) *Physical Literacy Throughout the Lifecourse*. London: Routledge.

Section 3

Outside the Box

The four chapters in this section shift the perspective from the curriculum and age phases to types of provision. The chapters represent a small selection of different ways that learning outside the classroom is manifested. This additional perspective seems an especially important aspect of any book on learning outside the classroom. An industry is currently emerging around provision of these experiences for schools, in which externally managed learning spaces are badged as Learning Outside the Classroom providers and in the process possibly being acculturated to mainstream schooling norms. This can be seen to have advantages and disadvantages, discussed in the following chapters.

11

Residential centres: desirable difference?

Tony Rea

Chapter objectives

- An appreciation of the possibilities afforded by outdoor education and activity centres; especially those centres that include a residential aspect

- An appreciation of the contribution these centres may have in the education of children aged 8–11

- An understanding of the theoretical underpinnings of the pedagogies utilised in some centres, and the relationship of these to learning in the primary school

- A demonstration of how residential centres' difference from schools may be threatened by a creeping neo-liberal agenda

To some readers outdoor centres may seem part and parcel of school life and of children's upbringing. To others, the concept may be new. Centres such as those described later in this chapter are well established, yet fewer children are gaining access to them due to their teachers' fears about litigation (Curtis, 2009), risk aversion (Furedi, 1997) and health and safety worries. For example, the *E.-coli* outbreaks amongst a few young children following visits to English farms where they were encouraged to stroke animals (September 2009) may have stopped visits such as those referred to in Waite and

148

Rea (2007). Furthermore, there is evidence that the experiences children have in centres are gradually changing, rendering them increasingly like school experiences.

In this chapter I will critically examine the changing landscape of centre-based outdoor education and the pressures society is placing on it. First I will explain the historical and cultural position of outdoor centres in the British education system, and provide an overview of the valuable work centres do using the theoretical construct of four 'pillars of knowledge' (UNESCO's International Commission on Education for the Twenty-first Century, quoted in Stoll, 1999). I will then critique those pressures that I consider are making centres more like schools, using the theoretical constructs of discourse and identity.

Much of the evidence I draw upon comes from my own doctoral research, which was an ethnographic study of an English residential outdoor education centre. Other material comes from published studies and unpublished PhD theses.

Outdoor centres: the historical and cultural background

The residential outdoor education where my study was conducted was originally a house on a country estate, and was gifted to an English Local Authority (LA) in the 1950s. This is not an uncommon occurrence. Other properties were purchased, converted or purpose-built. Outdoor centres may be in the public (i.e. owned and operated by LAs), private or charitable sectors.

The *raison d'être* of outdoor education centres lies in the thinking and developmental work of Baden-Powell (1930) and Kurt Hahn (1965). The types of activities undertaken in centres (see below) have a long tradition in the British educational system, strongly influenced by these two. Baden-Powell founded the scouting movement, whilst the theories of Hahn contributed to both Outward Bound and the Duke of Edinburgh's Award. Throughout Britain the numbers of state-run and private outdoor centres set up and run largely in the spirit of Baden-Powell and Hahn burgeoned during the 1960s to 1980s. The head of one such centre, Colin Mortlock, went on to write in favour of outdoor education, presenting arguments for adventure as a positive and resilience-building part of children's education, thus strengthening the position of the centres (Mortlock, 1984, 2002).

As we have seen in Chapter 10, the language of Baden-Powell, Hahn and Mortlock was principally about the power of adventure, and coping with adversity, to build 'character' in the individual. More recently, the language has changed to 'resilience' and ideas about self-concept. There is much recent research evidence that suggests properly planned and managed outdoor adventurous activities can encourage a growth in self-confidence and self-esteem (e.g. Rickinson et al., 2004) and readers may wish to return to Chapter 1 on theory for explanations of why this might be so.

During the 1990s and into the 21st century however, centres have been facing difficulties, for three main reasons:

1. Over-sensitivity towards health and safety issues and risk aversion in a society that seems quick to turn to litigation when accidents happen.

2. Cost and financial pressures.

3. Pressures on schools to raise attainment, and to demonstrate they are doing so; all part of the neo-liberalisation of British schooling (Ball, 2003).

There is a great deal of literature about neo-liberalism and education (for examples, see Ball, 2003; Wrigley, 2007). Summarised briefly, this is the process by which governments seek to impose 'liberal' notions of freedom to choose and consumerism onto schools, parents and children; transforming education into a commodity, the recent invitation to primary schools to become 'academies' being a classic case. In order to facilitate 'consumer choice', schools need to be clearly labelled and classified. This has led to the widespread use in England of school 'league tables' reporting examination outcomes to compare school performance, target-driven performance management for teachers and school managers, and a focus on impact in school inspections by Ofsted. 'Impact', based upon the assumption that a causal link exists between educational aims, objectives and pedagogy, and learning outcomes or benefits, became a mantra of late-20th century state schooling in Britain. I suggest throughout this chapter that this same neo-liberalism, and its emphasis on school effectiveness and search for impact, is leading to the over-formalisation of outdoor learning.

Hayes outlines the drawbacks of an over-formalised school curriculum that squeezes children's learning into 'predetermined packets' of time to meet learning objectives (2007: 151). He sees outdoor learning as a possible antidote to this. However, the effects of neo-liberalism has outdoor centres in a double bind: first it tends to restrict the numbers of children who attend centre courses as schools feel it may prejudice their attainment, second, it tends to allow schooling discourses to enter and dominate centres. This phenomenon is described in more detail later, where I also provide my definition of, and explanation of how I use the term 'discourse'.

Case Study
Activities and learning experiences in a 'typical' outdoor centre

My ethnographic study of a 'typical' outdoor education centre revealed the following long list of activities: rock climbing, orienteering, canoeing, coasteering, problem-solving games, fell walking, farm visits, surfing, beach games, rope courses, team-work games, river study, zip wires, ecology study, beach survival, gorge walking. Added to this, in a residential setting children may help to cook and clean, and will have to live together in dormitory accommodation, typically for a week.

The residential outdoor education centre I researched is owned and administered by an English Local Authority (LA). Children (typically aged 9–11) reside there for five days in groups of up to 34, accompanied by their teachers. The centre is staffed by the head and four other outdoor instructors (two of whom are qualified teachers) and support staff. Staff at the centre have defined six themes that all children are introduced to. These are:

1. *Making the future*, this relates to the centre's eco-centre status (Eco-Schools, 2002) and ethos.

2. *Caring, sharing* and (3.) *being a social being* relate to aspects of social learning, for example, teamwork and relationship nurturing.

4. *Adventure for life* and (5.) *learning for life*, are mainly about the acquisition of those skills and attitudes deemed to be necessary for a full and active participatory life style

6. *Risky business* is about doing things safely, emphasising risk assessment and risk management.

Both Christie (2004) and Nundy (1999) found it difficult or impossible to separate cognitive from affective areas of learning. For example, Nundy found that the residential aspect of the whole experience increased affective learning, which in turn impacted upon cognitive learning.

Residential centres place particular demands on younger children. For some, it may be the first time they have been away from home.

In my interviews with children following observations of them in the centre, I was initially surprised that they were much keener to talk to me about the residential aspects of the experience than they were about the outdoor adventurous activities. These interviews led me to think about attendance at residential centres more in terms of children's social and emotional development than the acquisition of knowledge or skills. For example, homesickness was a really strong theme in the interview data. My subsequent investigations and conclusions about it are that experiencing homesickness, living with and dealing with it, may be an important aspect of some children's learning. The experience may be valued by some children, parents and teachers as a process through which a child's resilience is developed; thus the residential experience may be seen as a 'rite of passage'.

Thoughts on theory

- Thinking back to the evaluative points raised in Chapter 1, *what* learning is afforded by such experiences? UNESCO's International Commission on Education for the Twenty-first Century (quoted in Stoll, 1999) proposed four fundamental types of learning, or 'pillars of knowledge', which was articulated with respect to outdoor learning by Davis, Rea and Waite (2006). The suggested pillars of knowledge are:

  - Learning to know
  - Learning to do
  - Learning to live together
  - Learning to be.

Consider how these might relate to the sorts of activities and aims in residential centres.

These 'pillars of knowledge' provide a potential lens through which to examine the work of residential centres further.

The first pillar: Learning to know – the cognitive domain

There have been a number of reports claiming the benefits of outdoor centres on children's cognition, or acquisition of knowledge. For example, Nundy (1999) investigated geographical learning at an outdoor centre compared to the classroom. He tested two groups of pupils on their geographic knowledge and understanding after they had been taught a specific topic. He found that fieldwork can lead to greater cognitive (and affective) learning outcomes than classroom-based activities. Nundy relates these gains to both place and pedagogy. He sees 'location' in which the experience occurred and 'key memory episodes' as being of primary significance: 'Students at the centre were able to recall, readily, novel events that happened during the week, such as the times they got wet or muddy' (1999: 194). The role of pedagogy including practical work is also highlighted. Children, he argues, have to be presented with 'challenges', be involved with group work and 'talk', and have the opportunity to control and re-construct their learning and thinking. Here we see an echo of the concepts found in Chapter 1, 'control', 'practical', 'challenge' and 'novelty', inviting both psychological and socio-cultural interpretations.

Christie (2004) found similar problems in separating cognitive learning from confidence when she investigated the impact of one week Outward Bound courses[1] delivered to an older age group, year 10 pupils, and found positive overall effects of the programme in terms of the students' self-perception of their academic skills. When back in the classroom, some students reported that they felt that they could speak out more in class, ask for help and work better with others. In terms of subject areas, they felt that they were doing better in English and French, as they were able to stand up and do 'speaking tests'. They felt that they had something to talk about (the Outward Bound experience) and to write about in essays. The students reported that their grades had improved and they felt more confident in their exams.

Buchanan (2010) reports on positive gains where primary-aged children are using number in a water-based outdoor activities centre, such as measuring boats to find the average width and length. Dismore and Bailey (2005), in a larger and more robust study of a programme somewhat similar to that reported by Buchanan, looked at a sample of about 700 Year 5 pupils who attended an outdoor adventure programme at a centre in Kent. Their findings also show some cognitive improvement in the pupils. At some schools they found an increase in pupil performance in both Qualification and Curriculum Authority (QCA) tests and optional Standard Assessment Tasks in English and mathematics when these were taken before, then after, an outdoor adventure programme that blended outdoor adventurous activities with the subject areas.

1 Outward Bound is a particular 'brand' of outdoor activity/education centre. Information about its background and approach can be found on the Outward Bound website www.theoutwardboundtrust.org.uk/ or see Hattie et al. (1997).

The second pillar: Learning to do – skills acquisition

It may be argued that because of the practical nature of the activities the children embark upon during their stay, centres do much to enhance the acquisition of new skills. But thinking back to the questions in Chapter 1, what *kinds* of skills does this argument refer to? Undoubtedly, the skills of the rock face, for example: knot tying, belaying, physical and dextrous manoeuvring, abseiling may be developed during some centre-based programmes, but the skills most favoured by the adults connected to those outdoor centres that I have been involved with are social skills.

The third pillar: Learning to live together – social skills development

Many would argue that greater benefits of programmes at outdoor centres are to be found in the affective domain, making contributions to personal and social aspects of learning, though others may see them as by-products. Pupils may mature and develop social skills during the residential and planned activities. They develop their understanding of others and appreciate the interdependence of participating and co-operating with others. Centres may have an effect on social learning. Rickinson et al. (2004) found evidence that residential experience in particular can lead to individual growth and improvements in social skills. Many of the problem-solving and team-building activities found in centres are designed to impact on this area of learning. However, I am cautious about generalising either in terms of the findings of Rickinson et al. or centres, which are far from homogeneous. Adopting a socio-cultural plane of focus, the outcomes observed in the research reviewed by Rickinson et al. may be seen as constructions of the groups and setting and the adult facilitator, and therefore specific to them.

The fourth pillar: Learning to be – self-awareness and greater autonomy

This aspect is concerned with the self, self-knowledge; it is about self-esteem and self-actualisation. It is also about individual judgements, values and morals and how these are moderated in cultural contexts. Moreover, it is about knowing one's place in the world, so far as that can be known, and so could include the concept of spirit and inspirational, spiritual and transcendental experiences. This clearly has strong roots in psychological theories of self-development.

In Rea (2008) I critiqued the trend of essentialising self-conceptual notions such as self-esteem, drawing on Brookes (2003). Many programmes based on outdoor centres are claimed to have had significant positive effects on the self-concept of those participating (see, for example, Ewert, 1983), by confronting participants with challenges which they 'overcome' as part of the programme. Furedi (2004) has criticised what he calls the 'turn to' therapy and its over-concern with self-esteem, partly because it positions people as vulnerable and deficient; whilst constructionists would argue that self-esteem is a contextually situated social-construction (Burr, 2003; Gergen, 1999). Brookes (2003) has also challenged a similar stable notion of 'character', arguing that individual behaviour in one situation may give little indication about behaviour in different situations. Thus, character and self-esteem may be considered contextually situated rather than essential.

There have been few studies of the place of spiritual development in the curriculum. Meehan (2002) conducted an analysis of curricular opportunities to address spirituality. Neither of them looked outside the classroom for opportunities to address spirituality. Creating a sense of awe, wonder and mystery inside the four walls of a classroom is difficult, but not impossible. The outdoors, however, can present teachers with a ready-made arena for pupils to experience elation, wonder, awe – all emotions that can have a profound effect on their spiritual development. (See also examples in relation to the Arts in Chapter 9.)

 Points for practice

- Reflecting on what you have read so far, especially on the first case study and the discussion that followed, think about how you might integrate a visit to a centre into your current practice.
- Which children might you take and why?
- Where would you go, and when?
- What aspects of the curriculum might you link with? Or is this an opportunity to depart from the curriculum?
- What do you think are the main reasons for taking children to a residential outdoor education centre?
- How might this affect what sorts of experiences you try to offer?
- Are there any drawbacks that you can think of from your reading of this and other chapters of the book?

Case Study

When a centre becomes a school

It is a bright sunny afternoon when 30 Year 6 children and their teachers and adult helpers arrive at the centre. There is a great deal of excitement as boys and girls pile off the coach and assemble around the 'garden' area at the back of the centre. They are quickly dispatched to their dormitories, not to unpack, just to dump their bags. Shortly after the children arrive they are told to go and sit in the lounge, one of only two spaces large enough to seat them all together, and less formal than the classroom.

Simon, the head of the centre, then introduces himself and uses a PowerPoint slide presentation to share the intended learning outcomes of the week-long residential with the children. They spend 45 minutes sitting and listening to Simon, asking and answering questions sometimes. Some of the children seem to be restless and not concentrating.

During the week, centre staff will de-brief the children numerous times following various activities, following the Kolbian cycle of reflection on experience (Kolb, 1984; see also Chapter 1) in a dedicated way. The learning objectives are referred to in briefings and de-briefing before and after many sessions and children are encouraged to write daily jottings on scribble pads or white boards, codified under the headings of the learning objectives. Free writing is not encouraged.

At the end of the week there is another extended period of time, in a large group sitting in the lounge, looking at the white board, re-focussing the children on the learning outcomes.

Why are centres becoming like school?

My research found that practices in the centre I observed were becoming increasingly like schools' practices. Centre staff followed the schooling orthodoxy of sharing with (or imposing on) children their intended learning outcomes. Though supported by some well-constructed PowerPoint shows and making use of interactive white board technology, unfortunately this fundamentally sedentary session often resulted in bored, restless young people and occasionally contributed to poor behaviour. As in Chapter 1, one might speculate about the mismatch of expectations of adults and children in this experience. They arrive in an exciting new place to be confronted with an imported pattern of interaction.

The reasons for this trend can be linked to the effects of a neo-liberal education agenda and the drive to raise attainment. Society's increasing risk aversion is also having some bearing. For example, Humberstone and Stan's (2009a) research found that both centre workers and adults accompanying children from their schools were disposed towards overprotecting children from risks. The trends towards risk aversion and neo-liberalism are in danger of adversely affecting what takes place in outdoor education centres.

Thoughts on theory

- The first three of UNESCO'S four pillars accept a traditional, acquisitional perspective of learning. Hager and Hodkinson (2009) term this the 'common sense' view of learning accepted by most people. However, if we take the view that 'learning' is a theoretical concept (Stables, 2005) we can accept that there may be great benefits in considering learning from other perspectives. Hager and Hodkinson have provided a useful overview of four different 'lenses' for understanding learning:
  - the propositional knowledge lens
  - the skills learning lens
  - the participation lens
  - the transformation lens.

Consider how the socio-cultural and psychological planes of focus discussed in Chapter 1 might relate to these lenses.

Like Hager and Hodkinson, we use the term 'lens' in this book as a metaphor for something that helps us to see – more clearly or differently. Lenses help us to shape our perspectives (the way we view things). One problem with metaphors and theoretical perspectives, however, is that they may become reified and thought of as having tangible existence, or, in social-constructionist language, as discourses, with rhetorical power. This is especially the case with the 'common sense' perspective of learning as acquisition, traditionally the predominant perspective in psychological learning theory. The discourse of acquisition has assumed a position of such power that this *discourse* is working to convince us that learning *is* acquisition, rather than helping us to further our understanding of a theoretical concept called learning. The first two lenses fit well within this perspective, but the last two are more problematic.

Another problem with the discourse of learning as acquisition is that it does not really help us to understand the fourth pillar: 'learning to be', self-awareness and developing greater autonomy. This fits better with Hager and Hodkinson's learning as a transformation lens, but may also be explained through thinking about learning as identity formation. Therefore, I now want to move away from the idea that learning is acquisition, to consider learning as identity.

The socio-cultural perspective of learning as identity is attractive in explaining UNESCO'S fourth pillar, as well as allowing us to look more critically at claims regarding acquisition. One problem seems to be that those who have written about learning as identity do not fully explain how it happens. I have found the philosophy of social constructionism useful in helping to explain learning as identity (for an introduction, see Burr, 2003; Gergen, 1999). Social constructionism is the philosophy that suggests reality, especially social reality, is socially constructed; that is to say, it does not exist outside of human social experience and discourse. A discourse is a system of words or texts that both create and continually re-form the concepts or phenomena they seem to describe.

Identity can be taken as meaning the discursive positioning of selves. This needs some explaining. Identity is unlike personality. Personality is a psychological concept that suggests the person we are is largely fixed and may be, to an extent at least, predetermined by biological factors. Identity, on the other hand, is a sociological term that in social constructionism suggests fluidity and transience. One may have different identities for different social settings – multiple-identities. Our identity is determined by the discourses that position us, and the discourses we use to position ourselves (Davies and Harré, 1990).

Examining learning at outdoor education centres critically

My research suggests that one of the major benefits of outdoor centres may be in providing alternative perspectives to children; providing them with different ways of looking at themselves and at the world. Constructionists (for example, Burr, 2003; Gergen, 1999) might call these alternative perspectives discourses. These 'new' discourses may include risk-taking, the outdoors, valuing nature, sustainability and ecology, informal and naturalistic learning, self-sufficiency and self-dependency, trust and reliance on peers, homesickness.

In summary, whereas there is evidence that centres are becoming increasingly like schools, research also suggests that schools might be yet better places for learning if they were able to adopt some of the discourses prevalent in outdoor centres.

Thoughts on theory

- How do the ideas of learning as transformation or as identity formation fit with your own perspectives (or lens) on learning?
- Are they useful to you as a teacher or potential educator?
- Are they any more or less useful than acquisitional perspectives on learning?

Case Study

When a school becomes an outdoor centre: Old Mill School

Set deep in heart of the rural midlands, Old Mill is a specialist school that accommodates the needs of around 90 pupils, all with learning difficulties. A large number of them have been diagnosed with autism or Asperger's syndrome. Many are funded by Local Authorities, some by their parents. Many of the children who currently attend Old Mill have specific learning difficulties.

The school is housed in an old mill that was renovated by the founder and the first cohorts of young people. The young residents are to be seen farming, fishing and involving themselves in crafts in the large grounds surrounding the mill buildings. Making things from natural materials, using traditional tools and preserving traditional skills, movements[2] and names; and doing much of this in the outdoors, are central to the ethos of the Old Mill.

Many facets of the ethos and practice at Old Mill School reflect and exemplify Rudolf Steiner's anthroposophic philosophical approach.[3] In addition the school believes that the pupils learn and develop through engaging with the environment by working with the variety of challenges that the natural environment and natural materials present. For example, green wood turning skills are practised. The wood is coppiced from sustainable woodland, planted and managed partly by the children. Clay is collected from a bank. It is processed by hand using traditional throwing methods, then glazed and fired in kilns made by the pupils.

2 By this I mean physical movements, especially big, slow, deliberate and rhythmic movements such as those involved in using a scythe or working a hand bellows. These are thought to have beneficial properties, especially useful in the management of some of the syndromes encountered by students at this college.

3 Anthroposophy is a spiritual philosophy founded by Steiner (see Steiner, 1995). It claims the existence of an objective, spiritual world. This spiritual world can be made accessible by developing a form of thinking independent of sensory experience. Anthroposophical ideas have been applied practically in many areas including Steiner Waldorf schools, special education (most prominently the Camphill movement), biodynamic agriculture, anthroposophic medicine (which thrives chiefly in continental Europe and North America, and has its own clinics, hospitals and medical schools) and eurythmy, a particular dance form that seeks to transform speech and music into visible movement.

Thoughts on theory

- How might Steiner's philosophy and educational theories evident in Old Mill School be theoretically linked to practice in good outdoor education centres?

- Can holistic approaches such as these be of any use in a mainstream system dominated by neo-liberalism and attainment?

- Educational activities here have a usefulness or purpose beyond their learning potential; a 'reality beyond the educational setting' (Chapter 1). Could mainstream schools learn from and apply any of the features relating to outdoor learning referred to here?

 Points for practice

- Consider what experiences you would wish a residential centre to offer children. What learning is associated with these? How do you know?

- Are there ways you could re-create some of these experiences locally within your own school community?

- Are difference and distance essential qualities for the contribution that residential centres make to children's learning? Are there other ways that excitement and self-challenge could be engendered?

- The Learning Outside the Classroom website has details of outdoor educators and centres with quality assurance badging. Consider also though how your knowledge of the children will provide key information to make the most of any visits.

 Summary

I have tried to explain the historical origins of outdoor centres and their cultural position in the British education system. Drawing on recent research evidence from my own work and that of others I have sought to provide both an overview of the valuable work centres do and a critical examination of the current landscape of centre-based outdoor education.

Broadly, I think that centres continue to provide a vital education in difficult circumstances, constrained as they are by three

(Continues)

(Continued)

principal factors: risk aversion and over-sensitivity towards health and safety issues, cost and financial pressures, neo-liberalism and the drive to raise attainment, which combine to make centres increasingly similar to schools.

To ameliorate the current situation I would make the following recommendations:

1. A bigger financial investment in centres so that all children can attend them.

2. Freeing them from schooling orthodoxy so that they can retain a difference from schools.

3. Allowing children at centres to act more independently, making their own risk assessments and learning from this about attitudes to risk and safety.

Further reading

Rea, T. (2008) Alternative visions of learning: children's learning experiences in the outdoors. *Educationalfutures: e-journal of the British Education Studies Association*, 2.

Waite, S. and Rea, T. (2007) Enjoying teaching outside the classroom. In: D. Hayes (ed.), *Joyful Teaching and Learning in the Primary School*. Exeter: Continuum.

12

School gardens and Forest Schools

Rowena Passy and Sue Waite

Chapter objectives

- An awareness of learning opportunities in school gardens
- An awareness of learning opportunities in Forest Schools
- An appreciation of how these might map onto your own intentions for children's learning

Outdoor learning for children follows a tradition dating back from educationalists such as Froebel and Pestalozzi, and has recently been enjoying something of a revival. There is a belief that today's children spend relatively little time outside in comparison with their forebears, and as a result are suffering from a condition that Louv (2005) has termed 'nature-deficit disorder'; children are losing contact with the natural world.

Learning outdoors, however, is not just about running about and getting muddy. Grahn et al. (1997) demonstrated that children spending large parts of their early education outside had better physical and social development, health and levels of concentration than children in traditional nurseries. Research with older children (e.g. Dillon et al., 2005; Rickinson et al., 2004) would seem to support their claims. In this chapter, we consider firstly school gardens and then Forest Schools as cases that seek to replace this missing ingredient in children's lives today.

School gardens and lessons for life

School gardens have a number of easily identifiable benefits as outdoor learning arenas. They are accessible and cost-effective, for they are dependent neither on travel nor on expensive technological equipment, and they can be accommodated in school grounds of all sizes. While those schools lucky enough to have acres of space clearly have an advantage, it is possible to create green areas in the most unpromising situations given a degree of imagination, energy and enthusiasm; almost all schools can create a garden of some kind.

School gardens have long been recognised as offering an important arena for learning. In 1905, for instance, the Board of Education extolled their usefulness as 'being of great service in illustrating object lessons and elementary science lessons' as well as providing 'manual instruction' and 'practical application' of classroom science (Jenkins and Swinnerton, 1998: 58). Nature Study was part of the curriculum through much of the 20th century, and in some cases school gardens provided a site for this; children studied the life cycle of creatures such as frogs and butterflies, grew vegetables (especially during the period of the two world wars), learned about pest control to protect their crops and drew pictures inspired by the changing seasons. In part intended to arouse a love of all things natural, Nature Study was also regarded as a means of developing children's sense of wonder and of imparting 'moral instruction', particularly for those who lived in rural areas who might otherwise be attracted to the 'lower' attractions of town life (Jenkins and Swinnerton, 1998: 63–4).

These claims – although nowadays generally reformulated – have a real resonance with contemporary attitudes to school gardens (e.g. Lepkowska, 2009; Miller, 2007; Ozer, 2007). Theoretical perspectives (e.g. Illeris, 2007; Jarvis and Parker, 2007) suggest that learning has cognitive, emotional and social components, and developments in understanding of the brain suggest that children need movement in order to learn effectively (Stein, 2007: 37). Gardens can provide these different components through activities that include growing vegetables and flowers, creating and maintaining wildlife habitats and establishing discrete areas that are dedicated to – for instance – 'peace', 'memorial' or sensory gardens.

The following case study illustrates how a garden might be used to provide different types of learning. It was undertaken as part of a research programme commissioned by the Royal Horticultural Society to evaluate the impact of school gardens, undertaken in the wake of establishing their 'Campaign for School Gardening' in 2007. The study provides an example of how strong and supportive leadership, combined with the energy and expertise of the TA gardening lead, can lead to a situation in which the garden is regarded by the head teacher as a 'key part of school life'.

The research consisted of two day-long visits to the school. The researcher was given a tour of the school grounds, observed lessons and a session of the gardening club, and undertook interviews with staff and pupils. The gardening lead kept a gardening diary in the months between the visits, and the school was given a disposable camera to take photos of memorable or interesting garden-related occasions. The intention was to explore how the garden was used, the perceived benefits and challenges associated with using it, and to tease out any perceived impact on children's learning and behaviour. The following narrative is compiled from these different data sources.

Case Study

Embedding the garden in school learning

It's Dig for Victory day. Year 5 are studying World War Two as part of their history curriculum and a number of pupils are getting ready to go outdoors, where they will prepare the soil for a garden in the way that citizens did all over the United Kingdom between 1939 and 1945. They are excited at the prospect and, once outside, set to work with gusto. With the Teaching Assistant's help, they measure the part of the grass that is to be converted to vegetable growing, fix lines of string to mark the edge of the plot, and then start to remove the top layer of turf with spades. It is hard work, and there are frustrations when stones make the work difficult. They chatter as they work, speculating on the way people managed the task in the 1940s and encouraged by the results of their own effort. They work with purpose – flagging only occasionally – and at the end of the session, there is a neat, rectangular patch of earth for growing vegetables.

Over the next few weeks, different groups of pupils from the same class continue the work by turning the soil over, digging in compost, planting and tending the plants as they grow. When the vegetables are harvested and prepared for school dinners, they experience a real sense of achievement.

Over the course of the year, each pupil has at least one session in the garden that is inspired by a particular curriculum area. The curriculum links are to topics directly related to scientific investigation, healthy eating, growing things, autumn and history – but also include art, literacy and

(Continues)

(Continued)

numeracy by inspiring drawing and providing data for writing reports on the local environment. The gardening club undertakes the continuous work of growing a wide range of fruit and vegetables, weeding and making compost.

And use of the garden involves the wider school community. The club for after-school and holiday care tends the garden during school holidays and eats the results. During the summer term, plants, vegetables and little herb gardens are sold at the school Town Square, a once-a-fortnight occasion where Year 6 organise the playground into market stalls to raise money for charity and the school. There are plans to keep chickens, so that the eggs produced can be made into cakes (with home-produced raspberry jam!) to sell. To support this work, local firms donate plants and materials to the school, while parents volunteer to help with jobs such as heavy digging or assisting with the gardening club. As the head teacher comments, the garden's 'influence and tentacles are spread everywhere'.

This case study illustrates the way in which a garden can be used in different ways to provide the cognitive (studying World War Two), emotional (the sense of achievement in growing vegetables) and social (working collaboratively) components of learning, and it clearly provides movement when children are engaged in tasks such as digging and weeding. What is particularly interesting, however, is the way in which the garden operates at a socio-cultural level. If we think of the school as a community (as discussed in Chapter 1), it is possible to see that the practices, norms and discourses that are related to the garden have a strong moral message. Gardening is inclusive, for everyone is expected to be involved in some way; growing plants from seed involves nurturing over time; handling tiny seedlings means being gentle and careful; knowledge can be shared, whatever the age of the giver and the receiver. But possibly the most important message is that of altruism – or, in terms of the Every Child Matters outcome, making a positive contribution (DCSF, 2008b). The garden thrives through communal effort in which all pool their expertise and help, and from which all share in the results – a message that is perhaps all the more powerful through being experienced repeatedly and in different aspects of school life. In the context of current anxieties over the sustainability of 21st century living, this may be a lesson for life in more ways than one.

Thoughts on theory

- The garden is 'part of the school' but what norms and practices characterise this space?
- How does this place affect the learning that can take place here?
- How can the school culture be supported by gardening?
- Thinking back to the discussions in Chapter 6 on mathematics, Chapter 8 on geography and history and Chapter 10 on the Arts, for example, how might this place enhance these curriculum areas? What other curriculum topics might be enriched by using the garden?
- What kinds of learning would **you** like to encourage through using the garden?

Points for practice

- Different gardens could be developed in your school grounds, such as a wildlife habitat, vegetable garden, pond, raised beds, willow classroom, sensory garden.
- Consider what learning might be supported by these different places in your planning. Include children in the planning process. Ownership is very important for the uptake of opportunities (Waite et al., 2006) and they have excellent ideas!
- Look for local schemes and national initiatives that might support your school garden. An Internet search or word with your Local Authority Outdoor Education Adviser will quickly throw up some ideas.
- Enlist the support of parents/staff with particular areas of expertise that you could draw on. Not only does this get a school garden but it also grows community spirit!

Forest Schools and dispositions for learning

We now turn to woodland settings. A Forest School provides a wilder context for learning and also reflects a contemporary drive for inclusivity and the recognition of individual needs, partly through high adult–child ratios (Davis, Rea and Waite, 2006; Maynard, 2007). It balances current extreme concerns about health and safety issues for children (Furedi, 2008) with intelligent management of risk and challenge.

Some principles that underpin Forest Schools have been identified:

▪ Forest School is for everybody; many work especially with children with social, emotional and behavioural difficulties of all ages in order to include them in school.

▪ Forest School is a process that builds on an individual's innate motivation and positive attitude to learning, offering them the opportunities to take risks, make choices and initiate learning for themselves; it is not outcome-led.

▪ Forest School is organised and run by qualified Forest School leaders; expertise is carefully developed through specific training.

▪ Forest School maximises the learning potential of local woodland through frequent and regular experiences throughout the year; it builds a relationship with place.

▪ Forest School helps everyone to understand, appreciate and care for the natural environment; it develops positive environmental attitudes and actions (Eastwood and Mitchell, 2003; Waite and Davis, 2007).

The physical surroundings

The site needs to be large enough for group activities with distinct areas for a camp, games, fire pit, work with tools and free exploration. As a rough guide the woodland should be about three times the size of the required area to prevent over-use of these sites within it. Reasonable vehicular access and permission from the land owner to light fires and use natural resources are also necessary. Tree cover from a variety of broad leaf species with a coppiced shrubby understorey is ideal, as it encourages a range of levels of looking and provides material for a variety of activities such as tree recognition, whittling and fire-making. The site should always be inspected for health and safety purposes before sessions to remove any major hazards. If the site is open to the public, an area can be marked by tapes as a safety measure but a private site is preferable to allow negotiated boundaries, i.e. where the children decide how far away they feel safe. On a visit to Denmark to see the source of 'the Forest School model', we saw children of about 5 allowed to roam for long distances through woodland adjacent to their kindergarten, to climb on top of building roofs and up trees as far as they felt comfortable. Considering such practices in a UK context tends to elicit gasps of shock as cultural attitudes to risk vary. The following case study is a composite story taken from research on six English Forest School programmes and our wider research on outdoor learning in early years and primary settings.

Case Study 🗁

Seeing the wood *and* the trees

The children made their way down the steep slippery slope to the wooded area on short little legs, aged as they were between 3 and 5 years. Despite some trepidation shown by the children, the accompanying adults did not 'rescue' them to avoid any risk of them falling over but instead encouraged them to manage the challenge themselves. At the bottom, a sparkling stream provided a pausing point while the children stomped in it, stirring up mud and testing the depth against their Wellington boots; in some cases, mistaking the depth and getting a soggy bootful! The adults were not worried about this; dry socks and shoes were waiting back at base.

In no great hurry to achieve the next thing, the group finally made it to the Forest School clearing. It was marked only by a ring of tree trunks and fewer standing trees. The children ran off into the woods in all directions, disappearing from sight amongst the trees. 'One, two, three, where are you?' called the Forest School leader and a chorus of voices answered. The children were familiar with the wood and knew the boundaries to keep within, although these were unmarked by physical barriers. The children turned over leaves and logs and exclaimed about the many creatures that lived beneath them. Others created stories about fairies and mossy palaces in their play.

Later, the leaders brought the children back together and in small groups amongst the trees, they created little dens for their 'forest friends', which they had whittled using sharp knives from small branches they had measured and sawn the previous week, and decorated with felt tips and natural things they found in the forest. A group of children speculated how the forest friends would manage within the woods and wove a complex story involving journeys by leaf down the stream to catch fish in the sea. Another told each other stories of their friendships with other 'real' woodland creatures, such as squirrels and mice. Some of the stories contained conflicts and fighting, and broken families, which the children worked through in the 'small world' play.

Many specific learning outcomes (the metaphoric trees) such as speaking, listening and story development were achieved in this outdoor experience, but the activities also addressed more holistic social and emotional aspects of learning (the metaphoric wood), where children brought their own experiences to the tasks and built self-confidence in their negotiation of physical, social and personal challenges. During the research we saw how children were not wrapped in cotton wool by adults but encouraged to find their own limits and comfort zones – a wet sock may help reinforce the children's awareness of their body and encourage personal responsibility (Davis et al., 2006). An important aspect was that boundaries were negotiated and so fitted with the Forest School ethos of respecting children's views. Taking account of children's feelings is extremely important for learning, as emotional engagement tends to make memories more lasting (Carver, 2003; Waite, 2007).

The adult's role was very much as facilitator rather than director of learning for many activities. The activity where children took it in turns to lead the group around the site to show off their favourite features enabled the children to learn social skills in how to keep the group interested and focused. The variety of activities available also ensured that different children found something to enjoy and engage in. The woodland context allowed children to let their imagination fly or to dash about using big movements when they chose what they did; while the more structured activities, where the adult needed to directly teach skills such as using a knife, provided a change of pace so that children focused carefully to master a task. The fact that sharp proper tools were used when the children learned to whittle wood or saw branches encouraged a serious approach to the tools' use. The squashed fingers that occurred in Chapter 2 from children becoming used to safety being managed for them were less likely to happen as they were involved in the assessment of risks and trusted to handle risky objects and their own boundaries relative to challenge and comfort. The pattern of periods of structure and freedom may also help children to learn to manage their behaviour and to concentrate for longer periods. We certainly noticed instances where concentration levels and engagement were such that deep learning appeared to be happening (Pascal and Bertram, 2001).

We also noticed many instances of language development during observations. Activities that particularly supported language were those where children were choosing their own activity. Low child–adult ratios also helped; staff often worked with two or three children and some provided a commentary on what the children were doing. However, on occasion this adult input suppressed the amount of child talk, and sustained talk was particularly noticeable when children were playing together without adult intervention or when the conversation was child-initiated. Teachers in our studies were impressed by the rich descriptive and speculative language in Forest School.

The amount of self-direction we observed perhaps increases the personal relevance of activities to the children's previous experience and enjoyment. It also means that children are able to work within their capabilities so that they tend to make positive associations with learning in this context. Skill development activities, for instance, were broken into small steps so that success was within each child's reach; this pedagogy may contribute to the child's sense of self-competence and self-confidence. Socio-cultural thinking might suggest that that success is situated and only associated with this context, making transfer of reified concepts such as self-esteem unlikely. However, from a psychological perspective, the simple and repeated experience of success may be helpful in building motivation for perseverance and a positive attitude to concentrated effort, especially for some children who may struggle to maintain this inside the classroom. The practice of creating small achievable learning steps may thus be a valuable pedagogical tool which practitioners can also apply back in their setting; breaking tasks into smaller sections can help a child's motivation as each step is successfully completed.

Sustained …

In the research from which our case study is drawn, Forest School programmes took place over six weeks with a morning or afternoon session each week regardless of snow, sun or rain. It was not a 'fair-weather only' activity. This consistency and repetition are important features in making the experience more durable and the learning more likely to be employed in other contexts. First, from a psychological perspective, repetition reinforces learning and, secondly, the changes that naturally occur in woodland provide many scenarios within which the pattern is repeated so the learning can be associated with more than a single context. In a socio-cultural sense, repetition also means that the children have an opportunity to become part of this new learning community with its particular norms for behaviour and learning. The difference between school and Forest School was something teachers and children commented on in our research so that Forest School was seen as providing a greater freedom for exploration and child-directed learning. Yet this perspective might also suggest that transfer of learning would be made more difficult by this contrast. A psychological explanation might be that transfer may occur through the intrapersonal effect of the different setting so that the child internalises the successes and positive attitudes experienced there and this changes their disposition towards learning.

Thoughts on theory

- What was your reaction to the story of Forest School?
- Forest School derives from Scandinavian *friluftsliv*, yet it is adapted in the UK to our cultural attitudes towards risk. See for example, Bentsen, Mygind and Randrup (2009) for a discussion of *udeskole* within Danish culture. The UK version emphasises small achievable steps to guarantee success. If you have some experience of Forest School, how would you describe its 'culture'? How does this compare to the 'culture' in your setting?
- What value might there be in introducing cultural expectations other than those that predominate within school into the children's experience through Forest School?
- Thinking of the theories of outdoor and adventurous education discussed in Chapters 1, 10 and 11, how important do you think the natural and wild is in the Forest School experience? Why might this be?

... and sustainable?

The question of whether Forest School can be imported back within mainstream settings is a contested one. Rea, in Chapter 11, suggests that evidence of improvement in social and emotional aspects of learning may be simply social constructions, specific to the group of people in that context. Furthermore, transport to remote sites has been shown to be a major barrier to continuation of Forest School experience (Waite et al., 2006). How might this and other potential barriers be overcome?

Forest School represented a rich alternative learning environment that pupils and staff both recognised in our studies but if it is only available as an occasional optional addition, it is unlikely to become embedded. Considering curricular opportunities in Forest School prior to the programmes, and planning suitable within-setting follow-up, enables closer integration with curriculum requirements or other intended learning in school or Foundation Stage setting. This addresses the concern in Chapters 1, 6 and 8 that there is a tension for teachers in meeting the curriculum requirements. Yet free play elements were the most valued by children, so balance between predetermination and freedom needs careful thought. Some theorists argue that it is the novelty from regular experiences that is part of the power of outdoor experiences (Broderick and Pearce, 2001). This returns us to the point in Chapter 1 that the *purpose* of the learning activity needs to be clear.

There are additional problems in transfer to those mentioned earlier and in Chapter 1. One class teacher identified many learning opportunities in the Forest School activities that she wanted to re-create back in school, but encountered difficulties in offering some activities with the lower adult–child ratios there. Some Forest School leaders are worried that untrained staff using the ideas might result in dilution of the principles of Forest School. However, these concerns must be set against practical obstacles for schools to afford the costs of Forest School conducted by external practitioners and the pressures of curricular demands on time and financial demands for transport to remote sites. Oxfordshire (Eastwood and Mitchell, 2003), for example, has created a programme of mainstream teachers being trained and seconded to Forest School, so that Forest School may gradually become integral rather than a bolt-on to mainstream school provision. Other sustainable models have been adopted in England, for example in Gloucestershire, Shropshire, Worcestershire and East Anglia (Knight, 2009) and many sustainable Forest Schools are well established in Wales and Scotland. Indeed these parts of the UK were amongst the pioneers of Forest School and education policies in these countries following devolution have tended to favour such learning outside the classroom.

 Points for practice

- Consider the key elements of the Forest School experience that would meet specific learning needs of your group of children.
- Create a balance of structure and small steps with more fluid child-initiated learning in your planning.
- Provide 'wilderness' and managed areas of garden in your school grounds for different learning purposes.
- In Forest School, boundaries are negotiated and flexible, dependent partly on the individual child's sense of adventure and risk. Early exposure to managing risk helps children to develop a capacity to set their own boundaries and challenges. Make sure that children have chances to take acceptable risk and develop their confidence and resilience.

Summary of similarities and differences

Our two case studies illustrate how forests and gardens have some things in common as spaces for learning, but also show how these commonalities are manifested in different ways in the two environments. Both encourage children to adapt to 'new' ways of learning that have their own practices and norms, for instance. Both, too, encourage children to learn new practical skills that foster confidence and a positive attitude to learning through success in employing these skills. In addition, children are experiencing learning in a 'real' (*life beyond the classroom*) context; wearing appropriate clothing, having a regard for safety and controlling body movement are all essential parts of making learning in forests and gardens a rewarding and enjoyable experience. In Table 12.1 we summarise some of the similarities and distinctions between Forest School and school gardens. Read down the table for commonalities and across the table's two right-hand columns for differences.

Table 12.1 Common and distinct features of Forest Schools and school gardens

Common features	School gardens	Forest Schools
	←————————————→	
Outdoors	Usually in school grounds	Usually woodland (at some distance)
Physical exercise	Man-made and tended	Wilder and more natural
Fresh air	Mainly adult-led	Choice and child-led learning
Repeated experiences	Minimised risk	Managed risk
Experiential learning	Accessible	Transport may be a problem
Small groups	Defined boundaries	Negotiated boundaries
Use of tools	Functional purpose (food)	Open-ended (skills)
Different relationship	Linked to school agenda	May be more dislocated from
between adults and children	and its community	school culture
Green spaces	Greater supervision	Greater freedom
Exposure to elements	Authentic jobs	Created activities
Social, personal and	Enthusiastic staff	Trained leaders
environmental awareness		
benefits intended		

Summary table devised by Waite, 2009

Some critical thoughts

There is evidence for the value of outdoor experiences as we have noted above, but research and practice in the field of outdoor learning tends to be conducted by enthusiasts and we need to acknowledge the subjectivity that this brings to our work. How differently might a member of staff who feared for her nail polish in the soil view the learning opportunities inherent in a garden! Yet it is partly through personal enthusiasm that outdoor contexts for learning are made effective and sustained. Indeed, the power of this enthusiasm applies to most areas of the curriculum. So, the support of head teachers in making time, money and energy available for these initiatives is critical to success for both Forest School and school gardens. Yet sustainability may be jeopardised by the programme being the 'baby' of one passionate member of staff; a team or whole-school approach is more likely to support continuation. How might others be convinced of the benefits? Keen staff often refer to their own positive memories of natural environments but continuing professional development, whether through the Forest School leadership training, RHS professional development or by visits to allotments, can have a significant impact on those who have not. Confidence and expertise is only built through active engagement with the outdoor contexts, another example of experiential learning through practice at an adult level. Others may question whether the curriculum can be adequately covered through these experiences. It is important to be clear about *what* you intend the experience to provide for the children. If it is mainly a social and intrapersonal benefit, that may still have important influence on the learning dispositions of the children for other desired outcomes. If it is to be a chance to learn about the environment, then first-hand experience may make class-based learning more memorable. If it is to develop language or inquiry skills, then a rich and changing environment offers many stimuli. If it is a particular element of the curriculum, then careful thought about what being outside will bring to that learning will increase its potential. You might also consider whether it may be that the time and space that these outdoor contexts provide is in itself an important antidote to the race to acquire facts and skills which sometimes characterises formal learning. As we have suggested in Chapter 1, it is for you to develop your personal theory to guide your uptake and use of the many different forms of outdoor experience for learning.

Summary

School gardens are accessible and productive but tend to be the province of one enthusiast while the Forest School movement is underpinned by specific training and pedagogical principles. Nevertheless, both may vary depending on the communities they serve. We hope that this chapter has helped you to consider how different additional resources and programmes might fit with your own view of learning and the advantages, disadvantages and differences that these two sorts of provision afford.

Further reading

Bentsen, P., Mygind, E. and Randrup, T. (2009) Towards an understanding of *udeskole*: education outside the classroom in a Danish context. Special edition *International Perspectives on Outdoor and Experiential Learning, Education 3–13*, 37 (1): 29–44.

Knight, S. (2009) *Forest Schools and Outdoor Learning in the Early Years*. London: Sage.

Useful websites

The Centre for Confidence and Wellbeing. A Scottish-based forum intended as a catalyst for change through research and support to develop confidence and well-being.
www.centreforconfidence.co.uk/index.php

Royal Horticultural Society Campaign for School Gardening. This nationwide education programme run by the UK's leading gardening charity teaches children the life skills of gardening, growing food, healthy eating and how to care for the environment.
www.rhs.org.uk/schoolgardening

13

Environmental education in the National Park: case studies on Exmoor

Dave Gurnett, Linda la Velle and Sue Waite

Chapter objectives

■ An awareness of possible curriculum enrichment through National Parks

■ An appreciation of what factors are memorable in experiences in National Parks

■ An appreciation of the ways in which theory can inform practice for use of National Park spaces

The designation of National Parks in the UK began during the 1950s. The National Parks are charged with maintaining a tripartite balance between conservation, recreation and enjoyment; at times, a challenging combination. Today, there are 14 National Parks in Britain, including Exmoor, an upland area of outstanding natural beauty in the south-west of England. Therefore most areas of the UK will have a National Park within reasonable distance. In this chapter, we use Exmoor National Park Authority (ENPA) as an exemplar of the way in which education and National Parks can work together. As the Education Manager for the ENPA, one author has 20 years experience of engagement with local and visiting schools and partnering the Field Studies Council, the Somerset

Wildlife Trust and the Somerset Rural Youth Project in inspiring projects. The involvement of children and community in Exmoor National Park (ENP) services has been an important priority since the park's inception. The 'lived in' landscape necessitates good communication with the community and ENPA has set an educational target of seeing every child during every year of his/her education on Exmoor, amounting to about 700 child visits annually, and an outreach target of a further 500 children from schools outside ENP. The Authority also owns a small residential centre, based on an old Exmoor hill farm, that is booked years in advance and sees an additional 1500 children a year.

Whilst clearly this contact alone may not change the children's lives, the activities undertaken may create a lasting memory that can foster a sense of belief in stewardship of Exmoor and can further prompt triggers to wanting to know more or take further action (see Waite, 2010 for an evaluation of the Exmoor Curriculum). Furthermore, this long-term perspective of regular engagement with the local young people in the Exmoor community helps to develop relationships and knowledge in the adult community that ultimately shapes the tripartite balance between conservation, recreation and enjoyment in future decision-making.

Pedagogical approach

The environmental education techniques described here are concerned with depicting the countryside *as it is*; as an immediate and real lived experience representing the relationship between animals, plants and people, both past and present. When sharing the countryside with children, a deliberate attempt is made to inspire them with its realities and intricacies, in the hope of creating some sort of lasting memory. This often includes direct sensual experiences, such as seeing, touching and feeling, where this is safe. By stirring the emotions through an environmental experience that involves either plants or creatures other than humankind and through accounts of past people's lives, the attempt is to turn a psychological key that creates memorable emotionally charged experiences (Gurnett, 2009). This approach is referred to as 'real experience environmental education' (see also Figure 13.1 below). It demonstrates and depicts the environment as it was and is, as opposed to a sanitised or anthropomorphised version. Real experience environmental education involves birth and death and the life process between the two; it does not make abstract the fundamentals of being but seeks to demonstrate these aspects through contextualised real encounters of cause and effect.

Thought on theory

- Consider this realist approach and the drama and story-mediated approach described in Chapter 8 and what these might mean for how learning in contexts beyond the classroom is conceived. It is worth reflecting how your own beliefs and values might shape the pedagogy you choose to employ and how the values of external partners, e.g. National Parks, might influence that.

As we saw in Chapters 7 and 8, in the approaches of Cornell (1989), Van Matre (1990) and Hodgson and Dyer (2003), the emphasis is on young adventurers entering an imaginary magical world and sampling the offerings through games and activities that generally position the child with an interface of 'something' physical (pen or pot) or intellectual (game rules or simulation) *between* him or her and the *real experience*, which could be seen as introducing an artificiality into authenticity. Selby, on the other hand, suggests that we bring birth and death into the curriculum, particularly when outside the classroom, firstly because examples are nearly always somewhere to be found and secondly because they help to explain the dynamic balance of life (2002: 88).

The use of environmental simulations and games proposed by Cornell (1989) can be a powerful introduction; however, if over-emphasised there may be a point when the game becomes the focal point and the message is lost. 'Unless information was directly embedded in the games, students found it difficult to recall any specific information four months after the field trip' (Knapp and Poff, 2001: 63). Yet stirring of the emotions through an environmental experience that involves creatures other than humankind creates lasting memories.

Sanitisation or anthropomorphism can have some simple instrumental usefulness as means to introduce a subject or to break down barriers when individuals feel uncomfortable with a natural or historic encounter. This might involve appealing to the children's greater familiarity with a plastic toy animal produced from a demonstrator's pocket and directly relating it to the 'real' encounter that we might see, or taking the whole group into a dark pine plantation where they are challenged by what they can't see and what it might have been like for people of bygone times or in different circumstances. The challenge is to relate children to the reality of the environment through its history and its flora and fauna and, if possible, humankind's impact on it through facilitating and guiding their first-hand experiences according to what 'crosses the path'. This serendipitous aspect of outdoor learning is discussed in Waite et al. (2006). The power of the tangible as opposed to a second-hand image is acknowledged:

> It is the rare exception that a vivid, provocative image can be found to explain a scientific concept that at the same time engages people emotionally. (Kollmuss and Agyeman, 2002: 12)

The Royal Society for the Prevention of Cruelty to Animals (RSPCA) suggests that cuddly toys, videos and computer simulations can be as effective as using real animals to teach respect and responsibility. Animals can be powerful communication tools, and are valued by children in learning how to care for things (Waite et al., 2006: 53). In many non-Western cultures people live close to nature, believing that respect should be accorded to nature, thus enabling their children from a young age to start piecing together the web of life, leading to an appreciation of ecological interdependency. When trying to inspire our children outside the classroom, the power of real experiences with positive or negative emotional connotations should not be underestimated. The case study of memorable experiences, discussed below, illustrates this point.

Case Study

Two thousand memorable experiences

A survey conducted in 2001 of memorable experiences of nearly 2000 9–12-year-olds receiving a broad range of environmental activities in eight different National Parks in the UK showed that animals featured prominently, with over 1000 reports of memories of wildlife, birds and dead animals (Gurnett, 2009). The question asked of the children was: what did you remember most? Other memories included natural views and the weather (about 400); there were about 300 reports of remembering facts, and smaller numbers (less than 100) mentioning food and being tired.

Further data were collected on memorable experiences from Exmoor National Park alone (samples totalling 946 children aged 7–11). These data were collected to qualify and extend the national data from 2001 surrounding children's memories after their visit to a National Park in England or Wales. Interestingly, wildlife/animal-life/bird-life in its many forms was again strongly featured as the most memorable experience (with nearly 300 mentions). Where the Exmoor data differed from the eight National Parks data was that there were almost equal numbers of reports of memories of their physical effort; through words such as being 'tired',

(Continued)

(Continued)

'exhausted', or 'it was hard work'. This emphasised not just the intellectual and emotional, but also the physical challenge of the learning experience for these children. (See Chapter 1, Figure 1.1 for the embodiment aspect of learning.)

Reliance on information that is largely second-hand about ecological and environmental issues removes a learner both physically and emotionally from the issue and is thus more likely to cause children conceptualisation problems when relating the simulation, or second-hand data to the real issue. Whilst using a prepared simulation activity is safe from an organisational, intellectual and fun point of view and often useful for a first foray into the countryside for teachers or leaders 'getting their bearings', it will never have the power of the lived experience, because of this visceral and emotional impact. Those activities most inspiring to the children always involve a sense of adventure, perceived risk and an experienced teacher who will go beyond the simulation game. (See Chapter 2 for a further discussion of risk.) For example, in the Autumn of 2007 more than 90 8–9-year-old children visited Exmoor, accompanied by teachers and other adults. At mid-morning snack on the edge of a thin pine wood about a kilometre from a small lane, the lead teacher thought it a good idea to let all the children go off and hide, count to one hundred, then all the adults would come looking for them. The event is still remembered by the children, as the whole wood was quiet and all the children had disappeared. The 'risk' that had been taken seemed to give the children a sense of adventure that tested their comfort zones and became a bonding, shared experience that the headteacher found amazing when the children relayed their stories back in school.

 Thoughts on theory

- Consider how this sort of 'freedom' and 'risk' might benefit children's learning. What do you think was the intention of this activity? How would you feel about doing a similar thing?

Historical aspects of places are important as discussed in Chapter 1 and 8 of this book. People have lived on Exmoor since before recorded history, and more recently, the area has provided a wealth of examples of the real-life balance between conservation, understanding, enjoyment and sustainable living. This resonates with the idea of 'emplacement' put forward by Howes (2005), whereby the social being engages with place. This sense of place can be used in various ways educationally (see also Chapters 1, 3 and 8, for example, and an embedded Exmoor community curriculum, Waite 2010). Another example of the way in which the cultural heritage of the area can enhance teaching and learning is seen in the West Somerset Mineral Railway Case Study, presented below.

Case Study

The West Somerset Mineral Railway, history and landscape

The West Somerset Mineral Railway (WSMR), a recently conserved 13-mile line, was constructed between 1857 and 1864 to transport iron ore from the Brendon Hills to the harbour town of Watchet on the Somerset coast, thence to be shipped to South Wales for smelting in the Ebbw Vale furnaces. At the peak of the WSMR's success more than 200 men from Somerset and Cornwall were employed in the mines and on the railway and new communities were formed along the line. Although built specifically to transport ore, the railway was opened to passengers in 1860. This bold industrial venture had a profound effect on what was essentially until that point a rural landscape and local economy. After 30 years the mines were closed due to the availability of cheap iron ore from overseas and the railway became economically unviable, eventually being dismantled and sold off in 1924 (Sellick, 1960). Since then the railway has remained a ruined reminder of Exmoor's industrial past.

In 2007 the West Somerset Mineral Railway Project was awarded a major grant from the Heritage Lottery Fund for conservation and interpretation of key sites and improvement of public access. This project included a significant amount of educational work in partnership with a variety of educational groups ranging from nurseries to college students to offer site visits and resources that linked to wider curriculum areas such as history, geography, environmental interpretation and media studies. Educational resources for the KS2 curriculum for 7–11-year-old school pupils[1] were trialled during field visits to the conserved sites. Their teacher commented, 'this exciting project has given the Year 5 (9–10-year-old) children an insight into West Somerset's industrial heritage'. The pupils enjoyed several site visits to the WSMR, including a trip to the recently conserved Langham Engine House, a 19th century building which originally housed an engine used to raise the iron ore to the surface and also to pump water out of the mines. As a culmination of the first term's work on the history of the railway and its workers the pupils wrote and performed a play, thus enacting their experiences and recreating the lives of local historic figures. (See also Chapter 8 for further

(Continues)

1 Pupils and their teacher, Sue Perkins, were from Danefield Middle School in Somerset

(Continued)

examples of how drama can be used to enhance outdoor learning in this area of the curriculum.)

Although no learning experience in environmental education can surpass the impact of a site visit, the WSMR Project can also provide teachers and learners across the country with very useful material to build a compelling narrative through virtual experiences through Web-based materials, including an innovative fly-over feature, which uses aerial imagery to transport the viewer the full length of the old railway, showing the extant sites and providing historical material. These are available at www.west-somersetmineralrailway.org.uk/ (accessed 30 November 2009).

 Thoughts on theory

- In the earlier case study and discussions in this chapter about the National Park's educational approach, direct experience was seen as fundamental to creating lasting memories. What role do you think *virtual* experience might have in children's learning? This question returns us to thoughts about what constitutes *authenticity* in Chapter 1.

The WSMR case study is an example of how a site of historical interest can provide a rich resource for a range of aspects of environmental education. Moreover, it demonstrates most graphically the crucial role that historic enquiry can play in environmental education. Skills of observation, recording, hypothesising, deducing and inferring are all exercised through the powerful narrative of a bygone local enterprise that flourished and faded, but has left behind its rich legacy of environmental, historical and cultural heritage. In planning for this themed topic, the teacher has enhanced and enriched the pupils' learning experience through practical field work, drama and role-play and through practising the traditional skills of the research historian.

 Points for practice

- Seek out local areas that have cultural and historical significance for children in your school as contexts for experiences that can address many different curriculum areas simultaneously. The more affective connections that are made to the children's existing knowledge and experience, the greater the likelihood that the learning points will be remembered.

(Continues)

(Continued)

- Experiment with recording using video and audio while learning outside the classroom; this can prove a valuable resource to develop a virtual outdoor experience to return to with the class or others in the school. Revisiting and working with memories will also help to make them durable.

- Develop strong sustained links with your local National Park and other outdoor organisations so that visits can productively combine expertise in the features of that place and your own expertise in knowing your children (see Chapter 14).

The Exmoor Model: real experience environmental education

To learn from real experiences, we need to understand ourselves as connected to places and people. This is discussed in Chapter 1 as a relational understanding of learning (see also Jarvis, 2009). For some, the 'connection' might have a spiritual connotation, such as a sense of awe and wonder. However, the nature of the connection is not necessarily for the teacher to define but for the individual to experience. Appreciation of a connection between human- and animal/vegetable/mineral-kind and the impact we humans can have on ecology are central in the Exmoor Model of real experience environmental education (Gurnett, 2009). Experience of the historical imprint left by people who have influenced the environment in times gone by adds weight and additional contextualisation to an appreciation of ecological interconnectivity.

Stories and mythologies certainly can have a role in creating an atmosphere, but we do not always need to invent circumstances to explain natural phenomena and we do ourselves no favours by dressing them up and either sanitising historical events or over-anthropomorphising nature. Perhaps the reason why the Western world has become so detached from its historic and natural environment is that it has hidden behind an artificial approach to environmental education that has failed to tell children about life, death, reproduction and consumption *as it is*: 'The roots of aesthetic sensitivity have existed long before the evolution of human culture' (Swonke, 2000: 260). (In Chapter 3, we also see that very young children seem to have aesthetic sense before it may have been socially constructed.) Emotional attachment, be it positive or negative, is used as an 'arousal increasing device' (Swonke, 2000: 262) to hold children's attention so that a message (or learning) can be conveyed. The message needs to relate to the experience and might be about the object of the experience; why it is where it is, how it relates to its habitat, or how it is looked after. What is important is that the learning content comes during or directly after the arousal, when interest is at its maximum and the children's focus is intense.

Accumulative psychological models, such as Kolb et al. (1981) relate well to the Exmoor Model (see Figure 13.1). This model only slightly differs in that it allows children to rejoin the learning situation at their own level after their many and varied day and residential experiences with ENPA education staff. A psychological perspective also underpins the role that memory plays in these experiences. Waite (2007) makes an interesting comparison between adult and children's memories of their outdoor experiences and learning. Children's recollection of residential experiences had a strong sense of challenge and achievement:

> This positive view [of the children] could be attributed to the experience being more recent, but this theory would not account for the strongly emotional content of the distant adult memories collected. Many of these shared positive emotional content with children's reports returning from their residential visit. (Waite, 2007: 343)

The Exmoor Model supports Waite's suggestion that memory for outdoor experiences does endure and often has an emotional component focused upon the first-hand authenticity of the learning. It can also be seen to invoke emotional attachments, as 'arousal increasing devices' (Swonke, 2000) to tune the children's senses – to hold attention – so that a message can be effectively conveyed. The Exmoor Model is the delivery framework that has evolved to tailor children's learning opportunities to the ENP's vision of communities with attitudes and behaviours that contribute towards sustaining Exmoor's special qualities.

In Figure 13.1 the solid arrows represent the dynamic cycle of the model; the broken arrows illustrate the fact that the process does not have to be completed and that different children can reach different points during the same activity. This model is cumulative and iterative and can be returned to at any stage of learning; each turn of the cycle brings the learner to a new, heightened level of potential emotional interaction. It represents the theoretical conception of how the learning of school communities on Exmoor can be influenced: as most children are seen many times during their schooling on Exmoor, their progression around the cycle can be repeatedly reinforced.

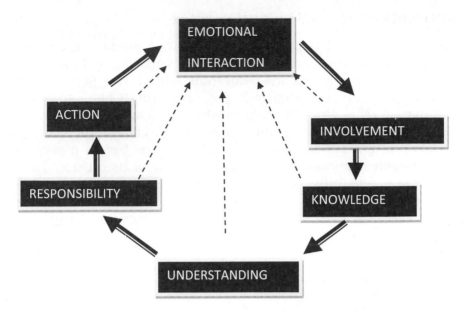

Figure 13.1 The Exmoor Model: real experience environmental education (Gurnett, 2009)

The fundamental issue is that behaviour needs consent and willingness to act and in environmental education, action is more likely after regular and coordinated visits than after single experiences (see also Chapter 14). The fact that ENPA has an educational target of seeing every child during every year of their education on Exmoor gives the children this chance of progressing with each turn of the cycle. The main lessons for facilitating children's experiences of environmental education in the field relate to the instrumental use of animals and historical evidence as communicating tools because of their immediate appeal to children and their relation not only to conservation issues, but also to the wider historical, geographical, and social curriculum (see Chapter 8). This appeal and desire to know more has the potential to act as a catalyst that might foster an interest or a practical interpretation.

The experiential component and a sense of ownership are considered very important in unlocking the imaginative and intellectual door for children (Davis et al., 2006; Waite, 2010). Wells and Lekics refer to 'participation with wild nature' (2006: 13) and Peacock to the importance of collaborative engagement (see Chapter 14.) This literature gives additional academic rigour to the 'Exmoor Model' and reinforces the necessity of real experiences that can be related to and accumulated, and that have a strong emotional and visual bias. The challenge is to make 'the experience' so memorable that 'future practice' might relate concretely or subliminally to the environment and thus re-engage the disassociation between 'belief' and 'practice'.

Implications for policy and practice

The Exmoor Model (Figure 13.1) represents a possible theoretical framework when working collaboratively with National Parks and schools. This model secures education within the heart of the process, but more importantly in the long term, it helps to ensure children develop into the adults who can have strong positive impacts within our communities and also affect how the National Park is run. Exmoor National Park Authority has been a pioneer in placing such importance on education as part of its mission. However, the determining factor of its influence is the willingness of enlightened teachers to keep prioritising real environmental educational experiences for their children. In the Learning Outside the Classroom manifesto, it is claimed:

> It is wrong to wrap children in cotton wool as they grow up. Trips and getting out of the classroom should be part and parcel of school life and always form people's most vivid childhood memories. (www.lotc.org.uk, accessed 30 November 2009)

But does the manifesto represent a massive step forward for education? Many teachers already share this passion and belief that it is important to engage children in learning outside the classroom regularly without the 'permission' that this manifesto represents. Nevertheless, given continuing pressure to comply with standards agendas (Waite, 2010), this official recognition may well help other teachers to take this step.

Our environment once offered all children the delights of the natural world; today it still can, but our lives have changed and become more structured, supervised and scheduled. If it were not for the commitment of teachers, such as those mentioned in this chapter and book, many children actually living *within* a National Park would probably not venture beyond the bus stop because the physical boundaries of their independent lives have shrunk. It is time this was changed. A substantial body of knowledge indicates that an empathy with the countryside, along with later positive environmental behaviours and attitudes, grow out of children's regular contact with the natural world. Thus stewardship in the form of accepted responsibility and subsequent action is engendered.

A lasting sense of care for the environment can be developed through the concept of biophilia, the association between historical memory and living organisms other than humankind. Many of the children observed during visits to Exmoor demonstrate this biophylic tendency to explore the natural and historic world; however, the key for its lasting effect is in promoting further opportunities for it to flourish. Imparting knowledge about responsibility for our natural and historic environment before a relationship with it exists is like building a boat before experiencing the sea.

Summary

In this chapter the development of National Parks as educational spaces within a historical and social perspective has been discussed, with specific reference to Exmoor National Park Authority (ENPA), its management and the role of education in its work. Two case studies illustrated an innovative model of 'real experience environmental education' based on school visits to Exmoor National Park; the first explored children's' memorable experiences of 'real experience' environmental education focusing on their response to living things; the second described the effect of pupils' and teachers' engagement with a historic industrial site, its story and multi-curricular learning opportunities. The model suggested involves engagement of learners' emotions and senses through a dynamic pedagogic cycle of increasing involvement, knowledge, understanding, responsibility and action.

Further reading

Cosmides, L. and Tooby, J. (1992) The psychological foundations of culture. In: J.H. Barkow (ed.), *The Adapted Mind*. New York: Oxford University Press.

Waite, S. (2010) *Contribution of the Exmoor Curriculum to Rural Young People's Educational Achievement and Environmental Awareness*. [Online] Available at: www.plymouth.ac.uk/researchcover/rcp.asp?pagetype=G&page=321. Accessed 1 June 2010.

White, R. and Stoeckin, V.L. (2008) *Nurturing Children's Biophilia: Developmentally Appropriate Environmental Education for Young Children*. [Online] Available at: www.whitehutchinson.com/children Accessed 28 December 2008.

14

Managed learning spaces and new forms of learning outside the classroom

Alan Peacock

Chapter objectives

- An awareness of macro- and micro-level influences in out of school learning contexts
- An understanding of what factors help to make out of school learning experiences successful

This chapter focuses on detailed evaluations of children learning in educational enterprises such as museums, botanical gardens, environmental centres and science centres, with a view to proposing what 'works best' in terms of promoting learning. A key theme will be the concept of macro- and micro-contexts, and the way these impact in many subtle ways on learning. Evaluations also indicate that successful learning outside the classroom depends on collaborative engagement, which implies ongoing cooperation between complementary professions with a focus on the development of effective planning and managing of experiential learning. International research will be referred to, indicating how a range of factors combines to affect the way young people respond to the experiences on offer, leading to analysis of how such settings can better promote learning, and the likely implications for teachers and host staff. Brief case studies will be included that show effective promotion of learning, drawn from programmes that involve partnership between teachers and other professionals.

Chapter 1 discussed the idea that communities, like teachers, botanists or museum curators, operate within a set of practices that have norms and goals that can be explicit or implicit. Participants identify with certain practices and as certain kinds of people. The idea of 'community' can therefore be a useful way to understand a particular situation, such as children and teachers working in a museum or botanical garden.

Learning spaces can then be seen as places in which different communities come into contact. Schools (teachers, children and parents) bring with them the practices, norms and goals of schooling with which they identify; host staff, referred to in this chapter as 'learning professionals', have their own disciplined knowledge and ways of working. There are generally accepted ideas that practical, 'hands-on', authentic experiences promote better understanding of concepts and skills. It is also accepted that the social dimension, where children and adults engage in enjoyable communication about the immediate experience, also contributes to the construction of knowledge. Chapter 1 has offered some theoretical explanations for these ideas. The challenge for effective learning away from the school classroom, then, is to manage the cooperation of different professionals in the managing of quality experiences for visiting learners. This chapter therefore reviews evaluation evidence which indicates what might be the 'best bets' in this respect.

 Thoughts on theory

Learning can depend a great deal on how the objectives are contextualised by those taking part. Imagine 16 10-year-old boys from a primary school on a rock-pooling expedition. It's a fine, sunny morning and they are all excited, since they have never been to this cove before. However, three boys (two of whom are known to have behavioural problems) have come without their Wellington boots. What happens? Much depends on who is hosting the visit. Their teacher, as well as wanting the children to carry out science observations, make drawings and ask questions, might also be conscious of health and safety issues, as well as maintaining behavioural standards; in effect, she is likely to be 'taking the classroom with her', so these three

(Continues)

(Continued)

might be asked to sit out the session on the rocks, to help them remember their footwear next time.

In this case, however, they are accompanied not by a teacher but by the National Trust warden (a parent and governor of the school) close to where the school was located. His perception is that they will come to no harm, and will be less trouble if fully engaged in the activity, so he lets them go into the water in their trainers. He is only able to take this line because of a long-standing tradition of collaboration between himself and the school staff. The boys produce wonderful colour drawings of shrimps they catch and observe; an example of learning being dependent on the specific context in which it takes place, or the *micro-context* of learning (see below).

- What kinds of arrangements between the two communities might work best to facilitate learning for children?
- What does this imply about the theories of learning that underpin the activity for the teacher or learning professional?

New forms of educational enterprise: learning spaces

In 1853, the Crystal Palace, originally built for London's Great Exhibition of 1851, was reconstructed in a park in Sydenham, South London, the centrepiece of which was a display of life-size concrete dinosaurs. Since then, other such museums, botanical gardens, zoological gardens, galleries, sculpture parks, national parks, nature reserves and theme parks have been established world-wide, unified by their aspiration to educate.

The educational function of such enterprises and sites has developed gradually over the years, and more rapidly in the past two decades. At the same time, a new generation of similar enterprises (interactive science centres, heritage sites, environmental/eco-centres, etc.) has developed. Examples of such educational establishments can be found world-wide; for a comprehensive list see www-2.cs.cmu.edu/~mwm/sci.html.

The explicitly educational function which such sites in the UK now share is apparent in their appointment of education managers, schools' liaison officers, communication assistants, explainers, guides, wardens, rangers etc. For simplicity, these will be referred to here as learning professionals (LPs). The facilities are mostly 'hands-on', in the sense that they encourage visitor interaction with artefacts and exhibits, and actively encourage visits by school parties as well as by individuals, families and the general public. They usually link their provision explicitly to the curricula of formal education, often through extensive websites with materials and activities to download, as well as through curriculum-linked guided (and virtual) tours and workshops.

In this chapter, all such forms of non-school settings for learning will be referred to as 'learning spaces'. The term 'space', rather than 'environment' is used in order to highlight the diverse nature of possible out of school settings. Learning spaces have been given a high profile in raising public awareness of environmental, scientific, social and cultural issues. Yet their effectiveness at communicating their messages to children has not been extensively studied. The physical layout – what will be called the *macro-context* – also varies enormously, in terms of size, location of buildings, plants, installations and other artefacts, and the ambience.

A range of studies does, however, suggest several possible reasons why it may be quite difficult for young people in particular to learn in the way the host organisation intends in such contexts. These reasons include:

- the structure and design of layouts and buildings which can often distract learners from focusing on explicit learning objectives;

- learners' preconceptions and the perceived significance of artefacts within these contexts (e.g. the idea that 'plants are boring');

- the affordances and constraints of specific physical arrangements, social groupings, artefacts, accessibility and localised distractions – what is referred to as *micro-contexts*;

- tensions between conflicting ideas of learning between LPs and school staff;

- the time available on each visit, and the potential for serial engagement.

In other words, within any given macro-context, there are many possible micro-contexts in which children and adults can attempt to engage in learning; and the specific nature of the micro-context can have a huge impact on what learning takes place. Some of the factors involved in this are discussed below.

The impact of micro-contexts

The following elements can all affect the micro-context in which learners operate:

- physical layout (pathways, spaces, artefacts, furniture)

- group size (from 1 to 30)

- space available (for discussion, writing, drawing)

- relevant objects (living things, rocks, machines, terminals)

- adult presence (teachers, parents, wardens)

- designated tasks (filling worksheets, listening, drawing, making, following trails)

- discourse (small group discussion, 1:1 questioning, teacher-initiated, child-initiated)

- signage (styles, size, location, cognitive demand)

- background distractions (noise, other groups, cafes, shops).

 Thoughts on theory

These aspects can be mapped onto Figure 1.2 in Chapter 1, according to *Place* – including physical layout; nature of space available, relevant objects and resources; signage and distractions – and *Others* – including group size; adult presence; and designated tasks. The discourse and nature of interchanges arise in interaction with the *Child*, co-constructing the possibility spaces for learning.

- Thinking of different micro-contexts, consider which elements can be changed and which are fixed. How might they be adjusted to lead to desired learning?

Roth et al. (1999), in a key article, show that group size, composition and location are strongly influenced by the layout and nature of the objects of interest (plants, installations, touch screens, sculptures etc.). In turn, group size and composition influence the nature of discourse, the roles individuals play and the extent to which individuals contribute. The presence or absence of LPs, teachers or experts in a group may also strongly influence the nature of children's dialogue. For example, it has been noticed that individuals interact differently with an installation depending on whether or not it is already being used. At unattended installations, visitors tend immediately to go 'hands on' without reading instructions; whilst if it is already in use, they pass the time reading instructions so that they are better informed when their turn comes (Hindmarsh et al., 2005).

Case Study

The Eden biomes

Wow! One half of Miss Grey's class enter the 'rainforest' biome under its huge dome, and start to strip off their coats, overwhelmed by the heat, humidity and sheer size. They struggle to hear what Miss Grey is saying – so much noise from the waterfall and the exclamations of older people all amazed at what they see – and are carried along the narrow path, unable to stop and talk to each other. Billy's glasses steam up. 'Can we breathe this?' he asks, watching the humidifier spray a fine mist of water close to his head. All this makes seeing and reading signs a real challenge. Meanwhile, in the Mediterranean biome with their teaching assistant, the other half of the class wander freely along the wider paths, asking the guides about the many kinds of citrus fruit trees, the seductive scents, and stopping to listen to the storyteller ...

Such observations in these different micro-contexts demonstrate that discourse is very different in the two adjacent settings. In small, widely dispersed groups, understanding can often be dependent on 'reading' some form of instruction in verbal, visual or symbolic form: and in the absence of a teacher or LP, our own observations indicate that children visiting as part of a school group rarely read the relevant information (perhaps since the 'classroom' norm is to read only when asked?). However, when visiting in family groups, younger children read signage aloud without prompting.

Points for practice

- You wish to focus on children learning about 'food plants' using both of these contexts, as well as the outdoor biome (called 'Wild Cornwall') which has such opportunities as a tea plantation and kitchen garden growing food for the restaurants. How might you go about planning a series of experiences for young learners, lasting for up to 90 minutes?

Designated tasks – i.e. the way LPs interpret their learning objectives – may be tightly or loosely structured, depending on the needs and preferences of visiting groups. But it is important to remember that the task structure can determine aspects like group size and where things take place. Schools may have a pre-set agenda and itinerary, often determined by teachers and reflecting the way in which the practices of school or classroom communities are organised; whilst parents with children typically do not follow structured learning pathways, but tend to respond to children's interests and explore serendipitously (Peacock, 2004). Thus the micro-context can have a major impact on how young people actually perceive the learning space, and therefore on what they can learn. This has to be taken account of in planning any programme for young people and crucially depends on effective partnership between LPs and school staff – what will be referred to below as 'collaborative engagement'.

New forms of learning

Many enterprises have already evolved a variety of ways in which they think their space can best be used by school groups. Most have produced materials, tasks, trails, workshops, websites and worksheets in one form or another, to be directed either by their own LPs, by teachers, by parents or by children themselves. Materials may be accessible through the Web in advance of visits. Such task structures will have implications for on-site artefacts to be used and may have significant impact on the nature of the discourse that ensues. Crucially, though, it is likely to be the way in which they alter the perspective of the group in any given micro-context that matters most.

Vare (2008) has noted that school groups tend to focus on strategies that rely heavily on delivery and dissemination of predetermined ideas, and that such approaches make children feel disempowered. In other words, they tend to 'take the school classroom with them' into the new learning space, and 'do school'. His research indicates, however, that in such settings most children actually perceive themselves to learn best through their own observations or through 1:1 learning. He therefore argues that effective learning happens in micro-contexts where a child is enabled to identify things that are both do-able and worth doing, and through making use of known and trusted people who have expertise, in this case, the LPs.

Our own interviews with children after their visits indicate that an important determinant of what they learn during engagement with artefacts is the way of knowing that they bring with them, often from their home rather than from previous experience in school (Peacock and Bowker, 2001). For example, children who were familiar with and had used maps with parents were able to orientate themselves to Mediterranean countries when shown a copy of the map of the different climatic zones at the Eden Project. Many pupils, however, had clearly no previous experience of using maps; hence most did not even notice or remember seeing them, despite their large size and key location.

The importance of collaborative engagement

The above demonstrates that learning spaces and their use by children can vary in many ways, as a consequence of the wide variation in potential micro-contexts. Some configurations, however, are more likely to lead to learning than others; and these may be particularly dependent on the way in which LPs, school staffs and other adults interact before, during and after visits to non-school learning spaces. What happens in any context can be closely linked to the perceived norms and expectations of these different groups of people; yet subtle tensions are not always apparent, and there are frequently attempts to impose the practices, norms goals and identities of the school setting on the learning space or *vice versa*.

There may be cogent reasons for this, to do with head teacher and parent expectations, notions of what constitutes school-work, curriculum pressures, concerns about effective management, health and safety issues, LP goals and control of children's time and behaviour. Learning professionals, often themselves ex-teachers, are very aware of these pressures and constraints. At the same time, they are aware that their objectives may be quite different, and that they are empowered to work in ways that teachers cannot. National Trust wardens and rangers, for example, are preferred by children when working outdoors as part of the NT Guardianship programme, because they 'know more than our teacher' and allow different ways of working; whilst these LPs themselves are aware that they can learn from teachers, for example about how to manage large groups or to communicate with a wide age range (Peacock, 2006).

What therefore becomes crucially important is the development over time of mutual understanding and collaboration between these different professionals – what we have called collaborative engagement. This involves:

■ modelling good practice in different contexts *(by LPs and teachers)*

■ facilitating collaborative needs analysis

■ collaborative planning between teachers and LPs

■ re-thinking of which particular learning spaces are most appropriate *(i.e. the micro-contexts)*

■ development of new, focused resources

■ team-teaching lessons, i.e. 'safe practice' for LPs and teachers

■ mediating critical reflection and problem-solving; safe feedback

■ promoting action research *(e.g. on resource management)*

■ subsequently revising school policies

■ on-going support; coaching for application.

Implications for LPs

The communities of practice in which teachers and LPs work are different in terms of their values, goals, language, personnel, resources encountered and location. LPs and teachers have therefore to help learners negotiate the transition from one community to the other, which many learners (and some teachers) find difficult because of the very different approaches to ways of knowing in each one.

Any structured learning space that is managed by LPs, be it a museum, an environmental centre or a stretch of coastline managed by the National Trust, incorporates an explicit 'curriculum' of ideas and objectives relevant to visitors in general, and school learners in particular. But this curriculum is not just a catalogue of key ideas; it is also an implicit set of practices, norms and goals – ways of being and knowing – which reflect the discipline(s) inherently at work in the space. To help learners make sense of a coastline, for example, a National Trust warden does not just need to know things; he or she also brings particular dispositions that have been learned through the experience of being a warden, and which allow him or her to know what is significant and what is not. Crucially, this way of knowing does not just affect what becomes known, it also affects the form of such knowledge. Put more simply, it means 'being a warden' rather than 'being a teacher' (see, for example, Chapter 13 on the Exmoor National Park).

Case Study

Collaborative engagement at Carymoor Environmental Centre

Mr Brown and his class have taken a 50-minute bus journey to visit Carymoor, a working landfill site in Somerset which also has 100 acres of capped landfill. The class see methane being extracted and burned to provide electricity for the national grid, toxic leachate being cleaned so that the water can go back into the river, recycling of glass, plastic and metal, and composting of green waste. The class know Sarah well; she belongs to the Somerset Waste Action Programme (SWAP) team based at Carymoor, one of six staff who have visited their class to do workshops on 'reduce, re-use, re-cycle'. They are excited about moving on to their silver award, after reaching the school's bronze award target for paper recycling; now they are targeting composting, so are particularly excited by how they do it at Carymoor. They even take a few bags of finished compost back to school for their garden. And these visits from their school have been going on now for several years, so a real partnership has developed between teachers, SWAP team and the 'Green Team' of Year 5 and Year 6 children who are the most vociferous in school about reducing waste.

Points for practice

- What aspects of a child's visit to such a site are likely to make the most lasting impact?
- How can a programme of learning about waste minimisation capitalise on this?
- How would you want to manage the various experiences (in school and at the centre) in order to optimise the curriculum impact?
- Present the children with a list of six things your council could do to reduce the amount of waste going to landfill, and give a rough costing for each. Ask the children to decide which should take place – but first, tell them that their budget is only half of the total needed to do all of the things. This generates debate and the important skill of agreeing on priorities, as real councils have to do.

Case Study

The Green family

'We've been here before, but think it's great for David and Laura, to see what really happens to all the rubbish we sadly throw away each week, especially all the packaging.' The Greens have their own objectives, born of previous visits, but also influenced to some extent by stewards, wardens or other staff, who may see it as their role to answer questions raised and thus fill gaps in their knowledge. However, they sometimes feel uneasy that at such venues there is currently little overlap between the goals of LPs and those of visiting families. Where there is overlap as part of an ongoing link between visitors and LPs, e.g. within the NT Guardianship scheme, the benefits of such partnerships are very clear. As Mr Green explained, 'We're amazed at how much of their school learning they bring with them when we go as a family, and how they want to demonstrate and reinforce this learning to us as parents.'

Thus the role of LPs crucially involves acting as a 'broker' between the hosts, visiting school groups and families, to model good practice as it relates to the learning space. At the same time, however, they must work with the aspirations of the school community in a careful balancing act – a highly demanding task in which the expectations of each community may well conflict at times. The benefit, where this succeeds, is the emergence of joint planning between school staff and LPs, and the re-working of programmes appropriate to both communities.

LPs are thus most effective when they actively assist learners to move back and forth as necessary between the communities of school culture, home culture and the sub-culture of the learning space itself. They will be able to help learners deal with the socio-cultural conflicts that might arise during their attempts at learning in the complex spaces and micro-contexts which they encounter. At the Eden Project, this involves focusing attention not simply on visible plants but on their uses as food, clothing, shelter, pharmaceuticals; the symbiotic relationship between plants and people; the importance of world trade in plants and its impact on development, and the 'can do' attitudes that develop 'action competence' in relation to big issues like sustainability. This necessitates carefully constructed tasks that require pupils to acquire the ways of working of a disciplined community, so that they not only identify with some of the key ideas but identify themselves as (young) botanists/ecologists etc.

Another good example of this is at 'Centre of the Cell' (www.centre-ofthecell.org), an innovative educational site located within the Institute of Cell and Molecular Science in Whitechapel, London, allowing children from schools to work alongside professional scientists addressing key medical and ethical concerns. Children are able to use professional microscopes, for example, to compare cells and tissues, to grow cells on a 'virtual lab bench' and discuss the ethics of stem cell research with professional scientists.

This approach has been summed up as follows:

> Rather than preparing students for life in a technological world, I work with teachers to create opportunities for participating in this world and for learning science in the process of contributing to the everyday life of the community. ... Early participation in community-relevant practices provides for continuous participation and a greater relevance of schooling to the everyday life of its main constituents. (Roth, 1996)

More and more young people are having the opportunity to learn in new contexts outside school, yet there is a wide variation in the extent to which their experiences result in the kinds of learning that professionals hope for. Collaborative engagement – the working together of professionals from school and host organisation over an extended period of time – holds out the best chance of guaranteeing such learning. Yet the context, and especially the specific micro-context in which these professionals work with children, is crucial, and the parameters have to be understood by all involved. Small variations, for example, of personnel, group size, timing, signage or artefacts – can make all the difference. This chapter has tried to point up the impact of this, in order to help teachers anticipate different outcomes. It has also illustrated the crucial role of joint planning and team teaching between professionals from both school and host enterprise. The hope is that better understanding will help to overcome any anxieties about taking learners out into more exciting and challenging learning spaces.

 Summary

This chapter touches on several important and successful examples of how school learning can mesh with the opportunities and objectives of other managed learning spaces. The opportunities exist in all areas, and are not as difficult to access as many (especially, at times, the media) have suggested. Few involve large amounts of funding; some, including most of these mentioned above, in fact support school visits in a number of ways. The key is to have committed staff, both in school and at the host venue, who understand the value of on-going collaboration in planning, preparation and organisation of visits, not only by children out of school but by host staff to the school. This symbiosis is what distinguishes progression in the use of learning spaces from the mere experience of 'school trips'.

Further reading

Alexander, R. (2001) *Culture and Pedagogy*. London: Wiley-Blackwell.
Capra, F. (2002) *The Hidden Connections: A Science for Sustainable Living*. London: HarperCollins.
Peat, F.D. (1995) *Blackfoot Physics*. London: Fourth Estate.

15

Making a difference: learning on a grand scale

Sue Waite

Chapter objectives

- An appreciation that learning outside the classroom contributes to curricular objectives both directly and indirectly

- An understanding that psychological and socio-cultural perspectives provide theoretical underpinning for learning outside the classroom

- An appreciation that learning outside the classroom may provide a strong foundation for lifelong attitudes to learning, community and nature

- An understanding of steps to support the development of whole school policy and practice in learning outside the classroom

A few years ago I was organising a conference with colleagues for a local authority with the title 'The Great Outdoors: Exploring Outdoor Spaces for Children Aged 0–14'. On one level this was a catchy cliché but it also neatly summarised our beliefs about what learning in outdoor contexts might offer, arising from our own practical experience and research we had conducted. The outdoors was 'great' in terms of being 'a really good thing' for children; 'great' expressed the wider world, which seemed a key element of its power to engage children's enthusiasm; 'great' also summed up for us the

201

conceptual breadth of 'outdoors' and encompassed the diversity of place. 'Exploring' encapsulated our ideas about the sorts of open-ended discovery learning that tended to happen in outdoor spaces. 'Spaces' suggested that these were places that were more open to different practices with less defined boundaries than schoolrooms. So our personal theories of outdoor learning included belief in psychological benefits for participants, socio-cultural understandings about the importance of engagement with life beyond the formal educational setting and an awareness of the complex role of place in relation to learning.

 Thoughts on theory

- What views of learning outdoors or in contexts beyond the classroom do you hold?
- How have the examples of learning outside the classroom, thoughts on theory and points for practice in this book informed your own thinking?
- What aspects would you regard as key to planning learning in different spaces?

In this final chapter I would like to return to the beliefs with which I ended the introduction of this book and which have been variously demonstrated through the practice and theory in its chapters:

- that learning outside the classroom is a 'good thing';

- that nature and community can contribute to children's education and lives now and in the future;

- that the politically shaped educational landscape may be beginning to acknowledge that schooling alone cannot *educate* a child.

I will suggest some of the ways in which learning outside the classroom throughout these fundamental years of learning from birth to 11 might make a difference to learning on a grander scale than narrow and short-term cognitive outcomes. Children's learning, physical experience, social interactions, emotional response and their well-being all contribute to the education of the whole child (Malone, 2008). I will draw together some ideas that run explicitly and implicitly through the pages of this book about *how* and *why* learning outside the classroom might be worthwhile and for *what*.

How does learning (outside the classroom) happen?

Models of learning

In this book, a number of models for learning have been put forward. This is because learning is a complex social construction and can be best understood by viewing it from a number of vantage points. In Chapter 1, Figure 1.1, the relationship between place and body is theorised as mediated by the mind through the social and cultural positions that shape the ways in which we perceive and behave. It makes the point that experience happens to particular bodies in particular places, so that we need to be cautious about how we generalise from the specific, but it also makes it clear that experiences are felt, known and embodied in relationship with others and both contribute to and are shaped by culture. It also implies the significant impact that the multi-sensory richness of many outdoor contexts has on the whole person.

In Figure 1.2 this relationship is focused on the role of the practitioner and others in teaching and learning by illustrating how pedagogies are created in the interaction between place, others and the learner. Without paying close attention to these contributory factors, the tacit nature of much pedagogical practice may encourage the reproduction of traditional roles and ways of interacting, thereby missing out on the chance for innovative practices. This understanding of the construction of pedagogy is then further elaborated for group learning contexts in Chapter 2, Figure 2.1. This model represents how skilful practitioners are sensitive to the individual temporal and situational learning needs of children and adjust their facilitation to maximise the development of independent learning that is self-regulated, personally meaningful and motivated. In Chapter 3, Figure 3.1, the concept of personal meaning is further illustrated through possible lines of direction (PLODs) linked to a child's schema. Although this practice is situated within early years education, finding personal 'hooks' for learning is also motivating for older pupils and valuable when planning learning outside the classroom for any age.

Then, in Chapter 6, we see how the different elements of understanding mathematics might be addressed by doing, using and knowing in a mutually supportive way (Figure 6.1), introducing the idea of different possibilities inherent in activities. This model highlights how learning outside the classroom that is not related to concepts in schooling (and vice versa) may be difficult to transfer between those contexts. Figure 6.2, on the other hand, shows how

exploration and 'real life' application might be supported by inter-
polated taught conceptualisation. Finding the right balance between
the abstract and the experience is a key factor in successful planning
of learning outside the classroom.

The abstraction of principles from experience is intrinsic to all learning, although this does not necessarily imply a cool conscious
rationality in the process. An equally valuable abstraction might be
through emotional involvement and the development of a caring
attitude to nature, as in Chapter 13, Figure 13.1, we see a proposed
relationship between knowing, applying knowledge and taking
action in environmental education being mediated and strength-
ened by emotional engagement. Indeed, this affective psychological
component of learning is a theme that has run throughout the book
alongside socio-cultural understandings of the way we learn. The
interaction of the personal, social and situational in learning has
been theorised by Peter Jarvis (2009); if you would like to delve
deeper into learning theory, I would highly recommend his book.

Place-based learning

Viewed from one position, ideas about learning can apply in any
place (learning as the abstraction of principles from and internalisa-
tion of experience) but from another perspective, temporal and
geographical positioning make each learning experience unique (this
learning can only be understood in relation to this place, this time
and these people). As Nick Pratt and I suggest in Chapter 1, it may
therefore be useful to consider learning using different planes of
focus; broadly psychological (principally at an individual and group
level) and socio-cultural (at a group, societal and political level). I
think both are important to develop a good evidential basis for the
widespread belief that learning outside the classroom is a 'good
thing'. We have considered, for example, how advantages of novelty
and different pedagogical approaches can be lost if classroom norms
and practices are simply taken outside with the class. Innovative
places and ways of relating can be seen as offering different communities of practice but they might also be viewed as appealing to
different individual learning styles.

The rich multi-sensory nature of outdoor experiential learning
opportunities can make them especially valuable and inclusive for
children with special educational needs such as visual impairment or
profound and multiple learning difficulties, as they incorporate a
range of sensory inputs. We have also commented how some Forest

School programmes have been found effective in working with children and young people who have social, emotional and behavioural difficulties. Another likely contribution to inclusive practice is the troubling of established classroom norms by moving learning outside. In secondary and further education, work-related learning capitalises on many aspects of learning outside the classroom discussed here. (See, for example, how the concept of vocational education applies also to young people with severe learning difficulties through opportunities to realise aspirations outside the classroom in Waite, Lawson and Robertson, 2006.)

Places are not empty spaces and will be imbued with cultural expectations. Good place-based education should include 'the history, folk culture, social problems and the aesthetics of the community' (Sobel, 2004: 9) and work to develop respectful and ongoing relationships with others and alternative learning spaces. Thus it embeds education deeply within its community, bringing exciting opportunities for building bridges between the school culture and that of homes, families, work and environment. Access to other cultures is one of the most exciting and potentially transformative aspects of learning outside the classroom.

We have also seen in the chapters of the book how extended learning can be developed progressively, starting with blurred boundaries between pedagogy inside and outside the classroom in the Foundation Stage, the gradual support for moving beyond comfort zones in subjects like physical education where the playground is just another classroom, through projects that combine key skills across subject disciplines, to highly charged rites of passage in residential experiences. Enabling this progression requires practitioners to be ready to embrace different sorts of teaching and learning approaches, such as exploratory, inquiry-based and self-regulated learning that are encouraged by less teacher-directed spaces beyond the classroom. Progression, however, does not mean that children no longer need engagement with the local and small scale after their early years but rather that attitudes gained in familiar contexts will prepare them well for an expanding range of different places and the learning experiences that they offer. So, there is a broadening too in the spaces used from internally run school grounds activities to activities that interact with community local projects and so on to more remote areas that unsettle established expectations, offering a myriad of learning opportunities in the wider world. This breadth of opportunity is supported by a growing cadre of external providers and schemes including Learning through Landscapes, Eco Schools, Growing Schools, the Field Studies Council, residential centres and numerous other third sector and private organisations, who are increasingly likely to be registered with and accredited by the Learning Outside the Classroom Council in England and Wales.

Why learn outside the classroom?

The 'real world' is frequently cited as a reason to take learning outside the classroom, but this concept is problematic, as we have commented earlier in Chapter 1. First, a child's world is bound up in schooling; much of their time is spent in school learning to become 'good pupils' (or not) in socio-cultural terms (Illeris, 2007: 220). However school culture may not resonate with children's experience at home and in the community and this may have consequences for how successfully the child can relate to it. In a recent study reflecting on differences experienced in school, one young woman suggested that 'In primary school they keep you repressed, they don't tell you about the world'. As she saw it, protection from 'reality' prevented responsibility until secondary school when real-life challenges such as taking GCSEs are faced (Boyask et al., 2010: 4). Her comment encapsulates the sense that real life is experienced by children both within and beyond the classroom. Her real life challenge is after all a school examination, but it also suggests that the wider world may be seen as separate from primary schooling. It also hints that challenge perhaps helps make something **real** for a person. Indeed, many outdoor learning experiences seem to include an element of difficulty, physical or emotional challenge (Beard and Wilson, 2007) or intellectual stretching through exploration and inquiry (Waite, 2007).

Yet, clearly difficulty alone may not be motivating, but rather de-motivating. Another frequently cited feature of outdoor experiences is enjoyment (Waite, 2007). In a recent survey of children for the DCSF (Tellus4), a quarter of children and young people did not think lessons were made fun and interesting. The researchers suggested that learning outside the classroom could provide further opportunities to make lessons varied and interesting for children and young people (Chamberlain et al., 2010). Variety is another important feature commonly associated with learning contexts beyond the classroom (Brierley, 1994). Varying the circumstances of learning might contribute to more flexible application of its principles. So that the socio-cultural idea of 'we do things like this here' is extended to 'things can be done like this in these situations'. Although almost half the respondents to Tellus4 (46 per cent) said they had enough chances to learn somewhere that was not in a classroom, a quarter (25 per cent) said they did not have enough opportunities to do so (Chamberlain et al., 2010). Clearly, as the all-party Children, Schools and Families Select Committee sixth report on Learning Outside the Classroom published on 1 April 2010 concluded, further structural support is required if provision for Learning Outside the Classroom is to increase. They call for more funding for it to schools, improved training through Initial Teacher Education and Continuing Professional Development and official inspection of provision by Ofsted to address the commonly identified barriers of finance, attitudes and performativity (Waite, 2009).

Table 15.1: Theoretical perspectives and contributions of learning outside the classroom

Psychological plane of focus	Socio-cultural plane of focus
Personal, intrapersonal and psychosocial contributions	*Interpersonal societal contributions*
Enjoyment/ motivation	Authentic applications
Engagement	Awareness of other cultural contexts
Memory	Criticality applied within and outside the school context
Personal relevance	Relevance to other aspects of child's life
Social and emotional aspects of learning	Social interaction/learning for whole life
Learning about oneself and others	Learning to become/learning to be
Self-regulated learning	Congruence between home and school
Collaborative learning	Becoming part of community of practice
Attachment to place and nature	Understanding of situated norms
Embodiment	Doing/active participation

These second two barriers are also pertinent to whether children perceive such experiences as meaningful. Adult attitudes that place emphasis on the attainment of nationally dictated standards create norms and practices that are focused on schooling rather than education in a broader sense and may thus be very different from learning experiences at home and in the community. How far does life experienced in classrooms reflect the life lived in all the other spaces and times occupied before, during and after the school years; *life beyond the classroom*? Relationship between what we know and what we experience is how we learn, so when congruency is disjointed and incompatible, the reality seen in the classroom may be seen as meaningless or irrelevant for other contexts (and vice versa) and thus impair the capacity to use knowledge generated in one context in another. How then can congruency between the classroom and the world beyond be managed? These concerns offer compelling reasons for the arrangement of opportunities to learn outside the classroom. Furthermore, they suggest that reassessment of teaching practices within and out of school contexts may help to mediate discontinuities by including sensitively attuned child-centred, place-based, exploratory and narrative pedagogies. The table on page 207 summarises some of the ways in which being outside the classroom supports learning seen through psychological and socio-cultural lenses.

What might be learned outside the classroom?

Purposes

In this book, we have given many examples of the sorts of learning that can happen in contexts beyond the classroom. Our focus has been largely in terms of the effects on children as they learn between birth and eleven years of age. We have emphasised the importance of clarity about what these purposes might be and aligning place and pedagogy to support those ends, and noted how this can present apparent conflicts if agenda are dictated rather than negotiated. However, the centrality of the child, which is endorsed by policies such as Every Child Matters, encourages broader and joined-up approaches to ensuring children's well being. It aspires:

> to make this the best place in the world for children and young people to grow up. We want to:
>
> • make children and young people happy and healthy
>
> • keep them safe and sound
>
> • give them a top class education
>
> • help them stay on track.
> (DCSF, 2008b)

The recent UK coalition government's initiative of academies in the primary phase is purported to increase schools' self-determination of curriculum and pedagogy. Yet schools will still ultimately be driven by the imperative to perform through the continuation of testing and without the support of local authorities and bodies such as the Qualifications and Curriculum Development Agency to disseminate best practice, they may even find breaking new ground more rather than less challenging (Passy and Waite, 2008).

We have shown evidence in the chapters that learning outside the classroom can keep children active and contribute to their health and well-being, that they enjoy outdoor experiences and visits to other learning contexts and that feeling positive about learning, especially learning that connects with other aspects of their lives, can help them stay motivated and engaged. There is also considerable evidence that risk and challenge, which are sought out and valued by children and are important parts of learning, are nevertheless being squeezed out of their experience by fear of injury and litigation. Learning outside the classroom, however, can offer opportunities for children to practise managing risk within agreed parameters and so to develop courage and perseverance. However, if a top class education is interpreted narrowly as being about acquiring certain parcels of knowledge, then learning outside the classroom's offer may be diminished and the apparent freedom for schools to decide may be restricted. The strength of learning outside the classroom lies particularly in the development of skills for learning and of knowing in a different way to learning as acquisition. For this reason, the main chapters address learning in broader terms than individual subject disciplines and also provide evidence of other effects that learning outside the classroom might have for children, schools and families as summarised in Table 15.2.

Table 15.2 Summary of possible effects of learning outside the classroom

Children	Schools	Families
Positive dispositions to learning	Creative pedagogies and cross-curricular study	Extended schools
Social and emotional aspects of learning	Improved behaviour through engagement	Parental support
Health and well-being	Better attendance	Every Child Matters – wraparound care
Authentic practical skills	Application of knowledge through using and doing	Community cohesion
Relevant to interests	Enrichment and extension of curriculum	Strengthened partnership with families and community
Attachment to place	Citizenship qualities	Care for community
Wider environmental awareness	Sustainability and positive environmental attitudes	Environmental awareness and action

Yet more important, however, is the foundation that learning outside the classroom in these critical years will provide for children's future lives. This foundation has the potential to 'improve the skills of the population ... to build a more economically competitive, socially mobile and cohesive society' (DBSI, 2010: DSO 5). By introducing children to learning in contexts other than schools, they gain a clearer understanding that the purpose of education is not simply bounded by the school and the goals assessed and measured within that, which tends to lead to an instrumental approach to learning. They also appreciate that learning happens and can be applied in many other contexts and is an opportunity to extend and develop interests, knowledge and skills. This disposition is key to becoming a lifelong learner ready to adapt to changes in working practices and social opportunities. Learning to be a pupil is what children learn best in school, but learning to be an inquirer, a scientist, an artist or a writer with a purpose is better supported by authentic activities and places.

Practical skills in applying and constructing knowledge are supported by working outside the classroom in naturally occurring though, crucially, well-planned ways. Key skills in communicating, being motivated and applying learning, working with others and problem-solving are developed within outdoor contexts, alongside personal development and interpersonal skills. Variety in contexts and inquiry-based learning will tend to support critical thinking capacity as different circumstances have to be accommodated, modifying knowledge and skills. They are also likely to encourage creative approaches and innovative thinking, as children begin to appreciate that 'answers' in learning outside the classroom are not 'right' or 'wrong' but complex and situated. By exploring this complexity, children's curiosity is piqued and this helps to develop lifelong learning dispositions.

Respecting and involving community and families in learning outside the classroom also opens the way for children and families to be more engaged with education and for formal education to take account of the whole child. It takes account of the fact that parents may not have positive attitudes to learning in schools and could offer a genuine attempt to redress the dominance of middle-class families in home–school partnerships (Reay, 2009: 59). This might then lead to improved participation and better educational outcomes for disadvantaged social groups (Warren and Hong, 2009). Reaching out into the community can also contribute to positive social behaviours for citizenship, such as schoolchildren gardeners helping the elderly in their community to maintain their gardens. Growing food in school teaches children about healthy living and, of course, these are skills that will become increasingly important in the future with the increased prominence and prioritisation of environmental issues. Environmental education that is embedded in practice in the local community has been shown to have lasting effects on environmental awareness and positive actions (SEER, 2000). Sustainability in education is necessary to securing our future.

With such grand prospects for learning outside the classroom affecting not only children's current schooling but also their future lives, it is perhaps rather daunting to know where to begin. Finding out where you are now as a school or early years setting is a good starting point. Readers may find it helpful to do an audit of their current provision using research reports of surveys of schools and early years providers with benchmarks against which they can compare their practice. This is available on the outdoor and experiential learning research network website at the University of Plymouth (www.plymouth.ac.uk/research cover/rcp.asp?pagetype=G&page=321 in the report *Current Practice and Aspirations for Outdoor Learning for 2–11-year-olds in Devon*).

Finally, involving children in planning outdoor spaces is another very important step in creating ownership and engagement with spaces (Clark, 2010) and in making sure they are fit for purpose. Adult and child perspectives on what constitutes a rich learning environment do not necessarily correspond. Some adults may focus more on appearance rather than function. The process of discussion can also be tremendously revealing about how children view learning (Waite et al., 2006).

The following points for practice are designed to support you in constructing your own plan for development.

 Points for practice

- Consult with children throughout the school (for example, through focused circle times, cross-age phase family groups, surveys) about what they value in learning outside the classroom.

- Consult with parents and the community about what help and ideas they would be able to offer and what they would like their children to have the opportunity to engage in.

- Consider as a staff what other aims you have for the children's education beyond the prescribed curriculum.

- As a whole school team, share this information and have an inset session to map out all the ways in which learning outside the classroom could bring motivation, enjoyment and learning to the curriculum and for the identified other purposes.

- Convene a learning outside the classroom (LOtC) group (including children and parents) to develop some of the ideas, provide support for the development and maintenance of resources and to create a shared understanding of approaches to risk.

- Consider the balance between small-scale local home-grown and external expert provision. Develop collaborative relationships with external providers to maximise a shared understanding of aims.

(Continues)

(Continued)

- Plan for learning outside the classroom opportunities several times a week throughout the school. Remember to include preparatory and follow-up work to encourage transfer of learning between contexts.
- Remember the mantra for clarity when planning learning outside the classroom:
  - *What* are we trying to teach/learn?
  - *How* will this best be supported?
  - *Where* is most likely to provide those conditions?
  - *Why* is this so?
- Create longer-term plans for progression across the curriculum and addressing the other identified purposes.
- Evaluate successes and challenges and feedback to group for further development.
- Celebrate successes with the community and draw in further expertise through volunteers.
- Include the community as much as possible as a bridge in developing community cohesion and partnership between home, community and school.

To conclude, in a recent study of an outdoor curriculum (Waite, 2010), two quotations about what experiential learning outside the classroom could achieve were juxtaposed:

> Tell me and I will forget, show me and I may remember, involve me and I will understand. (Confucius, c.500 BC)

And about 2,500 years later ...

> If we read a book in a lesson, we forget it; if we're out on a walk, we'll remember the walk and remember what we did. (Year 7 student, AD 2009)

I hope that this powerful and enduring message and the contents of this book will inspire you to employ new contexts and pedagogies to support children learning outside the classroom from birth to 11 and beyond.

Further reading

Jarvis, P. (2009) *Learning to be a Person in Society*. Abingdon: Routledge.
Reports on University of Plymouth outdoor and experiential learning research network. Available at: www.plymouth.ac.uk/researchcover/rcp.asp?pagetype= G&page=321

Useful websites

www.eco-schools.org.uk/about/   Eco-schools initiative

www.english-heritage.org.uk/education   English Heritage

www.everychildmatters.gov.uk   Every Child Matters

www.field-studies-council.org/index.aspx   Field Studies Council

www.field-studies-council.org/publications/index.aspx   FSC resources

www.gflscotland.org.uk/client_files/File/Curriculum%20Support/ACE%20
Primary%20Science.pdf   Scottish Curriculum for Excellence resource for
doing Science outside

www.growingschools.org.uk/   Growing Schools

www.lotc.org.uk/   Council for Learning Outside the Classroom

www.ltl.org.uk/   Learning through Landscapes

http//oeap.info/   Outdoor Education Advisors Panel (for latest guidance, especially on Health and Safety issues)

http://oeap.info/what-we-do/oeap-training   For training and access to outdoor
learning cards

www.OPALExploreNature.org   The Open Air Laboratories (OPAL) network aims
to create a new generation of nature-lovers by getting people to engage with
the natural world around them

www.teachernet.gov.uk/sustainableschools   Sustainable Schools

www.teachers.tv/series/getting-out-of-the-classroom   and   www.teachers.tv/
series/worth-the-trip   Educational trip planning

www.teachers.tv/series/learning-through-play   Welsh primary schools play-
based learning through outside environment and non-traditional methods

www.teachers.tv/series/using-the-environment   Ways to use the environment
(see also for libraries and museums)

www.teachers.tv/series/watch-us-grow   Examples of school gardens

References

Adams, E. (2008) Art and design education and the built environment. In: G. Coutts and T. Jokela (eds.), *Art, Community and Environment: Educational Perspectives*. Bristol: Intellect, pp. 125–144.

Adams, J., Worwood, K., Atkinson, D., Dash, P., Herne, S. and Page, T. (2008) *Teaching through Contemporary Art: A Report on Innovative Practices in the Classroom*. London: Tate Publishing.

afPE (Association for Physical Education) (2008) Manifesto for a world class system of physical education. *Physical Education Matters*, 3 (4).

Alexander, R.J. (2009) *Towards a New Primary Curriculum: A Report from the Cambridge Primary Review. Part 2: The Future*. Cambridge: University of Cambridge.

Armitage, M. (1999) What do you mean you don't like it? Interpreting children's perceptions of the playground as an aid to designing effective play space. 2nd International Toy Research Conference, Hamstad, Sweden. Unpublished conference paper.

Athey, C. (1990) *Extending Thought in Young Children: A Parent–Teacher Partnership* (2nd edn, 2001). London: Paul Chapman Publishing.

Atkinson, D. (2002) *Art in Education: Identity and Practice*. Dordrecht: Kluwer Academic Publications.

Baden-Powell, R.S.S. (1930) *Rovering to Success*. London, Herbert Jenkins Ltd.

Ball, S. (2003) The teacher's soul and the terrors of performativity. *Journal of Educational Policy*, 18: 215–228.

Beard, C. and Wilson, J.P. (2007) *Experiential Learning: A Best Practice Handbook for Educators and Trainers*, 2nd edn. London: Kogan Page.

Bentsen, P., Mygind, E. and Randrup, T. (2009) Towards an understanding of *udeskole*: education outside the classroom in a Danish context. Special edition *International Perspectives on Outdoor and Experiential Learning, Education 3–13*, 37 (1): 29–44.

Berryman, T. (2000) Looking at children's relationships with nature from a developmental perspective: towards an appropriate curriculum. In: P.J. Fontes and M. Gomes (eds), *Environmental Education and the Contemporary World*, Proceedings of the International Congress on Environmental Education and the Contemporary World, 19–20 October 2000. Lisbon, Instituto do Inovaçao Educacional.

Bertram, T. and Pascal, C. (2004) *A Handbook for Evaluating Assuring and Improving Quality in Early Childhood Settings*. Birmingham: Amber Publishing.

Bilton, H. (2010) *Outdoor Play in the Early Years: Management and Innovation* (3rd edn). London: David Fulton Publishers.

Bixler, R.D., Floyd, M.F. and Hammitt, W.E. (2002) Environmental socialization: Quantitative tests of the children play hypothesis. *Environment and Behaviour*, 34 (6): 795–818.

Bloom, J.W. (2006) *Creating a Classroom Community of Young Scientists* (2nd edn). London: Routledge.

Boaler, J. (2002a) The development of disciplinary relationships: knowledge, practice and identity in mathematics classrooms. *For the Learning of Mathematics*, 22: 42–47.

Boaler, J. (2002b) *Experiencing School Mathematics: Traditional and Reform Approaches to Teaching and Their Impact on Student Learning*. London: Erlbaum.

Boniface, M. (2006) The meaning of adventurous activities for 'women in the outdoors'. *Journal of Adventure Education and Outdoor Learning*, 6 (1): 9–24.

Bourdieu, P. (1991) *Language and Symbolic Power*. Cambridge: Polity Press.

Boyask, R. and Donkin, A. (with Lawson, H. and Waite, S.) (2010) Researching diversity for policy: Outcomes from a partnership project. Unpublished paper.

Boyes, M.A. and O'Hare, D. (2003) Between safety and risk: a model for outdoor adventure decision making. *Journal of Adventure Education and Outdoor Learning*, 3 (1): 63–76.

Braund, M. and Reiss, M. (2004) *Learning Science Outside the Classroom*. London: RoutledgeFalmer.

Brierley, J. (1994) *Give Me a Child Until He Is Seven: Brain Studies and Early Education*, 2nd edn. London: Falmer Press.

Broderick, A. and Pearce, G. (2001) Indoor adventure training: a dramaturgical approach to management development. *Journal of Organisational Change Management*, 14 (3): 239–252.

Brooker, L. (2009) 'Just like having a best friend'. How babies and toddlers construct relationships with their key workers. In: T. Papatheodorou and J. Moyles (eds.), *Learning Together in the Early Years: Exploring Relational Pedagogy*. Abingdon: Routledge, pp. 98–108.

Brookes, A. (2002) Gilbert White never came this far south: Naturalist knowledge and the limits of universalist environmental education. *Canadian Journal of Environmental Education*, 7 (2): 73–87.

Brookes, A. (2003) A critique of neo-Hahnian outdoor education theory. Part one: Challenges to the concept of 'character building'. *Journal of Adventure Education and Outdoor Learning*, 3: 49–62.

Brown, M. (2008) Comfort zone: model or metaphor? *Australian Journal of Outdoor Education*, 12 (1): 3–12.

Browne, N. (2004) *Gender Equity in the Early Years*. Maidenhead: Open University Press.

Browne, N. (2009) Identity and children as learners. In: J. Moyles (ed.), *Early Years Foundations: Meeting the Challenge*. Maidenhead: Open University Press, pp. 185–196.

Bruce, T. (1991) *Time to Play in Early Childhood Education*. London: Routledge.

Bruner, J. (1996) What have we learned about early learning? *European Early Childhood Education Research Journal*, 4 (1): 5–16.

Buchanan, K. (2010) Buoyed up. *Secondary Teachers*, January, pp. 10–11.

Bullock, A. (1975) *A Language for Life: Report of the Committee of Inquiry*. London: HMSO.

Burr, V. (2003) *Social Constructionism*. Hove: Routledge.

Cannatella, H. (2007) Place and being. *Educational Philosophy and Theory*, 39 (6): 621–632.

Carr, M. (2001) *Assessment in Early Childhood Settings: Learning Stories*. London: Paul Chapman Publishing.

Carver, C.S. (2003) Pleasure as a sign you can attend to something else: placing positive feelings within a general model of affect. *Cognition and Emotion*, 17 (2): 241–261.

Cazden, C. (2001) *Classroom Discourse: The Language of Teaching and Learning*, 2nd edn. Portsmouth, NH: Heinemann.

Chamberlain, N., George, N., Golden, S., Walker, F. and Benton, T. (2010) Tellus4 National Report. NFER/ DCSF RR218. London: DCSF.

Children, Schools and Families Select Committee (2010) *Transforming Education Outside the Classroom*. Sixth Report of Session 2009–10, 1 April 2010. London: HMSO.

Christie, E. (2004) Raising achievement through outdoor experiential learning? A case study of Scottish secondary school students. Doctoral Dissertation: University of Edinburgh.

Clark, A. (2010) *Transforming Children's Spaces: Children's and Adults' Participation in Designing Learning Environments*. London: Routledge.

Clark, A., Kjørholt, A. and Moss, P. (eds) (2005) *Beyond Listening: Children's Perspectives on Early Childhood Services*. Bristol: Policy Press.

Cornell, J. (1989) *Sharing Nature with Children 2*. Herts, UK: Exley Publications.

Coutts, G. and Jokela, T. (eds) (2008) *Art Community and Environment: Educational Perspectives*. Bristol: Intellect Books.

Csikszentmihalyi, M. (1979) The concept of flow. In: B. Sutton-Smith, *Play and Learning*. New York: Gardner, pp. 257–273.

Csikszentmihalyi, M. and Schiefele, U. (1992) Arts education, human development, and the quality of experience. In: B. Reimer and R.A. Smith (eds), *The Arts, Education, and Aesthetic Knowing: Ninety-first Yearbook of the National Society for the Study of Education (Vol. 2)*. Chicago: University of Chicago Press, pp. 169–191.

Curtis, P. (2009) Teachers put off school trips by litigation fear. *Guardian*, 2 October.

Davies, B. and Harré, R. (1990) Positioning: the discursive production of selves. *Journal for the Theory of Social Behaviour*, 20: 43–63.

Davis, B., Rea, T. and Waite, S. (2006) The special nature of the outdoors: its contribution to the education of children aged 3–11. *Australian Journal of Outdoor Education*, 10 (2): 3–12.

DBSI (Department of Business Skills and Industry) (2010) Departmental Strategic Objective (DSO) 5 (archived 7 April 2010). [Online] Available at: http://webarchive.nationalarchives.gov.uk/20100407184332/bis.gov.uk/abou t/objectives. Accessed 28 July 2010.

DCSF (Department for Children, Schools and Families) (2008a) *Early Years Foundation Stage*. Nottingham: DCSF.

DCSF (Department for Children, Schools and Families) (2008b) *Every Child Matters Outcomes Framework*. [Online] Available at: http://publications. everychildmatters.gov.uk/eOrderingDownload/DCSF-00331–2008.pdf. Accessed 8 November 2009.

DCSF (Department for Children, Schools and Families) (2009a) Learning Outside the Classroom (LoTC). [Online] Available at: www.dcsf.gov.uk/everychild matters/ete/school/learningotc. Accessed July 2010.

DCSF (Department for Children, Schools and Families) (2009b) *The New Primary Curriculum*. [Online] Available at: www.dcsf.gov.uk/newprimarycurriculum/. Accessed 24 November 2009.

DFE (Department for Education) (2010) www.education.gov.uk. Accessed 3 June 2010.

DfEE (Department for Education and Employment) (2000) *The National Curriculum. A Handbook for Primary Teachers in England. Key Stages 1 and 2*. London: DfEE.

DfES (Department for Education and Skills) (2003a) *National Standards for Under Eights Day Care and Childminding*. London: DfES.

DfES (Department for Education and Skills) (2003b) *Speaking, Listening, Learning: Drama – Key Teaching points*. [Online] Available at: http://nationalstrategies. standards.dcsf.gov.uk/node/88194. Accessed 3 March 2010.

DfES (Department for Education and Skills) (2005) *Education Outside the Classroom Manifesto Consultation*. London: DfES.

DfES (Department for Education and Skills) (2006a) Learning Outside the Classroom Manifesto. Nottingham: DfES.

DfES (Department for Education and Skills) (2006b) *The National Framework for Sustainable Schools* [Online] Available at: www.teachernet.gov.uk/sustainableschools/index.cfm.

DfES (Department for Education and Skills) (2007) *The Early Years Foundation Stage*. Nottingham: DfES. Also [Online] Available at: www.standards.dcsf. gov.uk/eyfs.

Dewey, J. (1934) *Art as Experience*. New York: Minton, Balch & Co.

Dickson, T.J. (2005) Facilitation: Is there a better way of doing it? Insights from learning styles analysis. In: T.J. Dickson, T. Gray and B. Hayllar (eds), *Outdoor and Experiential Learning: Views from the Top*. New Zealand: Otago University Press, pp. 250–255.

Dillen, L., Siongers, M., Helskens, D. and Verhofstadt-Denève, L. (2009) When puppets speak: dialectical psychodrama within developmental child psychotherapy. *Journal of Constructivist Psychology*, 22 (1): 55–82.

Dillon, J., Morris, M., O'Donnell, L., Reid, A., Rickinson, M. and Scott, W. (2005) *Engaging and Learning with the Outdoors*. The Final Report of the Outdoor Classroom in a Rural Context Action Research Project. Slough: NFER.

Dismore, H. and Bailey, R. (2005) 'If only': outdoor and adventurous activities and generalised academic development. *Journal of Adventure Education and Outdoor Learning*, 5: 9–20.

Doherty, J. and Hughes, M. (2009) *Child Development: Theory and Practice 0–11*. Harlow: Pearson Longman.

Doherty, J., and Bailey, R. (2003) *Supporting Physical Development and Physical Education in the Early Years*. Buckingham: Open University Press.

Donaldson, M. (1978) *Children's Minds*. London: Fontana Press.

Dorian, K.R. (2009) Science through drama: a multiple case exploration of the characteristics of drama activities used in secondary science lessons. *International Journal of Science Education*, 31 (16): 2247–2270.

Duncan, J., Bowden, C. and Smith A.B. (2006) A gossip or a good yack? Reconceptualizing parent support in New Zealand early childhood centre based programmes. *International Journal of Early Years Education*, 14 (1): 1–13.

Dyer, A.J. (2004) A sense of adventure. *Resurgence*, 226: 28–32.

Dyment, J.E. (2008) Green school grounds as sites for outdoor learning: barriers and opportunities. *International Research in Geographical and Environmental Education*, 14 (1): 28–45.

Easen, P., Kendall, P. and Shaw J. (1992) Parents and educators: dialogue and development through partnership. *Children & Society*, 6 (4): 282–296.

Eastwood, G. and Mitchell, H. (2003) The Forest School Evaluation: An evaluation of the first three years of the Oxfordshire Forest School Project. Unpublished evaluation: Oxford Brookes University.

Eco-Schools (2002) Eco-Schools home page. [Online] Available at www.ecoschools.org.uk. Accessed 23 July 2010.

Elstgeest, J. (2001) The right question at the right time. In: W. Harlen (ed.), *Primary Science: Taking the Plunge*, 2nd edn. Portsmouth, NH: Heinemann.

Engeström, Y., Miettinen, R. and Punamäki, R-L. (eds.) (1999) *Perspectives on Activity Theory*. New York: Cambridge University Press.

Ewert, A. (1983) *Outdoor Adventure and Self-Concept: A Research Analysis*. Eugene, OR: University of Oregon.

Fielker, D. (1997) *Extending Mathematical Ability through Whole Class Teaching*. London: Hodder & Stoughton.

Fisher, J. (2008) *Starting from the Child*. (3rd edn). Maidenhead: Open University Press.

Fisher, J.A. (2009) 'We used to play in Foundation, it was more funner': investigating feelings about transition from Foundation Stage to Year 1. *Early Years*, 29 (2): 131–145.

Fjørtoft, I. (2001) The natural environment as a playground for children: the impact of outdoor play activities in pre-primary school children. *Early Childhood Education*, 29 (2): 111–117.

Fjørtoft, I. (2004) Landscapes as playscape: the effects of natural environments on children's play and motor development. *Children, Youth and Environments*, 14 (2): 21–44.

Fleming, M., Merrell, C. and Tymms, P. (2004) The impact of drama on pupils' language, mathematics, and attitude in two primary schools. *Research in Drama Education: The Journal of Applied Theatre and Performance*, 9 (2): 177–197.

Forbes, R. (2005) 0–3 years: working with young children. In: L. Dryden, R. Forbes, P. Mukherji and L. Pound (eds), *Essential Early Years*. Abingdon: Hodder Arnold, pp. 66–96.

Furedi, F. (1997) *Culture of Fear: Risk-taking and the Morality of Low Expectation*. London: Cassell.

Furedi, F. (2001) *Paranoid Parenting: Abandon Your Anxieties and Be a Good Parent*. London: Penguin.

Furedi, F. (2004) *Therapy Culture: Cultivating Vulnerability in an Uncertain Age*. London: Routledge.

Furedi, F. (2008) *Paranoid Parenting*. London: Continuum Press.

Gair, N.P. (1997) *Outdoor Education: Theory and Practice*. London: Cassell.

Gallahue, D.L. and Ozmun, J.C. (2006) *Understanding Motor Development*. Madison, WI: Brown & Benchmark.

Garrick, R. (2004) *Playing Outdoors in the Early Years*. London: Continuum.

Garvey, C. (1991) *Play*. Glasgow: Fontana.

Gergen, K.J. (1999) *An Invitation to Social Construction*. London: Sage.

Glover, J. and Young, S. (1999) *Primary Music: Later Years*. London: Falmer Press.

Goouch, K. and Lambirth, A. (2007) *Understanding Phonics and the Teaching of Reading: Critical Perspectives*. Maidenhead: Open University Press.

Gottlieb, A. (2004) *The Afterlife Is Where We Come From: The Culture of Infancy in West Africa*. Chicago, IL: University of Chicago Press.

Grahn, P., Mårtensson, F., Lindblad, B., Nilsson, P. and Ekman, A. (1997) *Ute påt dagis [Outside in the Day Nursery]*. Alnarp, Sweden: Forlag Movium.

Gray, E. (1997) Compressing the counting process: developing a flexible interpretation of symbols. In: I. Thompson (ed.), *Teaching and Learning Early Number*. Buckingham: Open University Press, pp. 63–72.

Greenfield, C. (2004) Can run, play on bikes, jump the zoom slide, and play on the swings: exploring the value of outdoor play. *Australian Journal of Early Childhood*, 29 (2): 1–5.

Greenwood (formerly Gruenewald), D. A. (2008) A critical pedagogy of place: from gridlock to parallax. *Environmental Education Research*, 14 (3): 336–348.

Grizedale Sculpture Park [Online] Available at www.grizedale.org/. Accessed 23 November, 2009.

Gurnett, D. (2009) Environmental education and National Parks, a case study of Exmoor. In: Conference Proceedings of the Fourth International Outdoor Education Research Conference, La Trobe University, Beechworth, Victoria, Australia, April 15–18, 2009. [Online] Available at: www.latrobe.edu.au/education/assets/downloads/2009_conference_gurnett.pdf. Accessed 1 June 2010.

Hager, P. and Hodkinson, P. (2009) Moving beyond the metaphor of transfer of learning. *British Education Research Journal*, 35: 619–638.

Hahn, K. (1965) Harrogate address on Outward Bound. [Online] Available at: www.kurthahn.org/writings/gate.pdf. Accessed 21 November 2009.

Hall, T.M., Kaduson, H.G. and Schaefer, C.E. (2002) Fifteen effective play therapy techniques. *Professional Psychology: Research and Practice*, 33 (6): 515–522.

Harding, S. (2005) Outdoor play and the pedagogic garden. In: J. Moyles (ed.), *The Excellence of Play*. Maidenhead: Open University Press pp. 138–153.

Harlen, W. and Qualter, A. (2009) *The Teaching of Science in Primary Schools* (5th edn). London: David Fulton.

Harnham Water Meadows Trust (2010) [Online] Available at: www.salisburywatermeadows.org.uk/rosecottage.htm. Accessed 25 February 2010.

Harris, D. (2006) 'Open or Closed – That Is the Question'. Paper presented at the British Educational Research Association Annual Conference, University of Warwick, 6–9 September 2006. [Online] Available at: www.leeds.ac.uk/educol/documents/162090.htm. Accessed 21 November 2009.

Hattie, J., Marsh, H.W., Neill, J.T. and Richards, G.E. (1997) Adventure education and Outward Bound: out of class experiences that make a lasting difference. *Review of Educational Research*, 67 (1): 43–87.

Hayes, D. (2007) What Einstein can teach us about education. *Education 3–13*, 35 (2): 143–154.

Heath, S.B. (1983) *Ways with Words: Language Life and Work in Communities and Classrooms*. Oxford: Oxford University Press.

Heathcote, D. (1980) From the particular to the universal. In: K. Robinson (ed.), *Exploring Theatre and Education*. London: Heinemann.

Hincks, R. (2007) Joyful teaching and learning in science. In: D. Hayes, (ed.), *Joyful Teaching and Learning in the Primary School*. Exeter: Learning Matters, pp. 106–112.

Hindmarsh, J., Heath, C., vom Lehn, D. and Cleverly, J. (2005) Creating assemblies in public environments: social interaction, interactive exhibits and CSCW. *Computer Supported Cooperative Work*, 14 (1): 1–41.

Hodgson, J. and Dyer, A. (2003) *Let Your Children Go – Back to Nature*. Milverton: Capall Bann Publishers.

Holland, P. (2003) *We Don't Play with Guns Here*. Maidenhead: Open University Press.

Hope, G., Austin, R., Dismore, H., Hammond, S. and Whyte, T. (2007) Wild woods or urban jungle: playing it safe or freedom to roam? *Education 3–13*, 34 (4): 321–332.

Howes, D. (ed.) (2005) Introduction. *Empire of the Senses: The Sensual Culture Reader*. Oxford: Berg.

Hufton, N.R., Elliott, J.G. and Illushin, L. (2002) Educational motivation and engagement: Qualitative accounts from three countries. *British Educational Research Journal*, 28 (2): 265–289.

Huggins, V. (2008) An Early Years curriculum for boys. Unpublished paper: University of Plymouth.

Hughes, T. (1988) Myth and education. In: K. Egan and D. Nadaner (eds), *Imagination and Education*. Milton Keynes: Open University Press, pp. 30–44.

Humberstone, B. and Stan, I. (2009a) An ethnography of the outdoor classroom: How teachers manage risk in the outdoors. Oxford Ethnography Conference, St Hilda's College, Oxford, 22–23 September 2009.

Humberstone, B. and Stan, I. (2009b) Well-being and outdoor pedagogies in primary schooling. In: *Conference Proceedings of Outdoor Education Research and Theory: Critical Reflections, New Directions*. The Fourth International Outdoor Education Research Conference, La Trobe University, Beechworth, Victoria, Australia, 15–18 April 2009.

Hutt, S., Tyler, S., Hutt, C. and Christopherson, H. (1989) *Play, Exploration and Learning: A Natural History of the Pre-school*. London: Routledge.

Illeris, K. (2007) *How We Learn: Learning and Non-learning in School and Beyond*. London: Routledge.

Illeris, K. (ed.) (2009) *Contemporary Theories of Learning*. London: Routledge.

Jarvis, P. (2007) Monsters magic and Mr Psycho: A biocultural approach to rough and tumble play in the early years of primary school. *Early Years*, 27 (2): 171–188.

Jarvis, P. (2009) *Learning to Be a Person in Society*. London: Routledge.

Jarvis, P. and Parker, S. (eds) (2007) *Human Learning: An Holistic Approach*. London and New York: Routledge.

Jenkins, E. and Swinnerton, B. (1998) *Junior School Science Education in England and Wales since 1900: From Steps to Stages*. London: Woburn Press.

Keep Britain Tidy. [Online] Available at www.keepbritaintidy.org/. Accessed 23 July 2010.

Knapp, D. and Poff, R. (2001) A qualitative analysis of the immediate and short-term impact of an environmental interpretive program. *Environmental Education Research*, 7 (1): 55–65.

Kolb, D.A., Rubin, I. and McIntyre, J. (1981) Organisational psychology: an experiential approach. In: B. McCarthy (ed.), *The 4 MAT System*. Englewood Cliffs, NJ: Prentice-Hall, pp. 21–25.

Kolb, D.A. (1984) *Experiential Learning: Experience as the Source of Learning and Development*. Englewood Cliffs, NJ: Prentice-Hall.

Kollmuss, A. and Agyeman, J. (2002) Mind the gap. Why do people act environmentally and what are the barriers to pro-environmental behaviour? *Environmental Education Research*, 8 (3): 239–260.

Koshy, V. (2001) *Teaching Mathematics to Able Children*. London: David Fulton.

Kylin, M. (2003) Children's Dens. Children, youth and environment. [Online] Available at http://colorado.edu/journals/cye. Accessed 21 November 2009.

Laevers, F. (1993) Deep level learning: an exemplary application on the area of physical knowledge. *European Early Childhood Education Research Journal*, 1 (1): 53–68.

Laevers, F. (no date) Concepts and experiences at the level of context, process and outcome. Katholieke Universiteit Leuven/Centre for Experiential Education. [Online] Available at: www.european-agency.org/agency-projects/assessment-resource-guide/documents/2008/11/Laevers.pdf. Accessed 1 March 2010.

Lampert, M. (1990) When the problem is not the question and the solution is not the answer: mathematical knowing and teaching. *American Educational Research Journal*, 27: 29–63.

Lane, A. (2005) What is technology? [Online] Available at: www.open2.net/sciencetechnologynature/worldaroundus/whatistechnology.html. Accessed 26 February 2010.

Learning Outside the Classroom (2006) [Online] Available at: http://publications.teachernet.gov.uk/default.aspx?PageFunction=productdetails&PageMode=publications&ProductId=DFES-04232–2006/. Accessed 24 November 2009.

Lepkowska, D. (2009) Curriculum: Cultivating the mind. *Times Educational Supplement*, 30 October.[Online] Available at: www.tes.co.uk/article.aspx?storycode=6026463. Accessed 8 November 2009.

Lindon, J. (2005) *Understanding Child Development*. Abingdon: Hodder Arnold.

Lindstrom, L. (2006). Creativity: What is it? Can you assess it? Can it be taught? *International Journal of Art and Design Education*, 25 (1): 53–66.

Little, H. (2006) Children's risk-taking behaviour: implications for early childhood policy and practice. *International Journal of Early Years Education*, 14 (2): 141–154.

Louv, R. (2005) *Last Child in the Woods: Saving Our Children from Nature-Deficit Disorder*. New York: Algonquin Books of Chapel Hill.

Luff, P. (2008) Looking, listening, learning and linking: uses of observation for relational pedagogy. In: T. Papatheodorou and J. Moyles (eds), *Learning*

Together in the Early Years: Exploring Relational Pedagogy. Abingdon: Routledge, pp. 98–113.

Luff, P. (2009) Written observations or walks in the park? Documenting children's experiences. In: J. Moyles (ed.), *Early Years Foundations: Meeting the Challenge.* Maidenhead: Open University Press, pp. 185–196.

MacNaughton, G. (2000) *Rethinking Gender in Early Childhood Education.* London: Paul Chapman.

Malone, K. (2008) *Every Experience Matters: An Evidence Based Research Report on the Role of Learning Outside the Classroom for Children's Whole Development from Birth to Eighteen Years.* Report commissioned by Farming and Countryside Education for UK Department for Children, School and Families, Wollongong, Australia.

Martin, P. and Priest, S. (1986) Understanding the adventure experience. *Journal of Adventure Education*, 3: 18–21.

Maynard, T. (2007) Encounters with Forest School and Foucault: a risky business? *Education 3–13*, 35 (4): 379–391.

Maynard, T. (2007) Forest Schools in Great Britain: an initial exploration. *Contemporary Issues in Early Childhood*, 8 (4): 320–331.

Maynard, T. and Waters, J. (2007) Learning in the outdoor environment: a missed opportunity. *Early Years*, 27 (3): 255–265.

McKenzie, M. (2008) The places of pedagogy: or, what we can do with culture through intersubjective experiences. *Environmental Education Research*, 14 (3): 361–373.

McKenzie, M.D. (2000) How are adventure education program outcomes achieved? A review of literature. *Australian Journal of Outdoor Education*, 5 (1): 19–28.

Medwell, J., Moore, G., Wray, D. and Griffiths, V. (2007) *Primary English: Knowledge and Understanding.* Exeter: Learning Matters.

Meehan, C. (2002) Promoting spiritual development in the curriculum. *Pastoral Care in Education*, 20 (1): 16–24.

Mental Health Foundation (1999) *Bright Futures: Promoting Children and Young People's Mental Health.* London: Mental Health Foundation.

Miller, D. (2007) The seeds of learning: young children develop important skills through their gardening activities at a Midwestern Early Education Program. *Applied Environmental Education and Communication*, 6: 49–66.

Mills, J. (2009) *Music in the Primary School.* Oxford: Oxford University Press.

Min, B. and Lee, J. (2006) Children's neighborhood place as a psychological and behavioural domain. *Journal of Environmental Psychology*, 26: 51–71.

Mitchell, W.J.T. (ed.) (2002) *Landscape and Power.* Chicago: University of Chicago Press.

Moore, R. (1986) The power of nature orientation of girls and boys toward biotic and abiotic play settings on a reconstructed schoolyard. *Children's Environments Quarterly*, 3 (3). [Online] Available at: www.colorado.edu/journals/cye/CYE_BackIssues/CEVol3(3)Contents.htm. Accessed 26 July 2010.

Moore, R.C. (1995) Children's gardening: first steps towards a sustainable future. *Children's Environments Quarterly*, 6 (1): 1–4.

Mortlock, C. (1984) *The Adventure Alternative.* Milnthorpe: Cicerone.

Mortlock, C. (2002) *Beyond Adventure.* Milnthorpe: Cicerone.

Nabhan, G.P. and Trimble, S. (1994) *The Geography of Childhood*. Boston, MA: Beacon Press.

Neill, J. (2008) Enhancing life effectiveness: The impacts of outdoor education programmes (Volume 1). PhD Thesis, University of Western Sydney.

Nicol, R., Higgins, P., Ross, H. and Mannion, G. (2007) Outdoor education in Scotland: a summary of recent research. [Online] Available at: www.snh.org.uk/pdfs/publications/education/OCReportWithEndnotes.pdf. Accessed 24 November 2009.

Nundy, S. (1999) The fieldwork effect: the role and impact of fieldwork in the upper primary school. *International Research in Geographical and Environmental Education*, 8 (2): 190–198.

Nutbrown, C. (2006) *Threads of Thinking: Young Children Learning and the Role of Early Education*, 3rd edn. London: Sage.

Ødegaard, M. (2003) Dramatic science. A critical review of drama in science education. *Studies in Science Education*, 39 (1): 75–101.

Ofsted (Office for Standards in Education) (2009) *Making More of Music: Improving the Quality of Music Teaching in Primary Schools*. Manchester: Crown Copyright.

Ofsted (2010) Citizenship established – Citizenship in schools. [Online] Available at: www.ofsted.gov.uk/Ofsted-home/Publications-and-research/ Browse-all-by/Documents-by-type/Thematic-reports/Citizenship-established-Citizenship-in-schools-2006–09/(language)/eng-GB. Accessed 3 March 2010.

Ouvry, M. (2003) *Exercising Muscles and Minds: Outdoor Play and the Early Years Curriculum*. London: Routledge.

Ozer, E. (2007) The effects of school gardens on students and schools: conceptualization and considerations for maximizing healthy development. *Health Education and Behavior*, 34, 846–863.

Paechter, C. (2007) *Being Boys, Being Girls: Learning Masculinities and Femininities*. Maidenhead: Open University Press.

Page, T., Herne, S., Charman, H., Dash, P., Atkinson, D., and Adams, J. (2006). Art Now with the living: A dialogue with teachers investigating contemporary art practices. *International Journal of Art and Design Education*, 25 (2): 146–155.

Palmer, J. (1998) *Environmental Education of the 21st Century: Theory, practice, progress and promise*. p142. London: Routledge.

Pascal, C. and Bertram, T. (2001) *Effective Early Learning: Case Studies in Improvement*. London: Paul Chapman Publishing.

Passy, R. and Waite, S. (2008) *Excellence and Enjoyment* continuing professional development materials in England: both a bonus and onus for schools. *Journal of In-Service Education*, 34 (3): 311–325.

Pavey, F. and Wickett, K. (2008) A learner led learning environment. Commissioned by the Children's Workforce Development Council as part of the Practitioner-Led Research Programme, 2007–2008. Leeds: CWDC.

Peacock, A. (2004) Talking about plants and people; analysing children's conversations with their parents at the Eden Project. *Primary Science Review*, 84: 10–13.

Peacock, A. (2006) *Changing Minds: The Lasting Impact of School Trips*. A study of the long-term impact of sustained relationships between schools and the National Trust via the Guardianship scheme. Swindon: The National Trust.

Peacock, A. and Bowker, R. (2001) Thinking of Eden: Developing children's thinking about sustainability at the Eden Project. *Teaching Thinking*, 5: 22–24.

Penn, H. (2010) Does it matter what country you are in? In: S. Smidt (ed.), *Key Issues in Early Years Education* (2nd edn). London: Routledge, pp. 18–22.

Placek, J. (1983) Conceptions of success in teaching: Busy, happy and good? In: T. Templin and J. Olson (eds), *Teaching in Physical Education*. Champaign, IL: Human Kinetics, pp. 46–56.

Play Safety Forum (2002) *Managing Risk in Play Provision: A Position Statement*. London: Children's Play Council.

Porteous, D. (1990) *Landscapes of the Mind: Worlds of Sense and Metaphor*. Toronto: University of Toronto Press.

Powderham Castle (2010) Victorian Kitchen. [Online] Available at: www. powderham.co.uk/learning/victoriankitchen.ashx. Accessed 3 March 2010.

Pratt, N. (2006) *Interactive Maths Teaching in the Primary School*. London, Paul Chapman Publishing.

Pratt, N. and Berry, J. (2007) The joy of mathematics. In: D. Hayes (ed.), *Joyful Teaching and Learning in the Primary School*. Exeter: Learning Matters, pp. 97–105.

Priest, S. (1990) The Adventure Experience Paradigm. In: J.C. Miles and S. Priest (eds), *Adventure Education*. State College, PA: Venture Publishing, pp. 157–162.

Primary National Strategy (2007) *Capable, Confident and Creative: Supporting Boys' Achievements*. London: DCSF Publications.

Pullman, P. (2005) Common sense has much to learn from moonshine. *Guardian*, 22 January 2005.

QCA (Qualifications and Curriculum Authority) (1999) *The National Curriculum for England: Key Stages 1 & 2*. [Online] Available at: http://curriculum.qcda. gov.uk/key-stages-1-and-2/index.aspx. Accessed 23 July 2010.

QCA (Qualifications and Curriculum Authority) (2000a) *Curriculum Guidance for the Foundation Stage*. [Online] Available at: www.naa.org.uk/naa_17850.aspx. Accessed 3 February 2009.

QCA (Qualifications and Curriculum Authority) (2000b) *Music – A Scheme of Work for Key Stages 1 and 2*. London: QCA.

Rea, T. (2008) Methodology in outdoor research: approaches from an alternative discourse. *Journal of Adventure Education and Outdoor Learning*, 8 (1): 43–53.

Rea, T. and Waite, S. (2009) International perspectives on outdoor and experiential learning. *Education 3–13*, 37 (1): 1–4.

Reay, D. (2009) 'Class acts': Home-school involvement and working-class parents in the UK. In: R. Deslandes (ed.), *International Perspectives on Contexts, Communities and Evaluated Innovative Practices: Family–School–Community Partnerships*. London: Routledge, pp. 50–63.

Rennie, L. and McClafferty, T. (1996) Science centre and science learning. *Studies in Science Education*, 27: 53–98.

Rickinson, M., Dillon, J., Teamey, K., Morris, M., Choi, M.Y. and Sanders, D. (2004) *A Review of Research on Outdoor Learning*. Slough: NFER and King's College, London.

Rickinson, M., Lundholm, C. and Hopwood, N. (2009) *Environmental Learning: Insights from Research into the Student Experience*. New York: Springer.

Rogers, S. and Evans, J. (2007) Rethinking role play in the reception class, *Educational Research*, 49 (2): 153–167.

Rogers, S. and Evans, J. (2008) *Inside Role Play in Early Childhood Education: Researching Children's Perspectives*. London: Routledge.

Rogoff, B. (1990) *Apprenticeship in Thinking: Cognitive Development in Social Context*. New York: Open University Press.

Rose, J. (2009) *Independent Review of the Primary Curriculum: Final Report*. Nottingham: DCSF Publications.

Roth, W.-M., McGinn, M.K., Woszczyna, C. and Boutonné, S. (1999) Differential participation during science conversations: the interaction of focal artefacts, social configurations and physical arrangements. *Journal of the Learning Sciences*, 8 (3&4): 293–347.

Roth, W.-M. (1996) Art and artefact of children's designing: a situated cognition perspective. *Journal of the Learning Sciences*, 5: 129–166.

Salmon, M.D. and Sainato, D.M. (2005) Beyond Pinocchio: puppets as teaching tools in inclusive early childhood classrooms. *Young Exceptional Children*, 8: 12–19. [Online] Available at: www.sagepub.com/donoghuestudy/articles/Salmon%20Sainato.pdf. Accessed 21 February 2010.

Schafer, R.M. (1975) *The Rhinoceros in the Classroom*. Toronto: Universal Edition.

Schoenfeld, A.H. (1996) In fostering Communities of Inquiry, must it matter that the teacher knows 'The Answer'? *For the Learning of Mathematics*, 16: 11–16.

Science Council (2009) What is Science? [Online] Available at: www.science-council.org/DefiningScience.php. Accessed 2 February 2010.

SEER (2000) The Effects of Environment-based Education on Students' Achievement. State Education and Environment Roundtable: California Student assessment Project. [Online] Available at: www.seer.org/pages/csap.pdf. Accessed 5 January 2010.

Sefton-Green, J. (2006) New spaces for learning: developing the ecology of out-of-school education, Hawke Research Institute Working Paper Series, 35. [Online] Available at: www.unisa.edu.au/hawkeinstitute/documents/wp35.pdf. Accessed 1 August 2006.

Selby, D. (2002) The signature of the whole: radical interconnectedness and its implications for global and environmental education. *Encounter: Education for Meaning and Social Justice*, 14 (1): 5–16.

Sellick, R. (1960) *The West Somerset Mineral Railway and the Story of the Brendon Hills Iron Mines*. Newton Abbot: David & Charles.

Senge, P., Scharmer, C., Jawaorski, J. and Flowers, B. (2005) *Presence: Exploring Profound Change in People, Organizations and Society*, London: Nicholas Brealey Publishing.

Sherborne, V. (2001) *Developmental Movement for Children*. London: Worth Publishing.

Simon, S., Naylor, S., Keogh, B., Maloney, J. and Downing, B. (2008) Puppets promoting engagement and talk in science. *International Journal of Science Education*, 30 (9): 1229–1248.

Smidt, S. (2006) *The Developing Child in the 21st Century: A Global Perspective on Child Development*. London: Routledge.

Smith, P.K. (2010) *Children and Play*. Chichester: Wiley–Blackwell.

Sobel, D. (1995) *Beyond Ecophobia*. Great Barrington, MA: Orion Society Nature Literacy Series. Quotations in text from version available at: www.

eenorthcarolina.org/certification/beyond_ecophobia.pdf. Accessed 29 July 2010.

Sobel, D. (2004) *Place-based Education: Connecting Classrooms and Communities*. Great Barrington, MA: Orion Society.

Stables, A. (2005) *Semiotic Engagement: A New Theory of Education*. Lewiston, NY: Mellen Press.

Stein, J. (2007) The brain and learning, In: P. Jarvis and S. Parker (eds), *Human Learning: An Holistic Approach*. London: Routledge, pp. 32–49.

Steiner, R. (1995) *Anthroposophy in Everyday Life*. Hudson, NY: Anthroposophic Press.

Stephenson, A. (2003) Physical risk taking: dangerous or endangered? *Early Years*, 23 (1): 35–43.

Stewart, A. (2006) Seeing the trees and the forest: attending to Australian Natural History as if it mattered. *Australian Journal of Environmental Education*, 22 (2): 85–97.

Stewart, A. (2008) Whose place, whose history? Outdoor environmental education pedagogy as 'reading' the landscape. *Journal of Adventure Education & Outdoor Learning*, 8 (2): 79–98.

Stoll, L. (1999) Realising our potential: Understanding and developing capacity for lasting improvement. *School Effectiveness and School Improvement*, 10: 503–532.

Swanwick, K. (1999) *Teaching Music Musically*. Abingdon: Routledge.

Swonke, B. (2000) Visual preferences and environmental protection: evolutionary aesthetics applied to environmental education. *Environmental Education Research*, 6 (3): 259–267.

Sylva, K., Melhuish, E., Sammons, P., Siraj-Blatchford, I. and Taggart, B. (eds) (2010) *Early Childhood Matters: Evidence from the Effective Pre-school and Primary Education Project*. London: Routledge.

Sylva, K., Roy, C. and Painter, M. (1980) *Childwatching at Playgroup and Nursery School*. London: Grant McIntyre.

The Children's Society (2009) *Vision for a Good Childhood for All*. [Online] Available at: www.childrenssociety.org.uk/resources/documents/Admin/15484_full.pdf. Accessed 23 July 2010.

Thomas, G. and Thompson, G. (2004) *A Child's Place: Why Environment Matters to Children*. London: Green Alliance.

Thompson, I. (1997) The role of counting in derived fact strategies. In: I. Thompson (ed.), *Teaching and Learning Early Number*. Buckingham: Open University Press, pp. 52–62.

Tomlinson, H. and Arthur, M. (2009) Musical gardens. *Primary Music Today*, 42. [Online] Available at: www.primarymusictoday.co.uk/?PageID=43. Accessed 23 July 2010.

Tovey, H. (2006) The dangers of safety: perceptions of risk in outdoor play. Paper presented at 3rd Roehampton Educational Research Conference (ROERCE), Roehampton Institute, University of Surrey, 14 December 2006.

Tovey, H. (2007) *Playing Outdoors: Spaces and Places, Risk and Challenge*. Maidenhead: Open University Press.

Trawick Smith, J. (1998) School based play and social interactions: opportunities and limitations. In: P.D. Fromberg and D. Bergen (eds), *Play from Birth to*

Twelve and Beyond: Contexts, Perspectives and Meanings. New York: Garland Publishing, pp. 241–247.

Treffers, A. and Beishuizen, M. (1999) Realistic mathematics education in the Netherlands. In: I. Thompson (ed.), *Issues in Teaching Numeracy in Primary Schools.* Buckingham: Open University Press, pp. 27–38.

Tuan, Y.F. (1977) *Space and Place: The Perspective of Experience.* Minneapolis, MN: University of Minnesota Press.

Turner, T.N. (2003) Puppets to put the whole world in their hands. *International Journal of Social Education,* 1385 (14), 5.

van Matre, S. (1990) *Earth Education: A New Beginning.* Greenville, WV: Institute for Earth Education.

Vare, P. (2008) From practice to theory: participation as learning in the context of sustainable development projects. In: A. Reid, B.B. Jensen, J. Nikel and V. Simovska (eds), *Participation and Learning: Perspectives on Education and the Environment, Health and Sustainability.* New York: Springer.

Vygotsky, L. (1998) The genesis of higher mental functions. In: K. Richardson and S. Sheldon (eds), *Cognitive Development to Adolescence.* Hove: Erlbaum.

Waite, S. (2007) 'Memories are made of this': Some reflections on outdoor learning and recall. *Education 3–13,* 35 (4): 333–347.

Waite, S. (2009) Outdoor learning for children aged 2–11: perceived barriers, potential solutions. In: Conference Proceedings for International Outdoor Education Research Conference, La Trobe University, Beechworth, Australia, 15–18 April 2009. [Online] Available at www.latrobe.edu.au/education/assets/downloads/2009-conference-waite.pdf. Accessed 1 June 2010.

Waite, S. (2010) Final Report for Exmoor National Park Authority Sustainable Development Fund: *Contribution of the Exmoor Curriculum to Rural Young People's Educational Achievement and Environmental Awareness.* (January 2010). [Online] Available at: http://www.plymouth.ac.uk/researchcover/rcp.asp?pagetype=G&page=321. Accessed 1 June 2010.

Waite, S. (2011) Teaching and learning outside the classroom: personal values, alternative pedagogies and standards. *Education 3–13,* 39 (1) (in press).

Waite, S. and Davis, B. (2006) Developing undergraduate research skills in a Faculty of Education: motivation through collaboration. *Higher Education Research and Development,* 25 (4): 403–419.

Waite, S. and Davis, B. (2007) The contribution of free play and structured activities in Forest School to learning beyond cognition: an English case: In: B. Ravn and N. Kryger (eds), *Learning Beyond Cognition.* Copenhagen: The Danish University of Education, pp. 257–274.

Waite, S., Cutting, R., Cook, R. Burnett, J. and Opie, M. (2009) Learning outside the classroom: environments for experiential enrichment. In: C. Nygaard, C. Holtham and N. Courtney (eds), *Improving Students' Learning Outcomes.* Copenhagen: CBS PRESS, August 2009, pp. 239–256.

Waite, S. and Rea, T. (2007) Enjoying teaching and learning outside the classroom. In: D. Hayes (ed.), *Joyful Teaching and Learning in the Primary School,* Exeter: Learning Matters, pp. 52–62.

Waite, S., Davis, B. and Brown, K. (2006) Final report: Five stories of outdoor learning, July 2006. Report for funding body EYDCP (zero14plus) and participants. [Online] Available at: http://www.plymouth.ac.uk/researchcover/

rcp.asp?pagetype=G&page=321. Accessed 1 June 2010.

Waite, S., Evans, J. and Rogers, S. (2008) ESRC submission: Opportunities afforded by the outdoors for alternative pedagogies in the transition between Foundation Stage and Year 1 (RES-000–22-3065).

Waite, S., Lawson, H. and Robertson, C. (2006) Work related learning for students with significant learning difficulties: relevance and reality. *Cambridge Journal of Education*, 36 (4): 579–595.

Waller, T. (2007) 'The Trampoline Tree and the Swamp Monster with 18 Heads': outdoor play in the Foundation Stage and the Foundation Phase. *Education 3–13*, 35 (4): 393–407.

Ward Thompson, C., Aspinall, P. and Montarzino, A. (2008) The childhood factor: adult visits to green places and the significance of childhood experience. *Environment and Behaviour*, 40 (1): 111–143. [Online] Available at: http://eab.sagepub.com. Accessed 3 September 2008.

Warren, M. and Hong, S. (2009) More than services: Community organising and community schools. In: R. Deslandes (ed.) *International Perspectives on Contexts, Communities and Evaluated Innovative Practices: Family–School–Community Partnerships*. London: Routledge, pp. 177–188.

Waters, J. and Begley, S. (2007) Supporting the development of risk-taking behaviours in the early years: an exploratory study. *Education 3–13*, 35 (4): 365–377.

Webster-Stratton, C. and Reid, M.J. (2003) Treating conduct problems and strengthening social and emotional competence in young children (ages 4–8 years): The Dina Dinosaur treatment program. *Journal of Clinical Child Psychology*, 11 (3): 130–143.

Wellhousen, K. (2002) *Outdoor Play, Every Day: Innovative Play Concepts for Early Childhood*. Albany: Delmar.

Wells, N.M. and Lekies, K.S. (2006) Nature and life course: pathways from childhood nature experiences to adult environmentalism. *Children, Youth and Environments*, 16 (1): 12–15. [Online] Available at: www.colorado.edu/journals/cye/16_1/16_1_01_NatureAndLifeCourse.pdf. Accessed 19 February 2007.

Wenger, E. (2009) A social theory of learning. In: K. Illeris (ed.) *Contemporary Theories of Learning*. London: Routledge.

Whalley, M. and the Pen Green Centre Team (2007) *Involving Parents in their Children's Learning*, 2nd edn. London: Paul Chapman Publishing.

Whitehead M. (2010) *Physical Literacy Throughout the Lifecourse*. London: Routledge.

Wolf, M. (2008) *Proust and the Squid: The Story and Science of the Reading Brain*. Cambridge: Icon Books.

Woodhouse, J. (2003) Outdoor and adventurous activities. In: J. Severs (ed.), *Safety and Risk in Primary School Education*. London: Routledge.

Wrigely, T. (2007) *Another School Is Possible*. Stoke on Trent: Trentham.

Yorkshire Sculpture Park. [Online] Available at: www.ysp.co.uk/. Accessed 23 November 2009.

Young, S. and Glover, J. (1998) *Music in the Early Years*. London: Falmer.

Young, S. (2003) *Music with the Under Fours*. London: RoutledgeFalmer.

Index

Added to a page number 'f' denotes a figure and 't' denotes a table.

ability 16, 22
abstraction(s) 83, 84, 98
academy status 6, 52, 150
access to the outdoors 27–8
accommodation 11, 22
accumulative psychological models 184, 185f
achievements 3, 4, 16, 63, 107, 117
acquisition, learning as 2, 157–8
action competence 198
action-oriented place study 4
active learning 12, 55
activity theory 7
adult interventions 61
adult role 28–31, 169
adult-child interactions 30, 61
adult-directed activities 30, 56, 70t
adventure 149, 150
adversity 150
aesthetic sensitivity 183
affective learning 151, 153, 154
affordances, spaces and 60
altruism 165
animals 179, 185
anthropomorphism 178
anthroposophy 159
arousal increasing device 184
arts 109, 119–32
artwork, context and subjectivity 129–30
assimilation 11, 22
Association for Physical Education 135

attainment, focus on 156
attitudes, developing 25–6
audio recorders 72
authentic experiences 3, 69, 189
autonomy 154–5, 157
avoidance, of the outdoors 142, 144

Baden-Powell 149, 150
behaviour control 61, 62
belonging 17
biophilia 186–7
body, and learning 5, 6f
boundaries 169

Campaign for School Gardening 164
Centre of the Cell 198–9
challenge(s) 4, 22, 26, 29, 137, 139, 153, 166, 169, 206, 209
character 150, 155
child development
    relationship with nature 96–8
    see also cognitive development;
        physical development; social and
        emotional development
child-adult ratios 169
child-centred approach, arts
    education 127
child-directed learning 170
child-initiated learning 54, 70
child-led activities 12, 104
childhood, expectations and norms of 32
children's interests 37–43, 47–8, 72
child's perspective 58–9, 120–1
choice 62, 74
citizenship 117, 210

classrooms 10, 13, 60
co-constructors, children as 45
coalition government 6, 52, 118, 208
cognitive development 23, 109, 124
cognitive learning 152–3, 165
collaboration 130, 165
collaborative engagement 195–6, 197, 199
comfort zone model 138
'common sense' perspective, of learning 157
communities of practice 30, 68, 108, 138, 196
community, involvement of 210
community languages 66–7
competence 107, 135, 137, 138, 170, 198
computer simulations 179
concentration 38, 169
confidence 26, 117, 135–6, 173, 174
constructivism 5, 103
consumerism 150
context, artwork 129–30
contingent facilitation 30, 31f, 139
continuing professional development 174
continuity 51
control 10, 12, 31, 61, 62, 110, 153
cooperation 137, 154
costumes 68, 111
courage 209
creativity 38, 82, 110, 117, 137, 139
critical dialogue 110
cross-curricular studies 61, 109, 117
cultural heritage 181–2
cultural norms 7, 8, 10, 32, 58, 134
cultures
    beliefs and attitudes 37
    early learning environments 45–6
    environmental print 78
    and learning 3–4
    risk aware and risk averse 32
    see also socio-cultural plane
cumulative learning 10–11
curiosity 82, 210
Curriculum for Excellence 108

deep learning 169

designated tasks 194
differentiation 138–9, 140
digital cameras 72
discourse, micro-contexts 192–3
disempowerment 194
'doing' mathematics 84f, 85, 88, 93
'doing' science 104
drama 182
    benefits of 116–18
    pedagogy for outdoor learning 110–15

early learning environments 35–49
    children's culture 45–6
    children's interests 37–43, 47–8
    involving parents and carers 43–5
Early Years Foundation Stage 21, 27, 29–30, 36, 39, 50, 125, 135
Earthwalks 95–8
ecology 96, 128, 158, 179, 183
Eden Project 198
education, neo-liberalisation 150–1, 156–7
Effective Early Learning scale 38
embodiment 2, 135
emergent environmentalism 95, 109
emotional attachment 183–4
emotional development 23, 111
emotional engagement 169
empathy 98, 186
emplacement 109, 180
enabling environments 26–31, 37–8
energy 38, 95
engagement 2, 11, 12, 16, 115, 118, 180, 211
    see also collaborative engagement; emotional engagement
English and language 66–79
    activities 70t
    environmental print 72–7
    as a medium for learning 66–7
    role-play areas 68–72
    in support of equity 78–9
enjoyment 2, 12, 17, 25, 51, 95, 96, 117, 118
environment
    reducing impact on 102–4
    see also emergent environmentalism; indoor

environments; outdoor
    environments
environmental art 128–9
environmental education 210
    implications for policy and practice
        186–7
    pedagogical approach 177–83
    see also Exmoor National Park;
        Forest Schools; outdoor adventure
        centres; school gardens
environmental print 72–7
evaluations, of learning 188
events, artwork as 128–9
Every Child Matters 50–1, 165, 208
exercise play 29
Exmoor, historical aspect 180–2
Exmoor National Park
    involvement of community and
        children in 176–7
    real experience environmental
        education 183–7
experience(s) 14–15
    authentic 3, 69, 189
    direct 3, 4, 28, 69
    first-hand 17, 23, 102
    intersubjective 5
    macro level 16
    memorable 137, 179–80, 185
    real life 173
    relevant 3–4, 12
    see also outdoor experiences; real
        experience environmental
        education
experiential learning 1, 2, 5, 10, 11,
    204, 212
exploration 26, 27, 30, 58, 62, 98,
    110, 118, 121–2, 124–5, 170
extension of learning 25, 205

facilitating 16, 30, 139, 169
field study centres 117
fieldwork 108, 153, 182
Five Hour Offer 144
flow learning 96
focal planes *see* psychological plane;
    socio-cultural plane
Forest Schools 7, 138, 166–72
    compared to school gardens 172–3

physical surroundings 167–70
    principles underpinning 167
free flow, between environments 27,
    29
free play 57, 171
freedom
    of being in the outdoors 25
    in education 6, 52, 98, 150
    and learning 180
    through novel situations 15
freeze-frames 111
friendship groups 62
friluftsliv 171
frontier adventures 138, 139

games, environmental 178
gender stereotyping 47, 63
generalisations, mathematical 81–2
geographical information systems 116
geography *see* history and geography
Goldsworthy, Andy 128, 130
gross motor skill development 24, 25
group size/composition 192, 199

Hahn, Kurt 149, 150
hands-on 1, 2, 5, 10, 16, 17, 189
hazardous behaviour 32
health and safety 31, 148, 150, 166
hidden places 27
higher-order thinking 30
historic enquiry 182
historical interest 180–2, 185
history and geography
    drama 110–15
    landscapes 108–9
    social understanding of the world
        117–18
holism 5, 12, 41, 53, 108, 135, 160,
    168
homesickness 152, 158
horizontal mathematising 83, 88, 91,
    92f
hot-seating 111, 112

ICT, using 72, 91, 101, 116
identity 46, 158
imagination 61, 108, 109
impact, focus on 150

Impressionists 129
INCA study (2008) 51–2
inclusion 165
independence 61
independent learning 62, 107, 117
indoor environments 23, 27, 29, 37–8, 56
information sharing 44
integrative approach, to learning 109
interaction(s), with children 30, 61
interconnectivity 183
interdependence 154, 179
intersubjective experience 5
investigation 22, 104
involvement 38

key memory episodes 153
key people 62
knowledge
    learning professionals 196
    mathematics 84f, 85, 88, 93
Kolb's experiential learning cycle 11

land art movement 128–9
landscapes 108–10, 128, 129, 177
language development 169
    see also English and language
leadership 139
league tables 150
learning
    'common sense' perspective 157–8
    education and schooling 6
    evaluations of 188
    and experiences see experience(s)
    focal planes 5–6, 9
        psychological plane 5, 6f, 10–12, 15–16, 68, 71, 86, 170, 184, 207t
        socio-cultural 4, 5, 6f, 13–15, 68, 71, 77, 96, 154, 158, 165, 170, 207t
    using for different purposes 15–17
    see also outdoor learning
learning dispositions 32, 170
    mathematical 82–3, 86
learning opportunities 2, 7, 11, 172, 205
learning outcomes

Forest Schools 168
    sharing/imposing 156
learning outside the classroom
    arts 119–32
    auditing current provision 210–11
    barriers to 207
    developing a theory of 2–5
    English and language 66–79
    history and geography 106–18
    mathematics 80–93
    new forms of 188–99
    observation of natural behaviour 12
    physical education 133–46
    possible effects of 209t
    provision of different experiences 14
    purposes 208–12
    reason for 206–9
    relational model for 6–10
    science and technology 94–105
Learning Outside the Classroom
    Manifesto 3, 4, 36, 41, 137, 186
learning professionals 190–1, 192–3, 195, 196–9
learning spaces 189, 190–4
    collaborative engagement 195–6, 197, 199
    interaction of child, others and place 7, 62
    learning professionals 196–9
    micro-contexts 192–4
    new forms of learning 194–5
    school grounds as 103
Learning Stories 44
lifelong learning 26, 41, 210
listening 120, 125
'lived in' landscape 177
local communities, as learning environments 35–49
local contexts 7, 12, 109
Long, Richard 129

macro context, learning spaces 191
mathematical abstractions 83, 84, 98
mathematical activity 82–3, 84
mathematical dispositions 82–3, 86
mathematical ideas 83, 86, 88
mathematical thinking 82, 84–6
mathematics 80–93

defining 81–4
doing, knowing and using 84f, 85, 88, 93
role of the outdoors 86–91
mathematisation 83, 88, 91, 92f
matrices 96–8
meaning(s) 12, 16
media, awareness and criticality of 72
memorable experiences 137, 179–80, 185
memories 17, 96, 169, 184
micro-contexts, impact of 192–4
mind *see* psychological plane
mixed age-group classes 56
Mortlock, Colin 149, 150
motivation 12, 17, 25, 51, 170
movement 24–5, 29, 163
movement skills 135, 136
multi-sensory exploration 121–2
multiple identities 158
museums 117
musical activity 124
musical composition 122–3
musical development 126–7
musical exploration 122, 124–5
musical play 124–5
mystery 155
mythologies 183

narrative 112, 115, 117
  see also story-telling
national contexts, of learning 7
National Curriculum 54, 56, 98
National Parks 176
  see also Exmoor National Park
National Standards for Under Eights 48
National Trust wardens 195, 196
natural world 21, 22, 23, 24, 26, 28, 95
naturalistic learning 158
nature 96–8, 128, 179, 185
Nature Study 163
nature-deficit disorder 162
neo-liberalism 150–1, 156–7
noise 120
novelty 7, 15, 22, 153, 171

observation, of children 12, 39, 53, 63

observational skills 96, 99–100, 182
open-ended resources 29, 37, 63
orienteering activities 140
out-of-school learning 4
outdoor adventure activities 137–41
outdoor adventure centres 148–60
  cognitive benefits 152–3
  diminishing access to 148–9
  growing similarity to schools 149, 156–8
  historical and cultural background 149–52
  important role of 144
  learning at 158
  residential aspects 152
  self-awareness and autonomy 154–5
  skills acquisition/development 154
  typical activities/experiences 151
outdoor environments
  adult health and well-being 4
  changing nature of
    the challenge of 142–4
    and child's response 28
  EYFS guidance 21
  importance of 22–31
  mathematics 86–91
  non-judgemental nature 25–6
  reading 138, 144–5
  stimulation 86
outdoor experiences
  child development 23
  memories 184
  planning 28–9
outdoor learning 11
  external providers of 205–6
  holism in 5
  models 203–4
  over-formalisation of 150
  pedagogies of transition 50–63
    play-based and playful 57–8
    spaces: intentions and tensions 59–62
    understanding and use of spaces 52–4
  pillars of knowledge 152–5, 157, 158
  very young children 20–34

dealing with risk 31–4
in developed world 21
in developing world 20–1
importance of environment 22–31
outdoor spaces
  intentions and tensions 59–62
  teachers' understandings and use
    52–4
  variety in 29
Outward Bound 153
over-protectiveness 157
over-sanitisation 27
ownership 185, 211

parents and carers, involvement of
    43–5, 63, 210
'peak adventure' stage 137
pedagogy
  drama as 110–15
  environmental education 177–83
  place and learning 3, 5, 7–8, 103,
    153
  play-based 57–8
peers, reliance on 158
Pen Green Children's Centre 45
perceived risk 138, 139, 140
performance art 130–1
perseverance 209
persistence 26, 38
personalisation 15, 140
personality 15–16, 158
physical development 23, 24
physical education 133–46
  outdoor adventure activities 137–41
  outdoors and outside the classroom
    134
  overcoming barriers to outdoor
    learning 142–4
  physical literacy 135–6
physical experience, direct 28
physical literacy 135–6, 138, 145
physical movement 29
physical space, availability of 27–8
physical world, learning about 23–4
pillars of knowledge (UNESCO) 149,
    152–5, 157, 158
place
  as culturally constructed 5, 6f

historical aspects of 180–2
and learning 2–5, 7–8, 103, 153,
    204–6
see also space(s)
planning
  outdoor experiences 28–9
  starting with observation 39
play see free play; musical play;
    pretend play; role-play
play episodes, and different
    environments 56
play-based learning 51, 55–6
play-based pedagogies 56, 57–8
playgrounds 60, 134
plein air tradition 129
positive attitudes 170, 173, 186
possible lines of learning (PLOD) 40
power 8
power relationships 56
practical learning 1, 2, 5, 16, 153
Practice Guidance (EYFS) 21
pretend play 29
primary curriculum, INCA study
    (2008) 51–2
private spaces 61, 72
problem-solving 11, 86–7, 137, 139,
    154
process-oriented drama 110–12
productive questions 103
progression 205
proof (mathematical) 82
props 68, 111
psychological plane 5, 6f, 10–12,
    15–16, 68, 71, 86, 170, 184, 207t
public sculpture 128
pupil performance, outdoor learning
    153
puppets 111
purpose 16, 76
purposeful play 57

re-enactments 69
real experience environmental
    education 177–9, 183–7
real life experiences 173
Realistic Mathematics Education
    (RME) 83–4
reality 3, 158, 207

reflection 68, 69, 109
reflective practice 11
relational model, learning outside the
    classroom 6–10
relevance 3–4, 12
reliance, on peers 158
repetition 57, 170
residential centres *see* outdoor
    adventure centres
resilience 26, 149, 150, 152
resourcing/resources 4, 29, 36, 37, 63
respect 179
responsibility 31, 109, 117, 144, 186
risk 31–4, 137, 138, 139, 140, 180, 209
risk assessment 169
risk aversion 32, 148, 157
risk management 166, 209
risk threshold 137
risk-taking 32, 158
role-play 68–72, 115, 182
Romantic art movements 128
Royal Horticultural Society research
    163–4
Royal Society for the Prevention of
    Cruelty to Animals 179
rules 10, 14

sanitisation 27, 178
satisfaction 38, 138
scaffolding 133–4, 139, 140–1
scariness 29
schemas 38, 125–6
school culture 206
school gardens 163–6
    compared to Forest Schools 172–3
school grounds 61, 101, 103
school trips 61–2
schools
    as outdoor centres 159
    outdoor centres' growing similarity
        to 156–8
    see also Forest Schools
science, defined 94
Science Council 94
science and technology 94–105
    definitions 94–5
    developing a sense of belonging
        95–8

finding out about the world 99–101
reducing impact on environment
    102–4
scientific language 103
Scotland 108
sculpture 128, 129
security 4
self, centrality in learning 5
self-actualisation 154
self-awareness 154–5, 157
self-concept 150, 155
self-confidence 137, 138, 150, 169,
    170
self-dependency 158
self-development 154
self-direction 51, 170
self-esteem 135, 137, 138, 139, 150,
    154, 155, 170
self-protective instincts 33
self-regulation 22
self-sufficiency 158
sense-making 9, 69
sensitivity, to sound 120
sensori-motor stage/knowledge 22, 23
sensory deprivation 120
sensual experiences 177
Sherborne Developmental Movement
    140–1
simulations, environmental 178
situated social construction 155
situated understanding 14
skills
    acquisition and development 154,
        170, 209, 210
    transferred to outdoor context 144
    see also social skills
social action 98
social bonding 61
social constructionism 155, 157, 158,
    171
social dimension, knowledge
    construction 189
social, emotional and behavioural
    difficulties 205
social and emotional development 23,
    111, 124, 171
social reality 158
social responsibility 109, 117

social skills 115, 154
socially orientated activity 13–14
socio-cultural plane 4, 5, 6f, 13–15,
    68, 71, 77, 96, 154, 158, 165, 170,
    207t
sound gardens 126
space(s)
  becoming sensitive to 121–2
  different kinds of learning 3
  use of, process-oriented drama 112
  see also learning spaces; outdoor
    spaces; physical space
special educational needs 204, 205
spiritual development 124, 155
'standing back' 61, 107
state of flow 38
Steiner, Rudolf 159
stewardship 186
stories 183
story-telling 109, 112, 113–14, 115
structured play 57–8
subjectivity, artwork 129–30
sublime 128
success, learning through 139, 170,
    173
supervision 30–1
sustainability 158, 198
sustainability agenda 103

taken-for granted, re-evaluation of
    139
teacher-in-role 110, 115
teacher-pupil relationships 110
teachers, avoidance, of the outdoors
    142, 144
team-building 154
teamwork 139
technology

defined 94–5
introducing through role-play 72
use, at outdoor centres 156
  see also ICT; science and
    technology
timing, access to the outdoors 27
tools, use of 169
touch 120
transformative learning 8, 12, 158
transience, in artwork 128–9
transition, pedagogies of 50–63
transportable resources 29
trust 137, 139, 158

udeskole 171
understanding 14–15
unpredictability 7, 11, 24, 25

values 22, 109
variety, of learning contexts 206–7
vertical mathematising 83, 88, 91, 92f
Victorian Educational Visit 111
Vicuña, Cecilia 128
videos 179
vocational education 205

Wales 108
waterproof clothing 27–8
weather, overcoming difficulties of
    142–4
weather protection 63
well-being 4, 25, 38, 135, 136, 208
The Wind in the Willows 118
wonder 155
woodland contexts 169, 170
work-play distinction 60

zoning 61, 63

THEORIES AND APPROACHES TO LEARNING IN THE EARLY YEARS

Edited by **Linda Miller** *The Open University* and **Linda Pound** *Education Consultant*

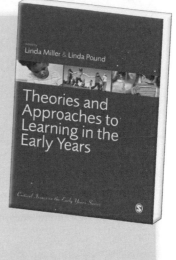

By focusing on key figures in early years education and care, this book considers the influential thinkers and groundbreaking approaches that have revolutionized practice. With contributions from leading authorities in the field, chapters provide an explanation of the approach, an analysis of the theoretical background, case studies, questions and discussion points to facilitate critical thinking.

Included are chapters on:

- Froebel
- Psychoanalytical theories
- Maria Montessori
- Steiner Waldorf education
- High/Scope
- Postmodern and post-structuralist perspectives
- Forest Schools
- Vivian Gussin Paley
- Te Whariki.

Written in an accessible style and relevant to all levels of early years courses, the book has staggered levels of Further Reading that encourage reflection and promotes progression.

CRITICAL ISSUES IN THE EARLY YEARS
December 2010 • 192 pages
Cloth (978-1-84920-577-1) • £65.00
Paper (978-1-84920-578-8) • £22.99

ALSO FROM SAGE

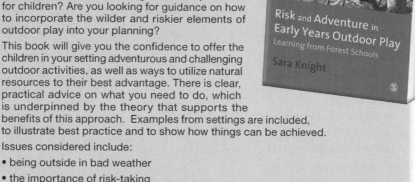

RISK AND ADVENTURE IN EARLY YEARS OUTDOOR PLAY

Learning from Forest Schools

Sara Knight *Anglia Ruskin University*

Do you want to create exciting outdoor experiences for children? Are you looking for guidance on how to incorporate the wilder and riskier elements of outdoor play into your planning?

This book will give you the confidence to offer the children in your setting adventurous and challenging outdoor activities, as well as ways to utilize natural resources to their best advantage. There is clear, practical advice on what you need to do, which is underpinned by the theory that supports the benefits of this approach. Examples from settings are included, to illustrate best practice and to show how things can be achieved.

Issues considered include:

• being outside in bad weather

• the importance of risk-taking

• the benefits of rough-and-tumble play

• observing and assessing children in this mode

• how these experiences improve children's learning

• explaining activities to parents, colleagues and managers

• ensuring health and safety requirements are met

• the role of the adult in facilitating these experiences.

Suitable for all students and practitioners working with young children from birth to eight years , this book will not only give you ideas for outdoor play but also help you understand exactly what you are doing, why it is educationally sound and developmentally important for children, and where it connects with the Early Years Foundation Stage in England, the Foundation Phase in Wales and the Curriculum for Excellence in Scotland .

April 2011 • 152 pages
Cloth (978-1-84920-629-7) • £60.00
Paper (978-1-84920-630-3) • £19.99

ALSO FROM SAGE

PROFESSIONALIZATION, LEADERSHIP AND MANAGEMENT IN THE EARLY YEARS

Edited by **Linda Miller** and **Carrie Cable** *both at The Open University*

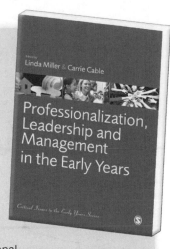

With the rapid change experienced by the early years workforce over recent times, this book considers what constitutes professionalization in the sector, and what this means in practice. Bringing a critical perspective to the developing knowledge and understanding of early years practitioners at various stages of their professional development, it draws attention to key themes and issues. Chapters are written by leading authorities, and case studies, questions and discussion points are provided to facilitate critical thinking.

Topics covered include:

• constructions of professional identities

• men in the early years

• multidisciplinary working in the early years

• professionalization in the nursery

• early childhood leadership and policy.

Written in an accessible style and relevant to all levels of early years courses, the book is highly relevant to those studying at masters level, and has staggered levels of further reading that encourage reflection and progression.

CRITICAL ISSUES IN THE EARLY YEARS

November 2010 • 184 pages
Cloth (978-1-84920-553-5) • £65.00
Paper (978-1-84920-554-2) • £22.99

ALSO FROM SAGE

OUTDOOR PROVISION IN THE EARLY YEARS

Edited by **Jan White**

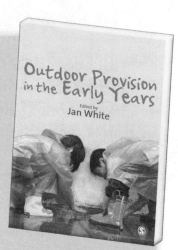

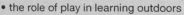

Outdoor education offers children special contexts for play and exploration, real experiences and contact with the natural world and the environment. To help ensure young children thrive and develop in your care, this book provides essential information on how to make learning outdoors a rich and valuable part of their daily life Written by a team of experts in the field, the book focuses on the core values of effective outdoor provision, and is packed with ideas to try out in practice. Topics covered include:

- the role of play in learning outdoors
- meaningful experiences for children outdoors
- the role of the adult outdoors
- creating a dynamic and flexible outdoor environment
- dealing with challenge, risk and safety
- including every child in outdoor learning.

There are case studies of successful strategies in action, covering the birth to five years age range.

March 2011 • 144 pages
Cloth (978-1-4129-2308-8) • £60.00
Paper (978-1-4129-2309-5) • £18.99

ALSO FROM SAGE